MANCHESTER FOURTEEN MILES

By the same author

THE FOOLISH VIRGIN
YOUNG MRS BURTON

Manchester Fourteen Miles

Margaret Penn

Cambridge University Press

Cambridge
London   New York   New Rochelle
Melbourne   Sydney

Published by the Press Syndicate of the University of Cambridge
The Pitt Building, Trumpington Street, Cambridge CB2 1RP
32 East 57th Street, New York, NY 10022, USA
296 Beaconsfield Parade, Middle Park, Melbourne 3206, Australia

First published 1947
First paperback edition 1981

First printed in Great Britain at the
University Press Cambridge
Reprinted in Great Britain by Redwood Burn Ltd
Trowbridge & Esher

British Library cataloguing in publication data

Penn, Margaret
    Manchester fourteen miles.
    1. Hollin's Green, Eng. (Cheshire) – Social
    life and customs
    2. Labor and laboring classes – England –
    Hollin's Green, Cheshire
    I. Title
    942.7′19   DA690.H734/   80–40707
    ISBN 0 521 28065 6

CONTENTS

CHAPTER I

THE FAMILY

"Stand up, child, and show respect to the Vicar!"

The girl addressed rose at once from the table, her face reddening painfully while the clerical figure in the doorway surveyed her with his cold, pale blue, prominent eyes.

She was a tall girl, well made, and going on for thirteen. She had a bright, clear skin, grey eyes, and very fine, straight chestnut-brown hair which was dragged back hideously from her forehead and tied hard back behind with a rusty black ribbon. Wrapped tightly round her middle was a coarse sacking apron, much too big for her, which fell down to and over her boots.

"All right, Hilda. Go on with your lunch," said the Reverend James Black, Vicar of Moss Ferry, not unkindly. He went out, and the girl was left alone again with his housekeeper, Miss Minnie Brown. Miss Brown was very small, with thick black hair and unusually bright brown eyes; she was in her middle thirties. When the Vicar's footsteps had died away down the tiled passage, she turned to Hilda, saying: "I want you always to stand up if the Vicar comes in when we are eating. It shows respect. Now finish your pudding and when we've washed up I'll show you how to lay the table for the Vicar's dinner. He likes to have everything done nicely, but you'll soon get into his ways."

They were eating in a very large bright kitchen. It seemed enormous to Hilda Winstanley, for it was even bigger than her Grandma's kitchen at Bridge Farm. And the smooth, shining, red-tiled floor, which she had just scrubbed with the energy of one in her first wage-earning job, made her think a little

I

disparagingly of Grandma Stringer's sanded, uneven flags. A flagged floor seemed so common after these handsome tiles.

Miss Brown chatted amiably to her while they cleared and washed up the dishes, and in her turn, gradually losing her awkward shyness, Hilda chattered back. Miss Brown expressed great surprise when Hilda volunteered with pride that, although she had all her life been a chapel-goer, she had nevertheless been baptised like a Christian into the Church of England, at St Margaret's, the village church.

"Then you should go to church, child, not to chapel. Wouldn't your mother let you go to church instead?"

"I don't think so, Miss Brown. They've always been chapel-goers at home; and our John hasn't once in twelve years missed going to Sunday School, twice every Sunday. And he's never been late, either. The Sunday School gave him a silver medal last Christmas to hang on his watch-chain. It says on it: 'Presented to John Winstanley, for regular attendance at the Kilnbrook United Methodist Sunday School for twelve years. Well done, thou good and faithful servant.'"

Hilda was both surprised and disappointed at Miss Brown's cold reception of this laudable achievement, for she only gave a disapproving nod that dismissed the subject and with it the entire chapel-going community of Moss Ferry and Kilnbrook, which was considerable. For the Vicar's housekeeper there was one Church alone, and the Reverend James Black was its sole accredited representative on earth. The United Methodists and the Primitive Methodists, the Wesleyans and the Baptists, the Congregationalists and the Presbyterians were all so many heretics, past praying for in spite of their numbers. It was a social crime to be a Nonconformist in Moss Ferry. Hilda was aware of this, hence her eagerness to explain the facts of her baptism. She

2

felt that it gave her a little lustre in Miss Brown's eyes, and already she was wondering if she could work on her mother to let her give up chapel-going and take to St Margaret's instead.

While she was folding up the tablecloth, a thin scraping wail echoed through the house, the like of which she had never heard before. It was a sound that gave no pleasure, and Miss Brown, seeing the puzzled look on her young helper's face, explained loyally but a little sadly: "That's the Vicar practising on his fiddle. He does it for an hour every day after lunch and he doesn't like to be disturbed. So try not to clatter about if you can help it, there's a good girl."

With her heavy-soled boots Hilda found this difficult, and in her anxiety not to offend began to walk on tiptoe, holding up the sacking apron to prevent herself from stumbling.

The kitchen now tidied, Miss Brown took her along the passage and showed her the dining-room.

Hilda stared about her in wonder. This room was even bigger than the kitchen. It had a beautiful mahogany table in the very centre, with a sideboard to match, and even chairs to match that, and the floor was covered with a thick soft red carpet. She had never been in a room like this before although she knew, from pictures in her annual *Chatterbox*, that well-off people did have such rooms and ate their dinners off tables just as splendid as the one here.

And the sideboard, which went nearly the length of the wall, made her eyes ache. It glittered all over with silver dishes and big glass bottles, and she wondered fearfully how she would ever learn which article was which.

Miss Brown gave her a red felt cloth to spread on the table, and on top of that a spotless, glossily starched, white one. At home they didn't have a cloth at all, except in the front room on Sundays

3

when there was company. For all other meals they ate at a big table in the kitchen covered with white american cloth, which was always wiped over after a meal and so was always clean and shiny. She was then initiated into the mysteries of a great many knives and forks and spoons. The Vicar seemed to require quite a number of them—a big knife and then a little knife, and a big fork and on top a spoon and a fork, and he had a little plate on the left-hand side with a clean serviette and a silver ring round it— (Miss Brown called it his napkin, of which Hilda made private note).

When the table was laid to Miss Brown's satisfaction and Hilda's undisguised admiration, she was told to fill up the coal scuttle. After this to sweep up the yard, and then, since it was nearly four o'clock and a Saturday, she might go home. She had shaped well, said Miss Brown, and great things could be expected of her. She must be sure to come every morning, except Sunday, from half-past seven until just on nine o'clock. Miss Brown said she would give her cocoa and bread and jam before she set off to school. For this work she would receive ninepence a week. It was the year 1909 in agricultural Lancashire, where a farm labourer's highest wage was eighteen shillings a week, and a roadman under the Council considered that a guinea a week gave him an exalted professional status. Ninepence a week, therefore, seemed to Hilda just if not generous.

In any case she was working of her own free will. She would not need to think of earning till her thirteenth birthday, when she left school. Her part-time services at the Vicarage had been asked for by the Reverend Black and his housekeeper; and her mother, though protesting that ninepence a week in return was not enough, had nevertheless made no serious attempt to stop her from earning it. Any road ninepence a week was not to be

4

sneezed at. It meant a fresh book every week, at tuppence a time, out of the Co-op. library at Daneshead; and she would still have sevenpence left for her own many other private uses.

And so, after putting away the sacking apron in the washhouse, she hurried home to show, proudly, her first week's wages.

*   *   *

"Our Hilda", as they called her at home, was not the child of Joe and Lizzie Winstanley, though she was nearly ten before she made this startling discovery. She began to hear things in the village and to ask questions about the visits which Lucy Stringer, from Bridge Farm in Kilnbrook, paid regularly every month to her mother, Mrs Winstanley. Nobody, however, seemed disposed to answer her questions. Her mother, when approached, always said the same thing: "Axe me no questions and Ah'll tell you no lies." Hilda was terrified of Lucy Stringer, who always stared so hard at her and asked her so many questions, and sometimes, when she wished to talk privately with Mrs Winstanley, remarked meaningly that little pitchers had big ears and hadn't Hilda better go out and play. Lucy brought new clothes when Hilda needed them, and repaid Mrs Winstanley any money she had spent on boots and bootmending for the child. Although she looked as if she were made of iron rods, she never left the Winstanleys without giving Hilda a penny to spend; nor did she ever go without sternly advising her always to be a good girl to her mother.

As soon as she was old enough to think about these monthly visits, Hilda began to connect them with some mystery concerning herself. It was, however, only through the malice of Sarah Dumbell, a notorious mischief-maker, that Hilda learnt excitedly that she was a "love-child". She had no real knowledge of what a love-child was, except that it was something people never liked to talk about openly. And it was Sarah Dumbell who told her that Lucy Stringer, the young woman from Bridge Farm, was in fact her aunt—her own mother's sister—and that her father, whom nobody in Moss Ferry had ever seen, was "a gentleman born". But he had not, Mrs Dumbell went on viciously, thought much of her mother; any road he hadn't wed her. Instead she had married George Huntley, who worked at the Stringer's farm in Kilnbrook. And Mrs Stringer, known to everybody as Grandma Stringer, was in fact Hilda's real grandmother. And she wasn't Hilda Winstanley at all, but Hilda Huntley.

When Hilda rushed home with this exciting news there was a fearful upset. Her mother reproved her sharply for listening to such a meddlesome Matty as Sarah Dumbell. Everybody for miles knew that all she lived for was to brew trouble. She was a shiftless, dirty, brass-faced woman with a grudge against them on account of her girl, Winnie, wanting their John and not getting him. "Ah'd as lief see our John lying stiff in 'is coffin as walking out wi' Winnie Dumbell," said Mrs Winstanley dramatically, and with a fine disregard for her eldest son's views about this. "And you be off now, our 'Ilda. Axe me no questions and Ah'll tell you no lies. Us'll see what your father has to say when he comes home. If you dunna behave yourself wi' your questions, he'll be taking t'strap to you." And she bustled about getting a tasty tea ready against the time her husband came in.

The threat of the strap had no terrors for Hilda. Never since she could remember had the man she had always thought of as her father shown her anything but affection.

Joe Winstanley was a farm labourer. He was a big-boned, good-looking man, with kind blue eyes in a red weather-beaten face. He loved his children impartially, and his wife had no fault in his eyes. He professed a great admiration for what he called Hilda's "book-larning", for she was the only one of the four

6

children with a passion for the printed word. Neither he nor his wife could read or write, and as soon as Hilda was old enough it fell to her to read the rare letters that came into the house. At Christmas, when she brought home her annual *Chatterbox* (given as a prize for good conduct in Sunday School), they listened happily while she read out stories and anecdotes. They both loved these *Chatterbox* readings, and once her mother cried when Hilda read out how Queen Alexandra, at a tea-party for poor people, took out her own beautiful lace handkerchief and spread it on her lap when she saw the other women had done this. And sometimes they asked Hilda to read them a chapter out of the big family bible, which they always called The Book. It was bound in padded black leather and had clasps which locked. When not in use it had the place of honour on a table under the front-room window, so that all who passed could admire it. It was illustrated with coloured pictures, and on the fly-leaf was written in her brother John's writing:

Joseph Winstanley, born February 28th 1864
Elizabeth Ann   „   „   July   17th 1870
John   „   „   October   12th 1888
James   „   „   September   1st 1890
Lily   „   „   April   26th 1898

And, as though she had been put in as an after-thought,

Hilda Winstanley, born June 14th 1896

*   *   *

When her father came in from work he saw immediately, from his wife's flushed and angry face, that something serious had happened to unsettle her.

"What's to do, Mother?" he asked mildly.

Mrs Winstanley, with Hilda listening intently, told him about Sarah Dumbell and her trouble-making. He looked very grave, and Hilda waited expectantly for what he would say. He sat down in his rocking chair by the window and started on his tea—his favourite dish of bacon and toasted cheese—before saying anything. He looked at his wife, and then at Hilda.

"Well, reckon she'll 'ave to know some day. If Sarah Dumbell's bin clacking it 'ad better come proper from us. What dost say, Mother?"

"Aye, Ah'll tell 'er. You 'earken to me, our 'Ilda. Us 'as had you since you were a babby, nobbut three weeks old. Your own mother went just after you were born, and your father, George Huntley, didn't know where to turn. Your Grandma at Bridge Farm said she would take you till she could find a good home for you with good people who would bring you up as their own. And your father was to pay five shilling a week, and your Grandma to find you in clothes till you was old enough to earn. She came to us, and as we only 'ad our John and Jim then, and could do with the bit extra, we took you. And we've brought you up same as our own, and that's God's truth if I never stir from this chair"; and she turned for confirmation to her husband.

"Aye," said Joe, nodding slowly and emphatically. "We never made no difference. What our own 'ad you've 'ad and allus will. And she's bin a good mother to you. And you keep away from Sarah Dumbell from now on. There was no call for her to go telling you owt." He poured himself another cup of tea, relieved that the business was out and done with.

"But what about my real father? Sarah Dumbell said George Huntley wasn't...."

Before she could get the words out, her mother gave her a stinging box on the ear that sent her half-way across the kitchen.

8

"George Huntley was your father. George Huntley and nobody else. And dunna you forget it. And no good 'e's bin to you either. It were nobbut three months after your mother 'ad gone afore he was off to Canada. And never 'eard tell of from that day to this. He was a real bad lot was George Huntley, going off that road wi'out a word to nobody, and your mother not cold in her grave. Your Grandma's paid for you all these years. Lucy Stringer brings me the money every month. Winter and summer. Wet or fine. She's traipsed here fair clemmed wi' cold, but it's allus bin paid to me regular every month. And your Grandma's never grudged you nothing. You've allus had a new frock for the Whitsun Walk, and new boots and a new 'at to go with it. Ah've bin fair put to it many a time to see our Lily 'ad the same. What one has t'other'll have, Ah've allus said; and what with your father's harvest-money and the bit extra at Christmas us've allus managed. And you can go and play with Elsie Entwistle for a bit now, but come in afore dark. And dunna you go talking about nothing. Axe me no questions and Ah'll tell you no lies. If everybody minded their own business there'd be no upsets. Sarah Dumbell'll come to a bad end. *And* that Winnie of hers. Traipsing after our John same as she 'as bin, the brass-faced hussy." And with this irrelevant finish she shooed Hilda out of the kitchen, and set about getting tea for when John came in from his work at the foundry in Daneshead.

*   *   *

John was the eldest of the Winstanley children. He was twenty, and ever since leaving school at thirteen had worked in the big iron-foundry at Daneshead. He worked in cast iron, chiefly at moulding. In the fireplace of the front room at home stood a superb pair of cast-iron stags which he had made specially for his mother; and on the kitchen mantelpiece was a pair of prancing horses, each ridden by a warrior, which he had also cast. Mrs Winstanley proudly explained to the uninitiated that one rider was going to the wars, and the other coming back from them. She treasured the stags and the warriors above all else in her home and blackleaded them each day till they shone like satanic mirrors.

Mrs Winstanley used to declare with pride that she had never known what it was to have a minute's uneasiness with their John, so it was a black day indeed when he came home from the foundry so early that she knew instantly something terrible must have happened. It had. For giving a back-answer to Jim Ormerod, the foreman, John had been sacked. Paid a week's wages and told not to come back; and after seven years of faithful service. He sat slumped down in the big rocking chair, while his mother fussed about the kitchen, fearful of pressing for all the details.

John was not so tall as his father, but he was well made and had his father's mild, good-tempered face. He was intelligent too, and mad about politics, football, and Edie Atkinson, his ugly, red-headed sweetheart in Daneshead. All the Winstanleys were very fond of him, and his foster-sister, Hilda, in particular. She took the greatest pleasure in doing for him any little service she could. She cleaned his Sunday boots, and brushed his Sunday and second-best suits, and was always willing to run down to Mrs Starkey's shop whenever he wanted a packet of Woodbines. John always had money in his pocket and thought nothing of giving her, on a Saturday, as much as twopence for spending-money. He paid generously for his keep at home, and his mother used to boast of his rare commonsense in having a tidy bit put by, though he had never meant it for such a rainy day as this.

Hilda's affection for him went deep, and for years she treasured above all else a present he had once brought her from Manchester. This was a "lady's companion"—a set of dainty sewing tools in a pretty blue imitation-leather case. They were so small and so delicate that for a long time she was afraid to use them. Now and then she opened the case and tried on the thimble, or cut snippets of paper with the minute scissors. And when her mother had company to tea she left the case lying open in a prominent place for everybody to admire. The fact that John had bought the present in Manchester gave it an added glamour, for Hilda had never yet been to Manchester. The signpost in the village said Manchester was fourteen miles away.

Mrs Winstanley gave him his tea and then filled a kettle so that he could have a good wash in hot water. The entire family washed at the kitchen sink, which stood alongside the big stone clothes copper. This was the first time Hilda could remember any of the menfolk washing after a meal instead of before it, and she sensed that there was something very wrong for John especially to eat his tea without ridding himself first of his working dirt.

He drank and ate moodily, going round and round in his mind for the best way of explaining to his mother what had happened at the foundry. For all his easy friendliness he was quick tempered. He got this from his mother, who could be very hasty when roused, and she was very often and very easily roused, as Hilda knew to her cost.

Finally, when the heavy silence had so got on her nerves that she had to speak, Mrs Winstanley said: "Ah wouldna take on so, lad. It'll settle itself. And there's other work to be had. There's allus t'soap works i' Irlam."

"Aye, Mother. But I don't like t'soap works. Iron's my job. I've allus worked wi' iron, and there's only t'one foundry in Daneshead. There's nowt else till Warrington. Tha knows that."

Mrs Winstanley did know it. And she knew too what getting the sack from the foundry meant to John. He had started there at thirteen, at five shillings a week. And now, at twenty, he was a first-class moulder and bringing home thirty shillings a week, and sometimes, on piece work, as much as two pounds. He had had slack times, of course, and even for a day or two been laid off; but this was final. Her mind could not cope with it and she sought uneasily for the right thing to say. She was afraid of upsetting his pride, but she could see only one thing to be done and she put it to him timidly: "Couldn't tha go back tomorrow and 'ave a word wi' Jim Ormerod? Ah know he's hasty but he's all reet at bottom. Tha's worked wi' him now for seven year and he's not going to let a bit o' quick temper lose him a good workman. Have a word wi' thi father and see what he says."

To her surprise John did not resent her suggestion. He had evidently been thinking that way himself, wondering how he could go back and eat humble pie. It would be hard, for he was as stubborn as Jim Ormerod, but it might be worth having a go at.

"Well, reckon there's summat to be said for it, Mother. Any road he canna eat me."

Mrs Winstanley's face brightened and she knew it was as good as over. Hilda, who had sat listening miserably, asked her brother if he was going to Edie's that night and should she clean his Sunday boots for him. And when was he going to bring Edie back home to tea. Why not the very next Sunday? Nervously she appealed to her mother to second this suggestion.

"Aye. You fetch her. Happen she'd like to go to chapel wi' us after."

John was embarrassed. His mother had not yet met Edie officially, and he himself never talked about her except to Hilda. He had an uneasy feeling that his mother wouldn't like her. For

Edie Atkinson was what Mrs Winstanley called a "goer", always one to be gallivanting about. However he promised to bring her the following Sunday, and his mother immediately started to plan what they should have special for tea in her honour.

*　　　　*　　　　*

The Winstanley's second son was called Jim and he had always been considered delicate. He was "chesty", and in the winter suffered horribly with bronchitis, which kept him away for weeks on end from his work at Endicott's farm. Doctor James, who had brought all the Winstanley children, and Hilda too, into the world, had always said that Jim must do none but outdoor work. His chest would never stand foundry work such as John did. The doctor never mentioned consumption, but it was more or less understood in the village that Joe Winstanley's second lad wouldn't be long for this world.

Jim was tall and big boned like his father, but in looks took after his mother, and he had her quick, easily roused temper. He was able to read and write, but, as his health had kept him away from school for long periods, he could only do these things slowly. He used to spend whole evenings reading *The Family Herald*, following the lines closely with his finger. *The Family Herald* was taken by John and was the only paper that came into the house until he scandalised his mother by taking in a Sunday newspaper—*The Referee*. Mrs Winstanley was afraid of newspapers. She said they boded no good for them that read them, and she was firmly convinced that they were written by no mortal agency, but by t'Owd Lad himself. Nobody in Moss Ferry ever referred plainly to the Devil. Even to the smallest child he was known simply and familiarly as t'Owd Lad, and great was the terror of any child threatened by its parents with the awful words:

"Ah'll tell t'Owd Lad about thee." The threat never failed of its effect, for t'Owd Lad, like the Lord Jesus, was known to have the power of being everywhere at once. Hiding in wait round every corner, ready to pounce at the first sign of wrongdoing and soar away with the offender into blackest night.

Between Jim and Hilda there was continual strife. With her book-learning she could always get the better of him in argument, and many and bitter were the fights they had. Sometimes as she watched him reading painfully through *The Family Herald* she would jeer at him unmercifully, provoking him to such a towering, lunatic and bestial rage that he would jump from his chair and pursue her with murder in his eyes. Only then, when she sensed the awful physical danger she was in, would she run to her mother for protection. Once, when in his rage he roughly pushed his mother aside in his desire to choke the life out of his sister, she had barely time to bound up the stairs to the little room which she shared with Lily. She managed to shoot the rickety bolt, and stood braced against the door, at which he was shaking and pounding. She could hear him slobbering, and quaked with terror lest the gimcrack fastening gave way.

She heard her mother come up and try to calm him down.

"Come away, lad! Tha knows she doesna mean it. It's only 'er way. Best to take no notice. Leave 'er be. Come on, do!"

He went downstairs, and Hilda, relieved but wretched, prayed to Jesus to make her a better girl. She knew very well her own wickedness and that she would, if ever he got his hands on her in one of his awful rages, be crushed like a blown eggshell.

When she felt that it was safe she crept down into the kitchen. Her mother, keeping a wary eye on both of them, threatened her with abduction by t'Owd Lad when she least expected it, and said it was high time her father took the strap to her if she didn't learn to behave. And if he wouldn't give her a good hiding then she would.

But although Hilda was always sorry afterwards for provoking her great lout of a brother, for the life of her she couldn't help doing it. With his laborious pothook writing, his slow reading and his dirty physical habits, he disgusted her. For though he washed himself just as thoroughly every night as John and her father, his clomping farm boots brought a strong smell of manure into the kitchen, and his corduroy trousers, which he tied just under the knees with a thick rope of straw, smelt of sour milk and other farm peculiarities. She could not understand why Jim should smell so horrible when her father, who also worked on a farm, never did. Joe always smelt natural—of bracken and hay and clean straw, and he always rubbed his boots well in the long sweet grass by the roadside, and scraped them on the iron scraper by the kitchen door, before coming in. Hilda never forgave Jim for disgusting her friend, Cissie Turner, when she brought her dinner to eat at the Winstanleys one day. Kilnbrook, where Cissie lived, was too far for her to go home for dinner, and she used to bring it to eat in the schoolroom. Mrs Winstanley, a friend of Cissie's mother, said the child was always welcome to eat with them. Hilda was excited at having a friend home and everything was going well till Jim clumped in with his smelly boots. She saw Cissie's face wrinkle at the offensive odour, and when she put away her unfinished sandwiches in her little basket Hilda could have died from shame. Cissie never came again, preferring to eat in the warm, clean schoolroom.

*   *   *

Lily, the third and youngest of the Winstanley children, was a horrible girl and Hilda disliked her nearly as much as she

disliked Jim, though they always went to school and Sunday
School together, and slept in the same bed in the little room at
the top of the stairs. For Lily too was a dunce, as big a dunce as
Jim. She was two years younger than Hilda, with a clumsy,
dumpy body and a fat, sallow, stupid face with round brown
button-eyes that never seemed to see anything. And she was
good—born good—and she was a tell-tale. If, as she often did,
she heard her sister, when their mother was out, trying to extract
pennies out of her moneybox with a knife (a feat at which Hilda
was quite expert), as soon as their mother returned she would
blurt out: "Our Hilda's been taking money out of her moneybox—she's taken a lot—I saw her"; and Mrs Winstanley would
confront Hilda and demand fiercely: "How much? Where is it?
Dunna you know it's as bad as stealing to take from your moneybox! Give it to me, this minute, *all* of it!"

And Hilda, who had extracted perhaps fourpence or fivepence,
would, with a great show of resentment, hand over two pennies,
having secreted the others in a place where even the prying Lily
would never find them. But Lily would stand there, maliciously
protesting that Hilda had stolen much more than twopence—
she had heard her take quite a lot of pennies, and she had been up
in t'orchard doing summat. Hiding them, she knew.

But Hilda, in spite of the Lord Jesus and t'Owd Lad combined,
would lie stoutly about this and, maddened beyond endurance at
her sister's sneaking ways, would lunge forward and pull Lily's
hair—seize a handful of it with all the force of which she was
capable, holding on as long as she could and thinking the clouts
her mother was giving her own head well worth it. The two girls
hated one another, but while Hilda was no sneak and only wanted
to be let alone, Lily was for ever prying and telling tales. She
would even call out to her mother on summer mornings when

she woke up to find Hilda reading some novelette that Elsie Entwistle's mother, who was a great reader and encouraged Hilda in this wickedness, had lent her. And Mrs Winstanley would shout back from her bedroom: "Put it away, our 'Ilda. No good will come of reading such wickedness. If you wants to read in the mornings you read in The Book, or you can 'ave your *Chatterbox*." And Hilda would shout back defiantly: "It isn't wickedness. Mrs Entwistle goes to chapel same as us, and she'd not lend it me if it was wicked. And you don't know what it's about either. If you could read it for yourself you'd see it isn't wickedness"; and secure in the knowledge that her mother had no answer to this challenge, Hilda would sneer at the treacherous, horrible Lily, calling her "Mardy, mardy, tell-tale, sausage fingers", until Lily, who was sensitive about her thick, podgy hands, would cry, and Hilda, unable in her contempt to bear even the feel of her sister's nightdress against her own, would stuff her pillow between their two bodies and lying flat on her back absorb the fascinating story of the golden-haired mill girl who had many trials and humiliations to bear before she married the boss's son and lived happy ever after.

*   *   *

Such were the five members of the Winstanley family at the house in School Lane: the house with the front room and the kitchen and three bedrooms. In the largest bedroom, with its big brass-knobbed bed, Mr and Mrs Winstanley slept. Hilda and Lily shared a little box of a room which only held their bed and one small chair. They hung their weekday clothes behind the door, their Sunday clothes being kept in their mother's wardrobe. John and Jim shared the third room, which was a fair size and at the back of the house.

The kitchen was fairly big too, and had a concrete floor covered with bright, home-made rag rugs, and there was a small but cheerful range on which all the cooking was done. In the centre of the room was a large square table covered with white american cloth, and against one wall a slippery horse-hair sofa on which Hilda and Lily always sat to table. One side of the table, underneath the window, was a big wooden rocking chair for their father; on the other side a smaller rocking chair for their mother; and on either side of the fireplace a solid Windsor chair. The clothes copper was in a corner by the fireplace, next to the sink at which they all washed in an enamel bowl. The window sill was covered with flowering plants, and on one wall was a very large oil-painting in a handsome gilt frame of an old lady wearing a goffered lace cap and a lace fichu. This was a fascinating picture, and Mrs Winstanley would point out to her company with pride that, no matter where you stood and looked at the old lady, she was always looking straight at you. This fact impressed itself deeply on Hilda and, when alone in the kitchen, she would walk round and look into the old lady's eyes. Sure enough, what her mother said was perfectly true: even if you stood right under the picture, even if you stood to one side of it, those eyes still regarded you. It was a pleasant old face, and her father had bought it for a shilling or two at an auction. It filled up the entire wall and gave life to the room. Indeed the old lady seemed to be part of the family, and when the picture was taken down for the annual turn-out and stood in the front room, the kitchen felt naked and cold until it had been hung up again.

At either end of the mantelpiece, which was high and wide, were John's prancing horses with various canisters in between— one for sugar, one for tea, and so on. The tea caddy was a Mazawattee one, with a picture of an old lady with a white shawl round her shoulders beaming at a steaming cup of Mazawattee tea. This canister had stood there ever since Hilda could remember; she loved the smooth feel of it and always rushed to spoon out the tea when she saw her mother warming the pot.

The front room (for only the gentry called them "parlours") was Mrs Winstanley's special pride, and contained all her best ornaments and furniture. It was never used except when they had company to tea, and only then on a Sunday. Once, however, when Hilda and Lily had the measles, Doctor James advised having their bed put into the front room because of its airiness and its being handier for Mrs Winstanley to look after them. Mrs Winstanley was scandalised, but Doctor's orders were Doctor's orders, and to their huge delight the two girls had their measles right under the front-room window, so that they could sit up, pink and spotted objects of interest to all who passed down the lane.

The principal piece of furniture was a very large and ugly mahogany cheffonier, with a looking-glass in it. At each side of the looking-glass stood the children's Sunday School prizes, and on coloured Berlin wool mats on top of the piled-up books were two vases of artificial flowers. In the middle of the room was a big mahogany table covered with a red chenille cloth edged with bobbles. There were six stiff mahogany chairs with horse-hair seats, and there was a very beautiful old grandfather clock with a blue and choppy sea painted round its dial and white-sailed ships sailing on it. On the window side of the fireplace was a big cupboard built up to the ceiling, and in this Mrs Winstanley kept her best tea service and various glass dishes and other crockery which she only used on special occasions. Underneath the window was a cheap wooden side-table at which Hilda, in summer, did her homework, and where she read in peace as often as she could until her mother, suddenly wanting something from the cupboard, would see her and say darkly and with her usual irrelevance: "Satan allus finds work for idle hands to do. Sitting cooped up in 'ere. Why dunna you go out and play with our Lily and Elsie Entwistle? They're playing hopscotch in t'lane."

And Hilda, deep in *From Log Cabin to White House*, one of John's Sunday School prizes, or *The Basket of Flowers*—one of her own good-conduct books—would scowl and answer back: "Can't you leave me be, Mother. I'm doing no harm to nobody." And Mrs Winstanley would reluctantly go away, puzzled and frightened and firmly convinced that Hilda would get no good out of such senseless behaviour. Some day she'd have to earn her keep same as everybody else, and what good then would all this book-reading be to her? And she would consult privately with Joe about it when the children were in bed. But he always sided with Hilda and argued that book-reading would do her no harm and he only wished he'd had a bit of schooling himself. So leave her be as long as she kept to her Sunday School prizes. Like his wife he was uneasy about the novelettes Mrs Entwistle lent her, and the book she got out of the Co-op. library at Daneshead once a week. They were both of them deeply suspicious of any but the prize books. They had no means of knowing what she was up to with other books, and sometimes would ask John if it was all right, and he, always ready to put in a good word for Hilda, would stick up for her and even defend Mrs Entwistle's novelettes, which were the same as Edie read in great quantities.

CHAPTER II
SOME RELATIONS

Hilda dreaded the afternoons when Mrs Winstanley's mother, Grandma Buckley, dropped in for a cup of tea. She usually came early, while the two girls were at school, and would do all her private talking to her daughter before they returned home.

Hilda's dread was not because Grandma Buckley was unkind to her, for, whenever she was sent on an errand there Grandma always produced something—a piece of cake or a peppermint drop or a Garibaldi biscuit. And if the cupboard was bare Grandma would then give her a halfpenny, or, best of all, rummage among her clothes and find an old black cape heavily beaded and tell Hilda she could unpick the beads and keep them. They were very tiny round black beads, and both Hilda and Lily would sit at the kitchen table on a winter night threading them for hours, seeing who could make the longest necklace. Hilda usually won at this for Lily was clumsy with her fingers; she would continually lose her needle or her thread would break, and then she would push the saucerful of beads towards her sister with a resentful sniff. No, Hilda dreaded Grandma Buckley's visits because she was a natural born moaner, and because she never washed her hair for fear of getting neuralgia. Instead she used to plaster it down from the centre-parting with water; and she would sit in the big rocking chair next to Hilda on the horse-hair couch, and all through her tea Hilda could smell Grandma's hair; it smelt musty, like water that had been standing for a long time. Both Hilda and Lily had their own heads washed every week in strong soda water, and Mrs Winstanley kept her thick black hair very clean also—washing it in soda water every two or three weeks.

Grandma Buckley was very tall and bony and she would sit in the rocking chair, her bonnet among the plants on the window sill, and her work-twisted old hands twiddling round and round over her black sateen apron as she moaned and whined. Nothing ever went right for Grandma Buckley. Before the children she never talked about her only son, Billy, though they knew all about him. He was a great trial in the family, though everybody in Moss Ferry liked him, drunk or sober. Like his sister, Mrs Winstanley, he was very dark—jet-black hair and a round, cheerful, red face—and he always had a halfpenny to spare for Hilda or Lily whenever they saw him. He never kept a job long because for weeks on end he would go on the drink, and when he couldn't buy one for himself there were always plenty who were ready to stand him a pint at *The Black Horse*. His mother felt it keenly that he never went to chapel, but spent the Lord's Day unabashed in the bar of *The Black Horse*, which no woman in Moss Ferry except the landlord's wife had ever seen the inside of. Hilda liked her Uncle Billy in spite of his godless ways, and the awful day when she had seen him being dragged through the white dust by the village policeman to the lock-up burnt itself for all time into her memory. Uncle Billy was fighting drunk that day, and in self-defence and for the honour of his house, the unhappy landlord of *The Black Horse* had been forced to send his wife to ask Ned Taylor, the policeman, to step over and have a word with Billy. Ned Taylor came and tried to reason with the now roaring Billy, who merely looked at him, stupidly, and then hit him flat on the jaw. Ned Taylor saw red. He nipped a pair of handcuffs out of his uniform and tried desperately to get them on Billy's hands. But Billy Buckley fought like a tiger, and though Ned appealed to the men in the bar to lend him a hand not one of them stirred. Not that they had anything against Ned

Taylor, who was only doing his job. But take a hand in getting Billy Buckley to t'lock-up? Not they! Finally the landlord, very shamefaced, offered his help. The handcuffs were slipped on and Ned began to pull his prisoner out of the bar. By this time all Moss Ferry knew what was happening and everybody was standing at their gates to see Billy Buckley took. Grandma Buckley was in a terrible state. She stood by the door of *The Black Horse* crying and twisting her hands and calling shame on her son, and worse shame on the landlord for having served him until he got into such a state. And she solemnly thanked the Lord Billy's father hadn't lived to see this day, and as it was she knew he was even now turning in his grave. And Billy's friends stood around sheepishly, wishing t'owd woman would go on home for she could do no good with her moithering. And then one of them saw Hilda coming up the road and sent her to fetch her mother. Hilda flew up School Lane and into the kitchen. It was a Saturday afternoon and Mrs Winstanley was baking bread, her sleeves rolled up as she pummelled the dough.

"Mother, it's Uncle Billy! Ned Taylor's taking him to t'lock-up and Grandma Buckley's there and won't go away, and Ned Taylor can't get him on to his feet and his head's all cut and bleeding. Jim Entwistle sent me to fetch you. Come on!"

Before her mother could stop her, Hilda was out of the kitchen and racing down to the dreadful scene outside *The Black Horse*. Her Uncle Billy lay on his back in the dusty road, the sun blazing down. Grandma was still crying, and Ned Taylor, aided by the landlord, was exerting all his strength to get the culprit on to his feet. But Billy wouldn't budge. No sooner did they get him up than he slumped back again. He was young and strong and drunker than any man in Moss Ferry had ever been, and though his hands were no use to him he fought with all his body. He kicked out with his heavy boots, he jerked his knees into the policeman's body and savaged like a bull at the landlord's chest. At last they gave up trying to move him on his feet. There was a deep cut on his head, and his face could hardly be recognised for dust and blood. There was froth on his mouth too. His bootlaces had come untied and his thick working jacket was ripped from shoulder to wrist down one sleeve. By this time his sister, Lizzie Winstanley, had arrived and made the first sensible suggestion yet.

"Best thing's to give 'im a sup o' water and then souse 'im wi' it. Throw t'bucket over 'im. It'll freshen him up and make him see plain. Now, Mother, no use taking on that road. Our Billy's a good lad at 'eart. Tha knows that." Then, turning fiercely to the little group of Billy's friends, "What are you all gawping round for as if you wor' crazed? Fetch me t'bucket o' water and bring a cup wi' it. And you go on home wi' Grandma, our 'Ilda. Set her down and make her a cup o' tea. Ah'll go to t'lock-up and see to our Billy, and have a word wi' Mary Ann Taylor."

The water was brought, and Mrs Winstanley knelt down beside the now exhausted Billy and urged him to take a sup.

"Come on, lad. It'll freshen thee up. And let's clean thee up a bit too," and she dipped the corner of her apron into the pail and wiped round the jagged cut in his head. She then flung the rest of the water over his head and face. It was drastic but effective, and after lying there sopping for a few minutes Billy sat up and looked miserably at the policeman, who again began urging him on to his feet.

Billy made a great effort and stood up, swaying top-heavily.

"Aw reet, Ned. Reckon you can tak' these off," and he held out his hands while the policeman solemnly unlocked the handcuffs. Mrs Winstanley took one of Billy's arms and Ned Taylor

24

the other. Lurching and swaying through the village, which looked on silently as though Billy Buckley were going to be hanged, they came to the little, red-brick lock-up which, not within living memory, had had an occupant till this day.

*   *   *

Neither that day, nor for many a day after, was anything talked about in Moss Ferry but Billy Buckley being took to t'lock-up, and how quiet he went after he had come to his senses wi' t'bucket o' water his sister Lizzie had flung over him.

The next day was a Sunday, and the lock-up being conveniently opposite Billy's home, his mother was allowed to go and see him whenever she felt like it and to take in all his meals. Mrs Winstanley had had her word with Mary Ann Taylor, the policeman's wife, and Mary Ann had promised solemnly that everything possible should be done for Billy's comfort while there. He slept heavily all Saturday evening and for the rest of that night, but on Sunday, when Grandma Buckley went in with his breakfast, he was up and washed, and feeling and looking very much ashamed. Mrs Taylor, with her husband's consent, had taken him in an early cup of tea. Both she and Ned liked him, and many a Saturday night Ned had deliberately paced the other way when *The Black Horse* was emptying and Billy Buckley was so drunk that it took half a dozen of his friends to hold him up and get him safely down the village street and plank him on the sofa in his mother's kitchen. Ned would never have laid the hand of the Law on him of his own free will. This had been forced on him and it was as much as he could do to look Billy in the face every time he unlocked the door of the lock-up to let in Grandma Buckley or her daughter. Mrs Winstanley went along Sunday afternoon with a currant loaf for the prisoner's tea and the firm resolve to give him such a talking-to that he'd never, so long as

25

he drew breath, bring such shame on them again. She had a sharp, nagging tongue, but a soft heart with it, and when she saw him so down—looking fair mazed as she put it—all she said was: "How's tha feeling, lad? Ah knows tha likes a taste o' currant bread so Ah've brought thee some. Joe Gibbon's bin having a talk wi' thi mother and he's coming along in t'morning wi' you and Ned to Warrington. He doesna think they'll do much to thee. Ned says it'll be a fine and Mr Gibbon says he'll put t'money down and tha's to pay him back when tha can. Mother's all for coming along, but she gets that moithered reckon she'd best stop 'ome."

"Aye, Lizzie. Dunna let 'er along. And it's reet good o' Joe Gibbon. Reckon Ah can pay 'im a bit every week like. There's not many Ah'd be beholden to as easy as Joe."

Joseph Gibbon was the farmer for whom Joe Winstanley had worked for many years. He was a good man, a great chapel-goer, and always ready to put his hand in his pocket when help was needed. He and his wife had wanted to adopt Hilda as their own when they first set eyes on her as a baby, but the Winstanleys had had her three months by then, and in their simple affection would have kept her out of their own meagre wages rather than let her go. The Gibbons had no children, and neither Lily nor Hilda, whenever they took their father's tea during harvest, ever came home empty-handed. Mrs Gibbon would always find a few eggs she could spare or a piece of home-cured bacon. And at Christmas there was a sovereign for their father, and a new half-crown apiece for Hilda and Lily. Mrs Winstanley, to whom the half-crowns were handed, would wrap each in many layers of paper and stuff it in the very toe of the stocking, among the nuts and little bags of sweets. And all Christmas day the girls would keep stroking and admiring them, and then, when the day was over, reluctantly drop their treasure into the red post office moneyboxes on the mantelpiece—one box scratched with an "L" and the other with an "H". And not till Moss Ferry's greatest day of the year—the annual school outing to Southport or Llandudno or Cleethorpes—would they see the light of day again.

Over his tea Billy consulted earnestly with his sister on the important question of whether he should go to Warrington as he was, in his working corduroys, or in his Sunday best. Lizzie, always a stickler for what was right and proper, said his Sunday best for that would show respect. And on Monday morning, in his stiff Sunday blue serge and black bowler hat and Sunday boots, polished by his mother till she could see her face in them, sitting red and villainous-looking by the side of Ned Taylor, with Mr Gibbon driving the trap, he was taken before the Bench at Warrington, and charged with being drunk and disorderly.

Moss Ferry turned out in force to wish him luck, and even Amelia Starkey, who kept the village store and hated Grandma Buckley like poison, called out encouragingly: "Never 'eed, Billy! Reckon us'll see thee again afore neet. And tha'll be wanting a screw for thi pipe," and with that she threw a great twist of black plug tobacco into the trap and hurried back into her shop, embarrassed by the grateful sniff which Grandma Buckley gave her.

And back before night he was. The magistrate, after hearing the charge, and the testimony of Policeman Taylor and Mr Gibbon that accused was of previous good character but acted mazed when he had had a drop too much, fined him five shillings, which Mr Gibbon promptly paid, Billy to pay it back at the rate of a shilling a week when he was in work again.

Nobody in Moss Ferry ever held it against Ned Taylor for

doing his duty and running Billy Buckley in, but had there been another pub even as far from the village as a three-mile walk, not a man but would rather have walked it than drink his pint again in *The Black Horse*.

*   *   *

Grandma Buckley had other children besides Billy and Lizzie. There was Annie, married to Jim Atkinson who worked on the railway at Kilnbrook and lived next to Cissie Turner. Annie was fair as her sister Lizzie was dark, and, though thin like her mother, she was a cheerful bustling woman and always pleased to see the entire Winstanley family for tea on Sunday before evening chapel. Hilda loved tea at Aunt Annie's, for it was a cheerful kitchen, and there were always jellies and hot potato cakes swimming in butter. She also liked her cousins, Joe and his younger brother, Fred. When tea was over, Aunt Annie would ask her husband to put on the phonograph and they would listen to sacred music until it was time to be off for chapel. Aunt Annie was the only member of the family who had a phonograph. It was an Edison Bell and a source of pride and wonder to all privileged to hear it. It had a great big purple horn that nearly blew you across the room if you got too near it when a record was on. The Winstanleys liked best to hear "Onward Christian Soldiers" or "From Greenland's Icy Mountains to India's Coral Strand", and they would all sing the words so loudly that the kitchen shook and rattled with the noise. Mrs Winstanley would help Aunt Annie to clear the table and wash up in the little lean-to at the back, and Jim Atkinson and Joe Winstanley, the two boys, Joe and Fred, together with Hilda and Lily and their brother Jim, would sit around and thoroughly enjoy themselves. Hilda never remembered her brother John coming to Aunt Annie's, because he was always at Edie's for tea of a Sunday and went with her to the Congregational Chapel in Daneshead afterwards.

And then there was Mrs Winstanley's eldest sister, Aunt Susannah, a tall, gaunt, consumptive woman who had one son, Georgie, and had seen nothing but trouble since she married that flibberty-gibbet of a chap, George Hankinson. Aunt Susannah lived in Manchester, in Ancoats, and did not often come to Moss Ferry because of the fare.· When she did, however, she would stop for quite a bit—sometimes for two and three weeks on end, bringing young Georgie with her, and Hilda would catch her talking earnestly with Grandma or her sister, Lizzie Winstanley, about George's goings-on and how this time she'd sworn never to go back to him, not if he came and asked her on his bended knees. Hilda could never find out properly what it was that her Uncle George had been up to, for whenever Aunt Susannah and her mother were speaking of Uncle George, and she came in unexpectedly, they would stop and look significantly at each other, and Mrs Winstanley would remark: "Little pitchers have big ears."

But Hilda liked her Aunt Susannah, who was smart in her talk and dressed quite differently from the women in Moss Ferry, and she would long for an invitation to go to Ancoats and stop a bit with them. Only Aunt Susannah never asked her. And she always went back in the end to Uncle George, and Grandma Buckley would shake her head and Hilda would overhear bits of talk between Grandma and her mother about Susannah having taken him for better or worse any road, and she was that set on him in spite of his carryings-on that it was no good meddling.

"She'd 'a done better to 'ave stopped i' sarvice," Grandma would say, and Lizzie would agree and give Grandma a warning look if Hilda or Lily came into the kitchen.

Youngest of all Grandma Buckley's family was Emma, who was in service in Warburton. Aunt Emma was at this time going on for thirty and had been walking out ever since Hilda could remember with Fred Rogers, who worked at the foundry in Daneshead with her brother John. Aunt Emma and Fred Rogers had been walking out together for so many years that it came as a thunderbolt to Moss Ferry when the talk got around that they were actually going to be wed at last. The whole Winstanley family was in a state of great bustle and excitement over the wedding, and Hilda and Lily were to go in their white spotted muslin frocks, which they had had new for the Whitsun Walk. Emma and Fred were to be married at the United Methodist Chapel in Kilnbrook by the Reverend Vane, who would be coming back with all the relations to Mrs Winstanley's for tea, Grandma Buckley's kitchen being considered too shabby for such an occasion. Mrs Winstanley scrubbed and polished her front room for days before this event, and Grandma Buckley kept coming over with cakes, and crying and moaning and whining to such an extent that she sounded as if she was preparing for Aunt Emma's funeral instead of her wedding. Joe and Lizzie and the children gave Fred and Emma a tea service for a present, which Mrs Winstanley went specially to Warrington to buy. Grandma Buckley bought them a set of bedroom toilet ware, and Uncle Billy had bought them a hearth rug. Aunt Susannah and Uncle George and young Georgie sent a handsome white marcella quilt (they were not coming to the wedding). Aunt Annie and her family gave them blankets and sheets; while Fred Rogers's family had pooled their resources and bought them a suite in green stamped velvet for the front room.

It was a lovely day for the wedding and the chapel at Kilnbrook was packed, for the whole neighbourhood loved a

wedding or a funeral or a christening. Everybody, including the
bride and bridegroom, walked to the chapel, and Hilda and Lily
sat with their mother and father and Grandma Buckley and Aunt
Annie and family in the front pew. They were all wearing their
Sunday best, and Grandma had a new bonnet with a purple
ostrich feather in it and she never left off crying. Even her other
daughters, Lizzie and Annie, cried a bit too, and Hilda felt quite
tearful herself when she turned round to watch Aunt Emma
coming up the aisle on her brother Billy's arm. Uncle Billy
looked very red and uncomfortable in his Sunday serge, but
Aunt Emma looked a treat. She had a grey cashmere frock with
a finely-tucked white satin front to it, and a white plush hat
with a pale grey ostrich feather curled round it, and Hilda noted
enviously the big gold watch which was pinned on to the front
of her frock with a gold lovers' knot bow. It was Uncle Fred's
wedding present, and that very night Hilda included in her prayers
a passionate request that such a watch might one day be hers.

James Bridge played the harmonium with proper wedding
music and all; Reverend Vane preached a grand sermon about
the duty of husband and wife and how they must help one
another in sickness and in sorrow; and Grandma Buckley kept on
crying and twisting her hands, and Uncle Billy fidgeted and
looked very unnatural. It was the first time for many years that
he had been to chapel, and he felt that all the people behind him
were nudging one another and remembering what had happened
when he was took to the lock-up. Hilda enjoyed every minute
of the sermon. She loved to listen to Reverend Vane's educated,
un-Lancashire voice and followed every word as though her life
depended on it.

When it was over, everybody waited till Fred and Emma had
got out, and then those invited to the wedding tea walked a little

31

behind them. Reverend Vane walked with Grandma Buckley, who was still crying and saying how she was going to miss Emma's bit of money which she had sent home every month, and she only prayed that Fred Rogers would turn out a better chap than that George Hankinson her Susannah had wed. Aunt Emma and Uncle Fred still walked ahead, arm in arm, and presently Mrs Winstanley, excusing herself to Reverend Vane, hurried past with Aunt Annie so as to get the kettle on in good time. Everything had been set out for the tea before Mrs Winstanley left for the chapel, and it was with pardonable pride that she welcomed everyone in and explained that she would na' be a minute brewing the tea. Fred and Emma sat at one end of the table, and the Reverend Vane sat at the other end between Mr and Mrs Winstanley. Hilda and Lily and the Atkinson cousins were at the table under the window, there being no room for them at the big table. Everybody was a bit nervous and tongue-tied first go, on account of Reverend Vane's presence, but he soon cracked a joke with Uncle Fred and then first one and then another loosened up, and by the time Mrs Winstanley was pouring out from one teapot and Aunt Annie from another, all of them, even Joe Winstanley, were talking.

There was a wedding cake—in three tiers—which Aunt Emma's missus, Mrs Dugdale at Warburton, had sent. There was a cold boiled ham and a big pork pie. There were jars of piccalilli and red cabbage and pickled onions. There were big cakes set out on Mrs Winstanley's best glass cake stands. There were several sorts of jellies and tinned fruit, and plates of white bread and butter and currant bread and butter. And when everybody had made a good tea and said politely that they had had an excellent sufficiency and couldn't find room for another mouthful, Mrs Winstanley, looking mysterious and important, went to the cupboard and proudly produced two bottles of port wine. Even the children were given a sip, and they all drank to a long and happy wedded life for Uncle Fred and Aunt Emma. Grandma Buckley was still crying, but in a tired sort of way as if it was too much trouble to stop, and Fred chivvied her and urged her to give over. Emma wasn't dead yet, said Uncle Fred, not by a long chalk she wasn't.

And then Reverend Vane said he must be going or he would miss his train at Kilnbrook. After he had gone, Uncle Fred and Aunt Emma set out for their new home at Daneshead. No one dreamt of such a thing as a honeymoon, for Fred had to be at the foundry next day. When the Wakes came on in August he would take Emma for a trip to Southport or Blackpool or maybe the Isle of Man—just for the day.

CHAPTER III
MORE RELATIONS

It was well known in Moss Ferry that Joe Winstanley's wife couldn't abide her mother-in-law, and so Hilda saw very little of Grandma and Granfer Winstanley, although they lived no more than half-a-mile away in the village. Lizzie's dislike of his mother worried Joe a good deal, for he was an only son and his mother had always done her best by him. It was true she had given him no schooling, but when Joe was a lad there was little schooling to be had anyway by the poor, and ever since he could remember he had always worked. He was no more than seven or eight when he started pea-picking at the farm on the Moss where his father worked; and he used to help at harvest-time and what with one thing and another there had never been any chance, nor, as his mother would say, any call for him to go to school.

Grandma Winstanley was a big, stout woman, good hearted but a slattern. There was always plenty to eat in her house, but Lizzie couldn't abide her slummockiness, and the two women never got on well, though for Joe's sake there was no open warfare. Very occasionally their father would take Hilda and Lily with him of an evening to see his mother and father, and the two girls would be allowed to play at "snap" while their elders talked. And Grandma always made them a mug of cocoa apiece and gave them a sugar "buttey" before they left.

Grandma Winstanley was the first person Hilda had ever seen lying dead, and she could remember going with her father to have a last look before they came to screw her down. She had

34

died naturally—just tired and worn out after her long hard life—
and Hilda was both terrified and astonished when with her father
she tiptoed up the stairs into the front bedroom and there was
Grandma lying so big and so still in her coffin. Her hands were
folded over her breast and she had a penny on each eyelid, which
made her look like a statue. And she didn't seem either old or
young. Her father kissed her and motioned Hilda to do the same,
but she was frightened and drew back and he did not press her.
She did, however, just stroke the folded hands, and shivered at
their icy coldness. Her father did not seem to be very upset
because anyway he was always slow and quiet, and his mother
had lived her time—she was going on for eighty. But when they
were at the bedroom door he looked back and said chokingly:
"Ah'm away now, Mother."

He said it quite loudly, just as he called out to his wife every
morning when he left home at six o'clock for his work: "Ah'm
away now, Mother," and her mother would call back: "Aw reet,
Joe." That was all, but this shouted-out farewell always gave
Hilda the comforting impression of deep, warm affection and she
loved to hear it. She half expected now, and she sensed that her
father felt the same, that the answer would come back from the
coffin: "Aw reet, Joe," but there was only silence, and holding
tightly to her father's hand they went down into the kitchen
where Granfer Winstanley was sitting, all slumped up and
miserable, in his rocking chair by the fire.

Both Hilda and Lily went to the funeral, wearing their white
muslin frocks with broad black sashes, and a black ribbon re-
placing the flowers on their white leghorn hats. And after the
service they all went back to Granfer's for a wakes tea, and just
as her mother had brought out port wine for Aunt Emma's
wedding tea, so Granfer Winstanley produced a bottle of port

wine now, only this time they didn't drink to anybody; it was just part of the funeral tea.

There had been a lot of talk between Joe and Lizzie about what was going to happen now to Granfer, and it was agreed between them that they could manage to find room for him in School Lane. Lizzie knew there was a bit put by and she reckoned Granfer would be able to pay for his keep. She put it to him: "Me and Joe's bin 'aving a talk, Granfer, and tha's allus welcome to come and live wi' us, tha knows. Us can put up a bed i' John and Jim's room. What dost say?"

"Nay, Lizzie. Reckon Ah can go on 'ere for a bit till Ah'm took. Now she's gone it winna be long, and Ah can do for mysen the little bit Ah wants."

*   *   *

Quite unlike Grandma Buckley with her crying, and Grandma Winstanley with her kind heart and untidy ways, was Hilda's real grandmother at Bridge Farm, Grandma Stringer. For she was big and stern and never, from the minute she got up in the morning till she was back in her bed at night, stopped working. She had a large red face that looked as though it were made out of rock, and on one side of her nose was a wart, which gave her an altogether terrifying appearance. But her forbidding looks belied her real nature, which was just as kind as Grandma Winstanley's had been, though her ways were different. She believed in work for everybody, young and old alike, and had brought up a fairly large mixed family of boys and girls on this principle. Satan never found work for idle hands to do at Bridge Farm, for Grandma saw to it that she got there before him; and not until they were all grown up and married did any of her children know what it was to sit comfortably before the fire in the daytime just doing nothing but sit and *be* comfortable. If every household and every farm and dairy task had been finished, then the girls might sit down and knit or sew in the afternoon, but not till tea was cleared did they dare sit down to read.

She had a good-natured, hard-working husband, but it was a sore trial to her that he couldn't keep off the drink. Granfer Stringer would take the produce to market at Patricroft, setting off with many stern injunctions from his wife to behave himself, and to be sure to put the money in the flannel bag which lay under his shirt. And he would set off with a cheerful, assuring, "Aw reet, Mother, never fear! Ah'll not lose a penny on it." And all day Grandma would fret and worry, wondering what he was up to and whether he'd have the gumption not to touch the market money. And every time he would come back, lying dead drunk in the wagon, with the market money safe in the flannel bag and his shirt buttoned up, but not a halfpenny left in his pockets. The horses would bring him home quite safely from Patricroft. Grandma would leave the gates open and sit in the kitchen listening, and sure enough there they were turning in from the road. She would clump out in her clogs, and Roger, her eldest son, would unharness and bed down the horses and help his mother drag his father from the wagon and sit him down to his supper, saying never a word to him, for it was no use to talk to him when he was like that. They would undress him and put him to bed, and Grandma would take the flannel bag and put the money away in the grandfather clock in the parlour— counting it to see that it was right. And the next morning the whole farm would tremble with her wrath, and Granfer would just sit there having his breakfast, ashamed and miserable and silent. He had a sweet nature, and thought there was no woman in Kilnbrook or anywhere else who was a patch on his wife, and he would swear to break himself of the drink. Through many years he swore this solemnly once a week but Grandma would snort and say: "Hold thi noise, do! What's t'good o' such promises? One o' these days tha'll be robbed, just see if tha isna. It's a mercy them horses has got more sense than thysen—great drunken gummut. A nice to-do for t'childer to see their father i' such a way. Why doesna take t'pledge, tha great softy?" And she would clatter about the kitchen, making a terrible noise with her clogs on the beautifully sanded flags. And Granfer would slink out, thankful she'd had her say and swearing to himself that he'd take heed and come home next market-day driving Prince and Jake as sober as a judge.

But he never did till after the awful thing happened—and somehow, somewhere between Patricroft and home, the flannel bag and the forty pounds in it disappeared. Then Grandma Stringer showed the stuff she was made of. When she found the bag gone and had searched his clothes and the wagon and satisfied herself that what she had dreaded for years had indeed happened, she made no reproaches next day. But she took him into the parlour, and placing his hands on the family bible said: "Will, swear on The Book tha'll never touch another drop from this day on to thy dying day," and so urgent was she, and so great his sense of sin and shame, that he promised what she asked. Grandma never once alluded to that lost forty pounds, and it was whispered in Kilnbrook that Will Stringer must ha' met t'Owd Lad himself and been feared out of his life, for he came home these days from Patricroft Market as sober as he went into it.

*　　　　*　　　　*

Grandma Stringer had seen more trouble than most women in Kilnbrook, and her husband's fondness for taking a drop too

38

much was the least of her trials. For out of her family of six children, two boys and four girls, two of the girls, Maggie (Hilda's mother) and Mary Ellen had early come to grief.

Maggie had been working for two years or so as a nursemaid in Warburton. She was small and dark and pretty, and everybody, even when condemning her, admitted to her "taking ways". There were always plenty of the lads eager for a chance to walk out with her, but until she left home to look after Mrs Farringdon's children she had never favoured anybody but George Huntley, who worked at Bridge Farm for her father. George was a good enough workman, but a good workman was one thing and a son-in-law another, and Mrs Stringer was bitterly disappointed that Maggie did not take up with one of the farmer's sons in the neighbourhood. There was Tom Hodson, at Risley Farm, who was set on the girl, and a nice enough lad too with a good healthy farm coming to him one of these days. Grandma pointed out these advantages to her daughter, stressing the important fact that Tom would be his own master should anything happen to Isaac Hodson and his wife. But Maggie would have none of him. She would listen to her mother resentfully, and finally announce that she'd take George Huntley or nobody, and where was the shame of being a farm labourer any road. Except that George was hired he did no different work from Tom Hodson, and he wouldn't always be hired either, for some day he planned, if she married him, to take her out to Canada and work up to a farm of his own. Grandma Stringer had made up her mind many a time to have a word with her husband about getting shut of George, but she was a good woman and a just woman, and when it came to the point she would feel that mean inside herself that she never approached Will openly on the matter. And any road, she argued to herself, it might be the very worst thing they could

39

do, for Maggie was turned twenty and once she'd got a thing into her head there was no getting it out again, and she'd walk out and be after George so soon as look at you. And that wouldn't do nobody any good, Grandma reflected sagely. If Maggie meant to take him, better let them wait and save a bit and have it all square and straight. She and Will might even manage enough to set them up in a little place of their own, for George could pay back, and the idea of letting a girl of hers go to Canada was something that didn't stand thinking about. Foreign parts was no place for a decently brought up girl to be off to.

When Maggie told her mother that Mrs Farringdon of Mount Pleasant, Warburton, wanted a girl as nursemaid for her two young children, and she'd like to have a try for it, to her surprise her mother said why not? She'd never been away from home and it couldn't do her any harm, and if she didn't like it she could always come back. So Maggie went to Warburton, and Mrs Farringdon took to her and it was settled that she should have the place. Grandma Stringer was pleased too, for Warburton was a tidy distance off and Maggie wouldn't be seeing so much of George Huntley, and who knows, thought Grandma hopefully, but what it'll come to nowt even yet. So Maggie took the job and it was understood that she would be home once a month, on her whole day out.

She liked the work of looking after the children and soon became a great favourite in the Farringdon household. On her days at home she had her mother and her sister Lucy listening eagerly as she described the style Mrs Farringdon and her family lived in, and the company that was always coming over from Manchester and Birkdale and Southport for the weekend. Sometimes they even had people from as far off as London. Mrs Stringer and Lucy were astonished—somebody fresh seemed to

be there every week. Mrs Farringdon sometimes made Maggie
a little present of a blouse or a hat, hardly worn as Maggie would
point out proudly; and though Grandma Stringer thoroughly
disapproved of a girl of hers wearing what she called "cast-offs",
she had to admit that Maggie knew how to carry a bit of style.
Not that there was anything wrong with the clothes her mother
bought her. Grandma was no believer in "shoddy", and when
the girls had a new frock she saw to it that the stuff was good;
she would make a special trip to Manchester for it, and in her
black bonnet and heavy sequined black velvet cape, was a formid-
able figure at the dress-material counter of Lewis's in Market
Street. The young man serving would take great pains in showing
her many rolls of cloth, and she would finger them for a long
time, and ask innumerable questions as to their serviceability
before deciding. If it was for a winter frock she would, in order
to satisfy herself that it was "nowt but wool", request the
assistant to snip a bit off and apply a match: if it wouldn't burn
then it was wool all right and not "shoddy", and Grandma
would give her order. If the material was for summer frocks she
demanded an assurance that it would wash and not ruck up under
the iron, and in spite of her country speech and downright ways
she was always given good service. Mrs Weatherhead, the dressmaker in Kilnbrook, always "made" for Mrs Stringer and her
girls, but Mrs Farringdon had everything made at Kirby Nicholson's in St Ann's Square, and of course everybody knew that
was one of the best shops in Manchester. Nobody could touch
them for style, and Maggie Stringer, coming home in one of
Mrs Farringdon's frocks, looked very different from what she
did in a frock of Mrs Weatherhead's making.

Gradually Mrs Stringer began to notice that Maggie was
altering in her ways. She was getting finicky, and to look at her

hands you'd think they were those of a lady. And her talk was altering too—getting soft and what her father would jokingly call la-di-da. Her mother sometimes felt uneasy and, apparently apropos of nothing, would say sternly: "Dunna you ever be nobbut a good girl, Maggie Stringer. We've brought you up decent, and decent you stop."

But Maggie would only laugh at her mother's solemn face and chaff her: "Oh, go on with you, Mother! What's to do now? The gentry's just the same as us, at bottom. No harm to them. Would Mrs Farringdon let me have to do with the children if I wasn't decent?"

There was no getting round this important fact and for a time Mrs Stringer was reassured, but she confided to her husband that she didn't hold with their Maggie's altering ways. Gentry was gentry and farm folk was farm folk, and there was no way over that as she could see.

"Dunna worrit yourself, Mother. Our Maggie's all right. She's a good girl."

"She'd better be," snapped Mrs Stringer, "after the way we've brought her up and all."

*   *   *

It was on Maggie's next day at home that her mother began to feel vaguely frightened and uneasy that all was not as it should be. She looked, as Mrs Stringer put it, "moithered." She couldn't get hold of anything definite, for Maggie was as cheerful and bright as ever, but her mother was not deceived. "There's summat wrong Will," she confided to her husband when Maggie had gone back to Warburton. "Reckon she'd best come home again. We can do with her here, any road. No call for her to be working for other folks if she doesna like it. Tha'd best stop

42

off on t'road to Warrington next market-day and have a word wi' Mrs Farringdon. Tell her our Maggie's wanted at home and she's to come back when her month's up. I'll write to Maggie about it."

Even to her husband Mrs Stringer felt she could not say outright what her worst fears were, but when Maggie came home at the end of the month she began to watch. There was one way—one certain way—of finding out what she dreaded to know. Maggie knew it too. She couldn't hide from her mother any longer that she would not need those thick squares of Turkish towelling for some time to come: it was for these that her mother had been on the look-out. No need to wait till it showed in her figure, though it wouldn't be long now before that happened, too—pull in her stays as tightly as she could.

Mrs Stringer tackled her quite quietly about it as they sat alone one afternoon sewing in the kitchen. "Reckon tha'd best out wi' it, Maggie. We've got to tell thi father and see what's best to be done. He'll be that cut up. I never thought a child of mine would bring such shame on us. We shanna be able to 'old up our 'eads again. Who is it? Will he wed thee?"

Mrs Stringer could not have explained how she knew it was not George Huntley who was responsible for Maggie's condition, but she did know and took it for granted that her daughter had been "led away" by one of the "gentry" at Mrs Farringdon's. Poor Maggie confirmed this and made it quite plain to her mother that there was no question of him marrying her. He had offered to help her with money, but at this information Mrs Stringer snorted: "Reckon 'e can keep his brass. That winna undo t'trouble. Well, summat's got to be done. I never bargained for *asking* George Huntley to marry a daughter o' mine, but that's the way on it now. If he's willing, you can both live wi' us till

43

t'child is born. Then you'd best be off to Canada if George is still set on it. I'll have a talk wi' thi father. Reckon we can manage enough to set you on your feet there. And give over crying, do. It canna be mended now. If George winna have you I don't know what's to do—time enough for crying then."

Mrs Stringer had to summon all her pride to tackle George, for though he knew she had nothing against him as her husband's workman, he knew too that she had looked higher for Maggie than a common labourer. But she made no bones about it once she got going. She told him the plain fact—that Maggie had been led away—that the chap was no good—and well, there it was. Was their Maggie good enough for him now, and would he father the child? She told him of their plans for helping the pair of them away to Canada and setting him up there on a bit of land of his own.

George didn't hesitate. He was sorry for Mrs Stringer for he knew what it had cost her to go practically on her knees to him, but he knew too that Maggie wouldn't end her days unwed. There were plenty of chaps willing to take her, good or bad.

He nodded assent. "Reckon she's not the first in Kilnbrook to be led away, but I'd like to get my boot on t'chap as did it. She's nobbut twenty, when all's said and done. Ay, I'll wed her if she thinks she can settle down along o' me. There wouldna be any but Maggie for me, any road."

And so there was another wedding at the United Methodist Chapel in Kilnbrook, and Mrs Stringer put a brave face on it and saw to it that everything was done properly. There was a slap-up tea for all who liked to come to it. Folks would know soon enough that Maggie Stringer had *had* to get wed, but thanks to George Huntley they wouldn't know anything else. She could still go to chapel and hold up her head, since it was accounted no

shame in Kilnbrook for a child to be begotten out of wedlock—
the shame was when there was no wedding to follow. That was
something almost unknown—something that didn't stand thinking
about. When a girl took to walking out with a chap it was taken
for granted that it was for good; that it would end in the only
proper way—at the altar. Nobody minded much how soon after
the wedding the child was born. Folks talked a lot, of course, and
nobody in Kilnbrook or Moss Ferry or Daneshead would ever
forget the famous occasion when Nellie Stubbs and Joe Dumbell
got wed in the afternoon and the baby was born that very night.
Nellie had stood there getting married with a stomach as big as
a load of hay, and nobody thought any the worse of her. It was
the excitement of the wedding that brought her on before her
time, and there wasn't a napkin so much as hemmed for the baby.
When the news got round that Nellie Stubbs's baby had arrived
and she hadn't had gumption enough to get a stitch ready, there
was a great rummaging in chests of drawers, and it was not
many hours before Nellie's baby was given more clothes than it
would ever be likely to wear out. But they came in handy, for
Nellie had one child close upon another, and though folk still
nudged each other when they saw her getting big as regular as
clockwork, and recalled what a near go she had had with her first,
there was no more respected chapel-goer in Kilnbrook than
Mrs Joseph Dumbell.

So the talk was no more than usual when Maggie Stringer,
now Mrs George Huntley, had her baby only five months after
her wedding, and had the child not cost poor Maggie her life,
nobody in Kilnbrook would have dared whisper that "it wor not
George Huntley's at all—summat had happened when Maggie
Stringer was in service at Warburton". For within three months
of Maggie's death, George Huntley, secret as the grave, went off

to Canada, and it was argued, though never openly, that no
decent chap would do a thing like that—go off and leave his own
flesh and blood to be reared by others. Grandma Stringer too
was secretly criticised for putting the child out to nurse. Folks
said she couldn't abide it and the talk got around that she and
Will Stringer had actually paid George's fare out to Canada, and
that, said Kilnbrook, was as good as proof positive that the child
was none of his getting. The gossip reached Grandma, but she
and her husband kept their own counsel. She had put the baby
out to nurse because, energetic though she was, she was past
fifty and felt she couldn't cope with the upbringing of another
child, and Lucy, the one daughter now at home, might well not
always remain single. She and Will gravely consulted together
on what was best to be done, and settled on asking Joe and
Lizzie Winstanley to bring it up. They would be paid five
shillings a week till it was old enough to earn its own living,
and Mrs Stringer would find it in clothes. Grandma stipulated
that they should rear it as their own for as long as they could.
Although she would never have admitted it, her commonsense
told her that some day it would be bound to find out, from
some busybody or other, that it was not a Winstanley. People
could talk as much as they liked, reflected Grandma, but none
would ever know for certain the truth about its begetting. Let
them clack. With George Huntley in foreign parts and not likely
to return, none could put a name to anything, and they couldn't
hurt poor Maggie any road.

*   *   *

Of Grandma Stringer's other children only Roger, her eldest,
and Lucy, walking out with Peter Morgan, remained at home.
There was Bella, married to a prosperous farmer over at Lymm,

46

with a young family around her and never occasioning her mother a moment's uneasiness. Bella was the ugly duckling of the family, but she was so good tempered and so kind hearted that nobody ever noticed her long, plain, horse-like face. And there was the beauty of the family, prettier even than Maggie had been, the eldest girl, Mary Ellen, married so unhappily that her mother, whenever she learnt the dread news that "another" was expected, almost hoped that Mary Ellen, like Maggie, would not get over it. Mary Ellen and her husband, Jonah Turton, and their continually increasing family, were so poor, owing to Jonah's liking for the drink, that they lived in a squalid, unhealthy, four-roomed hovel that nearly used to break Mrs Stringer's heart every time she entered it. Jonah earned good wages driving a traction engine for a firm of contractors at Daneshead, but when not at work he was hardly ever sober, and had it not been for her mother, Mrs Turton and the children would, many a time, have gone hungry.

Mary Ellen was the one member of Grandma Stringer's family in Kilnbrook that Hilda Winstanley really liked, and whenever Mrs Turton saw her passing she would warmly invite her to come and have a sit-down. Hilda, because of her liking for this as yet unfathomed aunt of hers, usually responded to the invitation, though the living room was so untidy and smelly that she was always glad to get out again. Children seemed to swarm everywhere. There was Sammy, the eldest boy, and, as Mrs Winstanley used to say, as nice a lad as ever drew breath. Then there was Janey, pretty and fair like her mother; then Martha, also a little beauty, and after her came the boy and girl twins, Rosie and Josiah. Sammy was his mother's favourite, and knowing this his father, when in drink and wanting to take it out of his wife, would, for no reason, beat him unmercifully. Jonah was a great, black-

47

looking fellow, and Hilda could never forget one awful Saturday afternoon when she had gone in there with Janey, and Mrs Turton had pressed her to stop for tea. Jonah sat at the table still in his dirt; filthy shirt open at the neck and showing his sweaty, hairy chest. Mrs Turton was bustling about the table, setting out what seemed to Hilda a very poor, very unappetising tea. Cracked cups without matching saucers; everything very coarse and the white american cloth stained with the remains of many previous meals. Sammy was sitting one side of his father with Janey next to him, while the younger children were spread around Hilda, who was not enjoying her tea one bit and wishing she could get away. Janey, turning round to take something from her mother, lurched against her brother, and Sammy could not save himself from jogging his father, who at that moment was drinking his tea. The scalding tea was spilt all down his naked chest and he let out a yell of rage like some wild beast. Hilda was watching Sammy. He went very white and the tears came into his eyes. Mrs Turton ran and snatched him to her, but Jonah seized him as though he were a rag doll, and unbuckling his heavy leather belt, beat him as though he were indeed made of rags and not soft young flesh at all. Sammy's screams were dreadful, and Hilda felt that they must surely be heard in Moss Ferry, half-a-mile away. Mrs Turton stood there like someone demented. The tears were pouring down her cheeks, and each time she made a desperate effort to stop that heavy hand her husband struck out savagely at her, bawling: "Tha can have some too if tha wants it."

She seized Janey, who, like the other children, sat cowering, and screamed at her husband: "Leave him be! He couldna help it. She did it! Give her some too! She did it I tell thee." And she pushed the terrified girl towards her father. To Hilda, sitting there ashamed and frightened on the sofa, it seemed a cruel thing to do, but she could not know that it was the only way to stop the beast. For of all his children Janey was the one, the only one, for whom her father had any tenderness. He let go of Sammy, and looking at his shrieking, half-mad wife, put Janey over his great knees and, with his hand this time, gave her a couple of smacks. Janey screamed, but she could not have been much hurt, and Sammy was free. He ran, shivering and whimpering like a puppy, to his mother.

Jonah, looking pleased with himself, buckled on his belt and sat down to finish his tea. Mrs Turton pressed more tea on Hilda, but she couldn't touch it. She felt sick and miserable. Apart from the lunatic rages of the schoolmaster with some of the children at school, she had never before witnessed such a savage scene. She got frequent boxes on the ear and smacks over the head from her mother, but never anything really serious, while her father had never once touched any of them. This was something utterly unknown. Jonah Turton, when he was beating Sammy, hadn't looked like a man at all. She didn't know what he did look like; she sat there paralysed with fear, itching to edge her way round the table and out to her own clean, kind, comfortable home.

She never went into Mrs Turton's again, but she never passed the cottage without feeling slightly sick as she remembered how she had left it that Saturday tea-time. Jonah Turton sitting there guzzling down his tea, all dirty with his work on the engine. Sammy whimpering against his mother. Mrs Turton, white and daft-looking, with her arms around him. Janey crying on the sofa, and the smaller children sitting hunched and frightened on the hearth rug; the squalid table, the general slummockiness, and the atmosphere heavy with evil which Jonah seemed to exude. It was a picture that burnt into her consciousness—a picture complete and framed that time never overlaid.

It was when she heard of things like this that poor Grandma Stringer wished Mary Ellen was out of it. She could not have her daughter and all those children at the farm, but for weeks at a time she had Sammy to stay with her so as to keep him out of his father's reach. And she kept the family supplied with milk and eggs and butter, and Hilda often saw her taking a great basket of newly baked loaves to the Turton's cottage. And many a time she paid the rent and set the children up in boots and clothes, for sometimes Jonah would stop away from home altogether, and but for her mother there would have been nothing in front of Mrs Turton but parish relief. Grandma Stringer up to now had always managed to save her from that final humiliation and disgrace.

One night Mary Ellen went to the farm and begged her mother and father and Roger to go back with her. Jonah was fighting drunk and she had locked the children in the back bedroom and slipped out. He had beaten her and she was fearful for her life; fearful too of what he might do to the children. They went back with her, to find Jonah lying on the sofa so dead drunk that nothing, seemingly, would ever waken him again. But Grandma Stringer woke him. She asked her daughter for a stout sheet and a darning needle and strong thread. While they stood around wondering what she was up to, she unbuckled that cruel strap. Then, with the men's help, she got the sheet underneath the unconscious Jonah, and firmly sewed him up, looking as though she wished it were his shroud. She sewed him up so tightly that he could not move hand or foot, and then, taking the strap, she set about him. She beat him till, in his agony, he rolled off the sofa on to the flagged floor, but still she struck at him. She went on and on—only stopping for a second to get her breath. He screamed for mercy. But still she went on. He was very much awake by this time and begged for help from his wife, from his father-in-law, and from Roger. But Grandma ordered them fiercely not to lift a hand. This was her job and she'd see it through. By gum, she would. The heavy brass buckle of the strap cut into Jonah's face and he was bleeding freely, but Grandma paid no heed. Mrs Turton, terrified that her mother would kill him, pleaded with her to give over, but Mrs Stringer was demoniac. Again and again and yet again she brought down the strap.

"That'll larn thee, Jonah Turton, to treat my girl like a dog. And her childer. And if ever tha lays a hand on her again, or on t'childer, Ah'll not answer for what happens to thee. Happen tha knows now what t'strap tastes like. And if tha doesna behave thyself from now on happen Ah can allus give thee a bit more, and Ah will too or my name's not Martha Stringer. Best get some water, Mary Ellen, and we'll give him a clean-up."

The two women set him free and tidied him up. Grandma Stringer tied on her bonnet and put on her grey woollen shawl that she always wore on weekdays, and facing him squarely repeated her threats.

"Tha're nobbut a great bully, Jonah Turton; reckon *Ah'm* not afeared o' thee. So put that in thi gullet and swallow it. And dunna you mind him, our Mary Ellen. If he touches thee again we'll have t'law on him as well—that'll larn him to mend his manners. Let's away, Will and Roger. Reckon she'll be all right now, or he'll answer to me for it."

And she stalked out, leaving her son-in-law sore and aching and, as she sensed he would be, very frightened. This was something she'd itched to do for years. She felt quite sure in her own mind that he'd never dare misbehave himself again. He was a bully nobody until now had had the gumption to stand up to, for although her husband and son had many a time wanted to give him a good hiding, they had always held back for fear it would be worse in the end for Mary Ellen.

Her instinct proved right, for though Jonah still drank heavily, still stopped mysteriously away from home for weeks together while Mrs Stringer practically kept the family in food, there were no more thrashings. Jonah would sit there sullenly, cursing his wife and cursing too that "owd gummut", her mother, and hinting darkly that he'd show 'em—the whole bloody lot—one o' these fine days; but for some time that was as far as it went. Eventually he disappeared for good—gave up his job at Daneshead and went to Manchester, people said. The three elder children were by then old enough to earn—Sammy on his grandfather's farm and the two girls in service—and Mary Ellen, with the bit these children were able to give, and the odd days she went out lending a hand here and there, and a plentiful supply of good food from the farm, lived her life in peace.

CHAPTER IV
MOSS FERRY

Moss Ferry was a small village, with only one street about half a mile long in which were the shops and most of the houses. The buildings faced the main Manchester road, and running down from the other side of the road were meadows which sloped to the River Mersey. This street had no name. It was known simply as "T'street".

The chief centre of interest in The Street was Mrs Amelia Starkey's general shop. Mrs Starkey was short, fat, dark, quick tempered but good natured, and she sold everything from paraffin oil to black treacle and jewel-studded back combs. Every child in the village always went willingly on an errand to Amelia Starkey's, for she never failed to give each one a sweet. At Christmas she made several enormous trays of black treacle toffee, which she kept in the lean-to outside along with the drums of paraffin, and occasionally a spurt of paraffin went over the toffee, but the children never minded this. At Christmas-time the child of every customer was taken into the lean-to and given a thick slab of the famous toffee wrapped up in newspaper. It was the best treacle toffee in Moss Ferry, and in spite of her long-standing feud with Grandma Buckley, Mrs Starkey always gave Hilda and Lily a very big slab indeed on account of Hilda's deep friendship with Elsie Entwistle, who was Mrs Starkey's favourite niece.

Mrs Starkey was important too because she was the mother of Annie Starkey, who was acknowledged by all to be the gradeliest-looking young woman in the district, and dressed

6

herself so smartly that to look at her you'd never think she had made the frocks herself.

One day the news got about that at the dance in the Reading Room that night Annie Starkey was to wear a wonderful new frock. It was a fancy-dress dance and of course only for grown-ups, but Hilda, who felt she would never sleep until she had seen this frock, begged her mother to let her go down to the Reading Room for a peep. Mrs Winstanley, who was as interested as herself in the wonder, agreed, and with Lily also they went down the lane and peered through the open door at the dance, which was in full swing. Presently they saw Annie, and she looked lovely—"a fair treat and no mistake" commented Mrs Winstanley admiringly. Annie had gone as "Winter" and her frock was of bright, moss-green velveteen, the full, swinging skirt edged round with white swansdown, which also trimmed the high neck and the wrists. And dotted here and there all over the frock were little puffs of swansdown with a glistening red bead in the centre to represent holly against the snow. On her bright auburn hair was a wreath of swansdown and real holly leaves with berries. The three of them, standing now unlawfully just inside the room, stared in wonder. Presently they were joined by others until quite a crowd had gathered, and even Joe, wondering what had happened to his missing family, came down and had a look. Everyone agreed that there was nobody in Moss Ferry to touch Amelia Starkey's lass for smartness, and nobody was surprised when "Winter" was given first prize—a silver-plated cake stand. Nobody noticed what the other fancy dresses even looked like, so startling was "Winter"—such a swirl of glowing colour in the lamp-lit Reading Room.

Mrs Starkey had also other claims to importance, for there was great excitement throughout the village when it became known that her cousin from America was coming to stop with her for a bit. Hilda knew all about America from her brother John's Sunday School prize, *From Log Cabin to White House*, and she was intensely eager to see this stranger from the other side of the world. She ran many an errand to the shop, but never seemed to see him, and he did not appear to go out much, or else he only went out when she was at school. But one afternoon, at tea-time, her mother sent her to get some barm for the bread-making next day, and coming in from the living-room to serve her, Mrs Starkey, as though divining Hilda's wish, left the door between shop and room wide open, and while she was waiting for the barm to be weighed Hilda was able to get a good look at the man from America. He sat at the table in his shirt sleeves, but it wasn't a working-man's shirt he wore. It was a soft, white shirt, and Hilda noted eagerly that he had pale blue elastic bands on the sleeves to keep them up. Also she watched him begin to eat his egg and was astonished at what she saw. He did not slice off the top, but tapped it with his spoon, and then picked off pieces of shell and put them on the side of his plate. He then did an even more astounding thing, and Hilda felt herself shaking with anxiety lest Mrs Starkey should finish serving her too soon. Instead of eating his egg out of the shell, like anyone in Moss Ferry would do, he emptied it into a cup, put a big knob of butter on top, added salt and pepper, stirred it vigorously, and spooned it up slowly and with evident relish. Hilda noticed that he had soft-looking hands, not working hands, and altogether he was an entrancing sight. Fancy eating an egg that road, and having pale blue bands on his sleeves too! Mrs Starkey now gave her the barm and Hilda paid, bursting to be off home to tell what she had seen. By next day everybody was talking about the man from America and his pale blue sleeve bands, and his unnatural way with a plain boiled egg, and for weeks Mrs Starkey's shop was invaded just about tea-time by Hilda's playmates, all praying that Mrs Starkey would leave the door open and that the man from America would be taking an egg to his tea and sitting in his shirt sleeves.

Besides Mrs Starkey's big shop, there was Fanny Wright's parlour-shop, where for one penny you could buy a whole quarter of a pound of American gums, and where also it was possible to get a ha'porth or even a penn'orth of sweets on credit. But Mrs Wright only allowed such generous terms to trusted customers, and then only to make sure of getting their regular Saturday trade, for her rival, Mrs Starkey, never allowed credit to any but grown-ups. Mrs Wright's was known as "the parlour-shop" because she had simply turned her front room into a shop, and she only sold sweets and, on Saturday nights, fish and chips.

The little room was crowded to suffocation on fish-and-chip night, for fish and chips was a real treat, and though you mightn't be able always to afford fish, it was wonderful to get a ha'porth of chips in a three-cornered bag, sprinkle them freely with salt and vinegar, and dawdle home, savouring them slowly so as to make them last as long as possible.

Mrs Wright had a rival in the fish-and-chip trade: Annie Cooney, who had also turned her front room into a shop. Mrs Cooney, however, sold nothing but fish and chips—fish on Saturday nights only, and chips every night of the week. Between them they did a roaring trade, though Mrs Wright was the wealthier of the two on account of the American gums and the credit system.

There was only one other shop which the children patronised. This was a proper sweet and cake shop kept by two maiden ladies, whose great speciality was marzipan potatoes any one of which *might* contain a threepenny piece. They were a halfpenny each and once Hilda found a threepenny bit in hers, but once only throughout many years. The effect of getting it was so stimulating, however, that she bought a marzipan potato every week of her childhood after that, dividing her Saturday penny between the marzipan potato and two ounces of Mrs Wright's American gums, for she felt she must have some compensation for expending a whole halfpenny on her weekly gamble with the marzipan. If it had not been for the financial possibilities of the potatoes, none of the children would have patronised the Miss Askells's shop. They were a pair of cold, uninterested ladies who kept themselves very much to themselves and led a mysterious life of their own in the dark parlour behind the shop. Nobody could ever find out where they originally came from, and in extenuation of their stand-offishness it was rumoured that they had come down in the world. They had none of the cheerful friendliness of Fanny Wright or Amelia Starkey or Mrs Cooney, and relied mostly on passers-by for their trade. But in spite of their reserve they kept the shop going, and although Hilda remembered them as always having been there selling cakes and marzipan potatoes and aniseed balls at sixteen a penny, neither she nor any other child ever stopped a second in the shop once the transaction was accomplished.

Then there was Mr Raike, the butcher, with his big tree trunk of a chopping block, and on Saturday mornings Mr Raike sold hot pease pudding—a tremendous great slab for a penny—and hot faggots at a halfpenny each. Mrs Winstanley used to assert that Mr Raike made the faggots out of the bits he chipped off the block, but she would always let Hilda and Lily buy a faggot apiece and a basin of pease pudding for their Saturday dinner. Saturday was her day for baking bread and she had no time for other cooking. The kitchen on that day was very pleasant to be in, with the big bowl of dough rising in front of the fire, and the smell of the loaves as she tipped them out of the oven. And for tea she would make teacakes while the oven was "right", and they would have these split open with butter or golden treacle on them. Mr Raike also made black puddings shaped like horseshoes, but the children seldom got more than a taste of these as they cost tuppence apiece, and made a tasty tea for their father once a week. Mrs Winstanley used to pop them into the oven to hot up, and with a baked potato they made a nourishing and appetising meal.

There was also a boot-and-shoe shop—quite a big, handsome place with a real plate-glass window. Hilda had been in it once or twice, but only to buy thick leather laces for the heavy boots her father and brothers wore to work. When new boots were wanted, Mrs Winstanley would make this the excuse for a Saturday night out at Daneshead. Daneshead was a fair-sized place and had lamps in the street and quite a lot of big shops, including the Co-op. with the library which Hilda visited once a week. Also Aunt Emma and Uncle Fred had lived at Daneshead since their wedding, and were always glad to have Lizzie and the children pop in for a cup of tea.

In the village there was a cobbler too—Tom Holroyd—whose wooden leg went clump, clump, clump over the stones. And it was a continual joke among the children how Mrs Armstead, who did the Holroyd's washing and was a bit simple in the head, was always getting moithered because Tom Holroyd never seemed to have a real pair of stockings to be washed. The cheekiest of them would shout after her: "Found t'other stocking yet, Mrs Armstead?" and then run for life out of her reach.

Tom Holroyd had a grown-up daughter, Maudie, who had passed all her examinations and was now a teacher in the village school. And he had too a well-educated son, married and with two children, with a good job under the Government in India. These two children, with their mother, once spent over three years in Moss Ferry and came to the village school. They openly despised it, but they were not old enough to travel alone to Manchester or Warrington. Hilda had a passionate envy of both girls because of their ladylike ways and superior clothes. They wore sailor suits of fine navy-blue serge and sailor hats with H.M.S. Ramillies on them, and thin, black cashmere stockings and refined-looking black shoes even on weekdays. Hilda was never bought anything but strong, laced boots for weekdays and buttoned kid boots for Sundays; it was not until she was thirteen that Mrs Winstanley, in a moment of weak affection, let her have her own way and bought her a pair of brown kid shoes for Sundays. She was even prouder of this first pair of shoes than she had been of her "lady's companion", for this she could only show off in the house, whereas her shoes were visible to all when she walked to chapel. She wore them for several Sundays before venturing to disturb their newness with anything but a duster, and then she read in one of Mrs Entwistle's novelettes that banana skin was the best thing to clean brown leather with. But her mother said no—bananas were not easy to come by—best to get some proper brown polish at the bootshop at Daneshead—penny a tin.

And having started a minor revolution with the shoes, the next thing she longed for passionately was a pair of kid gloves, for up to now she had worn either cotton gloves or mittens in the summer, and then only of course on Sundays, and thick warm woollen gloves knitted by her mother in the winter. But here Mrs Winstanley was adamant.

"Kid gloves, indeed! Whatever next! Reckon tha'll have to wait a bit afore I buys kid gloves for childer. Besides, they winna wash. Now give over moithering, our 'Ilda. No use keeping on about it. Ah've said 'no' and Ah *means* 'no'."

But Hilda persisted tirelessly. She had got her brown shoes through worrying, and she would get her kid gloves the same way. Her whole forces were now concentrated on the acquisition of a pair of real buttoned kid gloves. She used even to try to get Lily to cry for kid gloves too, but Lily snapped at her and said she didn't care what she wore and why didn't she give over about it.

Hilda jeered at her. "No, *you'd* never look like a lady if you had hundreds of pairs of kid gloves to wear—you fat lump you. Mardy, mardy, tell-tale, sausage fingers."

Lily showed unexpected spirit. "Reckon Ah dunna *want* to look like a lady if it means looking like you, our Hilda. And you've no call to go giving yourself airs. Reckon you'll have to work same as anybody else when you leave school, and you canna work in kid gloves that Ah know of."

But Hilda got the gloves all the same as a Christmas present from Grandma Stringer. When Lucy Stringer came to pay the money at the end of November and inquired confidentially of Mrs Winstanley what Hilda would most like to find in her stocking, Mrs Winstanley mentioned the worrying time she had been having over the gloves. She explained that it wasn't that she didn't want Hilda to have them, seeing she was so set on them, but that they were not serviceable; a Christmas box, however, was different. So it was agreed that Grandma Stringer would buy the kid gloves for Hilda and Mrs Winstanley another pair for Lily, so there should be no jealousy. Hilda was wild with excitement over them. They were soft, dark brown nappa and fastened with two buttons, and she wore them, as in the case of the brown kid shoes, for Sundays only. In the winter they did not keep her hands warm like the woollen ones, but this did not matter as she had a lovely fur muff (Grandma Stringer's present the previous Christmas), and she loved the smooth shape of her hands in the new gloves when she held up her hymn-book, and hoped passionately that the Reverend Vane had noticed them as well as everybody else in chapel.

*　　　　*　　　　*

The country round Moss Ferry was flat and green and un-interesting—just plain wide fields with no woods and few trees to break the dullness—but it was redeemed from downright ugliness by the view to be had when looking over towards Cheshire, which was well wooded and slightly hilly. There was also the River Mersey which ran at the bottom of the fields that spread away below the village and formed the boundary between Lancashire and the softer, greener, mistier Cheshire. Moss Ferry was proud of the fact that it was the Mersey itself—a real, God-made river—that flowed at the bottom of its fields, rather than the straight, cold, man-made Manchester Ship Canal, of which the rest of the county was so proud. Quite important ships sailed up the Mersey—ships with big funnels and queer, gay, foreign flags, and if you stood in the village street you would see the ships go sailing up the river, looking as though they were gliding effortlessly straight through the fields, for the river itself could not be seen because of its steep banks.

The village children used to bowl their hoops down the long straight high road that ran out of the village parallel with the river, and one of the most exciting things that could happen on a cold winter's day was to be lucky enough to be out with a hoop when a ship was coming up river, for then the children would form themselves into a row, like race-horses at the starting-point, and at the word "Go" the race with the ship would begin, and it was considered shameful to let the vessel ever get for a moment ahead. Hilda had an iron hoop with an iron hooked stick, though the better-off children had wooden hoops and wooden sticks, and the wooden hoops were more exciting to manage as they bounced along so lightly that it required great skill and agility to keep up with them. But the wooden hoops wore out in time, whereas the iron ones, which were made by the local blacksmith, lasted from generation to generation, and outlived by many lives the ships they had so often raced.

Hilda and Lily and Queenie and Elsie Entwistle and Alfie Hogben and Susy Hodgson and Lily Gibbon and the school-master's many daughters would sometimes, in school playtime, agree to meet at a given point on the road on a Saturday morning with their hoops. They would wait patiently for a ship to appear and then the big race would start, and sometimes last for nearly an hour. They would race through the village street, away past the Wilverton Bridge and beyond it for a mile or so until the winner was well ahead of the vessel, and then, if they were very lucky, there might be an equally exciting race back to the starting-point with a ship coming down the river. Hilda's and Lily's iron hoops had been raced by their brothers hundreds of times; they were worn to a thin, smooth brightness and flashed along like the rim of a new moon. Their hooked iron sticks shone with an equal lustre.

Winter or summer this was the most exciting, most energetic game played in Moss Ferry, but they all liked it best in winter—the colder and bleaker the day the more fun they got out of it. Sometimes the more adventurous of them, after the race, would go down the fields to the river itself, although this was forbidden ground to every child in the village. Hilda and her special friend, Elsie Entwistle, had a small private piece of river bank to themselves, and they would clamber at great peril down this until they were on a flat strip of sandy soil by the water's edge. As the ships sailed past, it was very stirring to watch the waves lapping up the banks; and one day the sailors on a big foreign ship waved to them and laughed and shouted unintelligible words and then flung a great bunch of bright green bananas on to the bank. They had never seen green bananas until then and tried to eat one, but found it hard and bitter. They dared not take the bunch home and so give away where they had been. There was no place to hide it safely, so reluctantly, when the ship and the waving sailors were out of sight, they pushed it into the river. After the gift of the bananas, Hilda and Elsie made frequent illicit excursions to their little beach, but though other sailors waved and smiled and called out greetings in strange tongues, no other gifts came hurtling to them over the water.

CHAPTER V

THE SEASONS

"Sports like these
With sweet succession, taught e'en toil to please."

Things in Moss Ferry were happening all the year round: right on from Christmas to Christmas there was one entertainment after another.

Christmas Eve was very special with its Treat in the Sunday School. The Superintendent and his wife, together with the teachers and the farming folk, worked hard to make it go with a bang. It began with a great tea. Long trestle tables ran the entire length of the room, and those who possessed such treasures as white damask cloths and sparkling glass vases lent them generously for the occasion. There were piles of bread and butter and hundreds of glass dishes with every known sort of home-made jam. There were plates of buttered buns and scones; huge pound cakes, so heavy with rich dark fruits that they tasted like toffee. And to finish there were jellies, and apples, oranges, figs, dates, bananas and sweets. All who could afford to, gave something towards the tea. From the farms came the rich yellow butter and the milk and fruit cakes; from the poorer people the sugar and the tea, given in pounds and quarter-pounds respectively. Mrs Winstanley, who had to count every halfpenny in her weekly purse, always proudly managed both tea and sugar and a batch of scones and buns. Mrs Starkey contributed several immense slabs of her famous black treacle toffee. The teachers waited at table, and saw to it that every child was stuffed to capacity and a bit over, and when all had finished the Superintendent stood up, and the guests too, and gave thanks to God for their good tea.

One Christmas Mrs Cooper's little boy, who had only been allowed half of a banana because he was a sickly little boy with a weak stomach, caused a great commotion by shrilling out, passionately and resentfully: "*I'm* not going to thank God for only *half* a banana." There was a dreadful silence and the Superintendent stood there looking very stern, and Mrs Cooper made things worse by smacking her son soundly over the head so that he began to scream and kick and his mother had to take him into the vestry. Nobody laughed, and the Superintendent, black as thunder, said: "Oh Lord we thank Thee again for our good tea, and we ask Thee humbly to pardon that one of our number who has offended against Thy law. Watch over him, oh Lord, and set his feet in the paths of righteousness, for Jesus' sake, Amen."

After this the rest of the evening went with a swing. First of all there were games. A tug-of-war between the boys and girls, then hunt the slipper and postman's knock. Then some of the children would recite, and one year, Hilda Winstanley, dressed in one of Grandma Buckley's black bonnets and with a grey shawl round her shoulders and a long black skirt of her mother's, an empty port wine bottle grasped firmly in her hands, caused quite a sensation by giving a rollicking imitation of an old woman who liked a drop too much. They clapped her and stamped their feet until she recited the last three verses again and finished by taking a long pull at the bottle and staggering off into the vestry in a state of apparently advanced drunkenness.

None of the grown-ups joined in the games, but sat happily round the room watching their children and enjoying themselves every bit as much as the young people. In the centre of the room was an enormous Christmas tree laden with presents, and the big moment of the evening came when the Superintendent

announced that the present-giving was to take place. He had a
list of all the children's names and slowly read out each one, and
when he had selected the present and handed it to the child he
solemnly shook hands, or in the case of the very small children
gave them a hearty kiss. Hilda used always to pray specially for
many nights before the Christmas Treat that she would be given
the fairy doll at the very top of the tree, but it was always given
to the poorest little girl in the room, and the other girls, irrespec-
tive of age, would crowd round her and ask if they could have
just a hold of it—only for a minute. The owner of the fairy,
trembling with pride, would agree, and the fairy doll was passed
from one girl to another, and held on high by each to be admired
for its beautiful pink and white face and golden shining hair and
stiff white muslin skirts.

After the present-giving there was still more to follow, for
Mr Gibbon, the kindest and wealthiest of Moss Ferry's farmers,
always gave a Lucky Dip to the Christmas Treat, and it was a
wonderful thrill to plunge your hand into the soft bran and grope
around till you got hold of a parcel. One year Hilda pulled out
a lovely string of bright blue glass beads, which she wore for
years with every Sunday frock she had, no matter whether the
blue matched her frock or not. Nobody in Moss Ferry ever
thought about "matching". A necklace was a necklace and that
was all there was to it.

When all the presents had been given, the whole company
knelt and recited the Lord's Prayer after the Superintendent.
After this they linked hands and sang Auld Lang Syne round the
Christmas tree, and then joined into little groups and walked
cheerfully home through the snow-covered lanes, singing "Chris-
tians Awake" and "While Shepherds watched their Flocks by
Night" and other seasonable hymns; and all, young and old,

looked forward to the next Christmas Treat as though it were only just round the corner and not a whole year ahead of them.

*   *   *

After the Christmas Treat came the Tea and Social given by the members of the Band of Hope, of which virtuous body Hilda Winstanley was an ardent supporter. She had been "saved" by Sister Muriel, who stayed one weekend with Mr and Mrs Gibbon, and came to the Sunday School specially to enlist for Jesus all such sinners as Hilda and her friends. Sister Muriel had preached a very moving sermon at morning Sunday School, exhorting passionately all present to believe in the Lord Jesus and thereby make sure of having Life Everlasting. When she had finished and all were kneeling, Sister Muriel moved round and spoke to each child in turn, and presently she got to Hilda. She put an arm round her and whispered about Jesus, and urged her now, while there was still time, to take the pledge and join the Band of Hope. Kneeling there caressed by Sister Muriel, who smelt so sweetly of scented soap, Hilda promised earnestly that she would never, so long as she lived, take a drop of strong drink, and that she would use all her powers of persuasion to convert any of her friends who showed a weakness for such potions. When Sister Muriel had been to each child she invited them to come to the table and solemnly sign the Pledge, which, she explained, would be a sacred binding oath only to be broken with the certain knowledge that eternal damnation would follow. They would burn for ever and ever in the Lake of Fire. At these terrible words Hilda shuddered, but all the same bravely wrote her name in the exercise book. Sister Muriel then pinned a rosette of blue silk moire ribbon on to her coat, which she was to wear always as a sign that she believed in the Lord Jesus and had been saved for the Life Everlasting.

She was now a full life-member of the Band of Hope, and went every Tuesday night to a meeting in the vestry of the Sunday School, where they sang hymns and read the bible—each member taking it in turn to read—and prayed earnestly for all poor misguided souls who were not yet saved. Lily was too young to be a member, for she was only eight, and so Hilda went alone to the weekly meetings right through the winter, sometimes falling in with other members coming from Daneshead. In her zeal she was brave enough, although she did not really like being out alone in the dark, empty lanes. One night, when passing a big, ugly, redbrick house standing far back from the road in a thick shrubbery, where some "gentry" lived who kept themselves so much to themselves that Hilda had never even seen them, a great dog bounded out of the drive, snarling and barking at her and barring her way to the chapel. Hilda screamed, and stark fear overwhelmed her, for, though the dog made no attempt to attack her, whenever she made a movement to press on her way it snarled and she could see its white teeth even in the darkness. She prayed feverishly for some of her Daneshead friends to come up the lane, but they must have been in front of her and were probably now safe in the warm vestry room. She stood there crying, not daring to stir. The dog began to sniff at her clothes, and Hilda, summoning all her courage and all her faith in the love of the Lord Jesus, and remembering the coloured picture in the family bible of Daniel safe in the lions' den, ventured to stroke it. The dog resented the caress and ungraciously snarled again and made as if to spring. Then Hilda, forgetting Daniel and the Lord Jesus and everything but her imminent peril of being torn to pieces alive, screamed so piercingly for her mother that even the thick walls of the house were penetrated and she heard footsteps running towards her down the drive. A gentleman appeared and took hold of her and said it was all right. Nigger, he explained, was only a young dog and there was no harm in him. She ought to have kept quiet and gone her way without taking any notice of him said the gentleman, unreasonably it seemed to Hilda. It was taking notice that had caused the trouble. "Don't you know", asked the gentleman sternly, "that you should never be afraid of an animal? They always know if you are and then they enjoy frightening you all the more."

Hilda was not impressed by this sensible advice, accompanied as it was by the generous gift of a penny, and, though she never missed her Band of Hope, she never passed the big house again without trembling lest the dog should be waiting specially for her. When she got near the spot she began to walk on tiptoe, crouching as far into the hedge on the other side of the road as she could, and ready to strike at the beast with the big stick her father had given her to "wallop" him with, if he showed his teeth at her again.

*   *   *

The winters in Moss Ferry were hard and long, and at Christmas there was usually deep snow lying inches thick, and the pumps were frozen for days and even weeks on end. To get water for making their breakfast cocoa and porridge, Mrs Winstanley would put a great iron pan on the fire and shovel into it heaps of clean snow from around the back door. And every morning it was Hilda's task to go to Bartholomew's farm down the lane for the daily milk. In spite of the bitter cold she enjoyed this errand and would go off cheerfully, wrapped tightly in her mother's thick grey woollen shawl, and wearing clogs as she always did in bad winter weather. The way to the farm was slightly down hill, and if there had been a hard frost overnight she could slide all the way in the deep ruts made by the farm carts, making it a point of honour to reach the farm gates without once having stopped sliding. Coming back she had to be careful because of the can of milk, but managed to avoid monotony by clomping and stamping in the centre of the road, enjoying the crisp sound of the crunching snow under her iron-tipped clogs.

Though Moss Ferry and Kilnbrook had never heard of the word "pagan" and, had they known its meaning would have been deeply shocked at being identified with "the heathen", their way of celebrating the passing of winter and the appearance of spring was, though organised by the chapel, purely pagan. For, when the first daffodils were showing, the chapel gave a Daffodil Tea, at the modest price of sixpence a head and half-price for children, and of all the social functions held throughout the year this one had the largest attendance. The Sunday School was transformed into a blaze of yellow, for there were daffodils everywhere. Vases of them all the way down the long trestle tea tables, and great pots of them placed at intervals round the room. The tallest of the girls acted as waitresses, and wore white muslin aprons worked with daffodils in green and yellow cotton, and each girl had a daffodil pinned on to the bib of her apron and another tucked into her hair. Every man had a daffodil in his buttonhole, and when tea was over there was a solemn and expectant hush and all eyes turned to the vestry door through which would emerge the girl chosen that year to recite some wonderful verses about thousands and thousands of daffodils fluttering and dancing beside a lake. When the door opened a murmur of pleased admiration ran through the room, for the girl, in a cunningly-made frock, looked, they said, as like a daffy as two peas. One of the older girls was always chosen to make sure that the verses were recited word-perfect, and in due course the coveted honour fell to Hilda Winstanley. The good-natured Annie Starkey made the frock for her out of green and yellow sateen—a petalled skirt of daffodil-green and a bodice of yellow sateen with a ruching of green sateen round the neck and sleeves. With this she wore white cotton stockings and white canvas shoes, and the inventive Annie had made miniature daffodils out of sateen and sewn them on the front of the shoes. Her hair-ribbon was of green and yellow silk, and as a finishing touch she held stiffly in front of her a big bunch of real daffodils tied with yellow ribbon. The recitation was a great success and she was clapped loudly for an encore, obliging by gravely reciting the entire poem all over again. People kept on coming up to her and her mother, saying what a treat it was to hear such grand verses recited so feelingly. They congratulated Annie Starkey, too, on her smartness over the frock, and made flattering remarks about Annie's cleverness in thinking of the daffys on the shoes. Mrs Weatherhead, Kiln-brook's professional dressmaker, got very red and jealous of all the praise given to her amateur rival, feeling that a slur was being deliberately cast upon her reputation as a real dressmaker who had served her proper time as an apprentice and now had apprentices of her own under her.

*   *   *

Perhaps the most exciting event of the year in connection with the chapel was the great Whitsun Walk, which took place annually on Whit Sunday afternoon. The Walk was not confined to the members of the Kilnbrook United Methodist Chapel, but was joined in by every Nonconformist chapel in the neighbourhood. Only the proud Church of England held icily aloof and looked down its disapproving nose at the heathen in their Whitsun blindness. And of course the Roman Catholics were not even regarded as heathen, but as entirely non-existent so far as God was concerned.

For weeks ahead all the scholars in all the Sunday Schools looked forward eagerly to the Walk, and at every service on the Sunday preceding it, prayers were offered for a fine Whit Sunday. And the prayers were always answered, for nobody could remember the Walk taking place on any but a fine, warm, sunny day. On this one day of the year the Primitive Methodists and the Wesleyan Methodists, the United Methodists and the Congregationalists and the Baptists forgot their natural animosities and became as one in their proud desire to make of the Walk an unforgettable spectacle. It was unwritten law that all the girls should be dressed in white from head to foot, and all the boys turned out as smartly as could be afforded. The Winstanley household buzzed with excitement for at least a month before the Walk was due. Lucy Stringer always brought along a length of crisp spotted white muslin to be made up into a frock for Hilda. And a white leghorn hat trimmed with a wreath of white and yellow marguerites, or glazed red cherries, according to the fashion. On her white frock Hilda wore a broad blue silk sash, and had white cotton stockings and white kid shoes and long, white, lace-tipped mittens. And Mrs Winstanley, at great and sometimes real sacrifice, saw to it that Lily had just the same. There was no Sunday School on Whit Sunday morning, for Sunday dinner had to be eaten early so as to be in time for the Walk.

At half-past one the different sections of the Walk met at the beginning of the road to Daneshead, and by two o'clock the procession was formed. The Sunday School teachers arranged the children according to size. First the little girls, and then the little boys, with the bigger children behind. Then came the teachers themselves, and behind them the parents. At the head of each denomination walked the Superintendent of the Sunday School carrying the chapel banner, and at the first wave of the leading banner the Walk began, slowly and proudly, to the big Congregational Chapel at Daneshead. When the Kilnbrook and Moss Ferry part of the procession arrived outside the chapel it halted until the Daneshead procession came into view. The two processions then united and filed impressively into the chapel. Settling into their places took a little time, but when this was arranged satisfactorily the service started with a rousing hymn sung by the Anniversary Choirs of all the chapels. It was a magnificent sight—the big chapel filled with girls and women in white frocks and white hats and a gay variety of coloured silk sashes, with here and there a black sash to indicate mourning. The men all wore their Sunday serges, and looked very stiff and unreal and respectable. The Congregational Chapel at Daneshead was famous for the big gallery that ran round three sides of it, and Hilda liked it best when the United Methodist procession was shepherded into this gallery and she could look down on the body of the chapel and the choir. They never had a local preacher for the Whitsun Gathering, but an important minister from Bradford or Manchester; and because he was a stranger and came such a great distance, he was listened to with more respect and attention than they gave to their own familiar ministers. The chapel had very long, round-headed windows of brightly coloured glass—red and green and puce and orange—and the sun shining through these turned the white frocks into red and green and puce and orange too. Everybody sang the hymns with loud enjoyment, but the big moment of the afternoon came when the congregation was hushed and the choir stood up and sang the

Hallelujah Chorus. The choir consisted of men and women, boys and girls, carefully selected from the different chapels for the purity of their voices. The choirmaster raised his hand and they were off.

Hallelujah! Hallelujah! Hall-e-lu-jah!

It was well worth waiting a whole year for and the grown-up part of the congregation would cheerfully have heard it all over again. As the great paeans of praise rolled out, Grandma Stringer, sitting below with her family, nudged her husband and whispered that Sir Charles Hallé himself could have found no fault with such a rendering. And, whispering back, he agreed as one privileged to know, for it was his special pride that in his younger days he had sung more than once with the Hallé Choir in the Free Trade Hall at Manchester.

The wonderful afternoon was over all too soon, but for some there was yet more enjoyment to come. All lucky enough to have relations at Daneshead went there for tea as a matter of course. Now that Uncle Fred and Aunt Emma lived at Daneshead, the Winstanleys and the Atkinsons and Grandma Buckley were all asked to tea. Afterwards they went back to the Congregational Chapel for the evening service, and then the Sunday of the year was really over. They walked slowly home, tired but happy, and the children consoled themselves by reflecting that any road they had their new Whitsun clothes to wear from now on every Sunday right through the summer.

*   *   *

One night after evening chapel, the lay preacher, Mr Headley, gave out a piece of news that caused tremendous excitement among his congregation. This announcement was none other than the proposed formation of the Moss Ferry and Kilnbrook Mutual

Improvement Society, to be held in the Sunday School vestry on the evening of every third Friday right through the winter. Mr Headley asked all those in favour to show same in the usual way, and although many of the congregation, like Joe and Lizzie Winstanley, could neither read nor write and had no idea what a Mutual Improvement Society was, every right hand shot up instantly, and some of the younger people, like Hilda and her friend Elsie Entwistle, waved their upraised arms about so as to make quite sure Mr Headley saw them and noted their grateful approval. For this was something real. A Society where folks would talk and ask questions and be told all sorts of useful and interesting information.

Mr Headley smilingly surveyed the forest of upraised arms, and announced that the motion was carried unanimously and a committee would at once be formed to get the Society in being without delay. All, he emphasised, were welcome, and there would be no charge beyond a small entrance fee to cover the cost of lighting and fuel. No members would be admitted under the age of twelve, and all members would be expected, in strict rotation, to read a Paper to the Society, and a debate would then follow. It was not, however, compulsory for a member to read a Paper. Some folks, observed Mr Headley diplomatically, were better at listening than talking, and there was every bit as much to be said for a good listener as there was for a good talker. For, he continued kindly, where would the talkers be if nobody had the gumption or patience to listen to them? This masterstroke put everybody at ease and, going home with Lily and her mother and father, Hilda was full of plans for the astonishing Paper she would read to the Mutual Improvement Society when it came round to her turn. Joe and Lizzie regarded her fondly, and even the ill-natured Lily made no disparaging remarks, for she was actually quite proud of her foster-sister's superior learning. Hilda caused a sensation when she revealed that already she had decided on the subject of her Paper. She had got it from one of her *Chatterboxes*. Her father laughed and said: "Ah reckon tha'll do it aw reet, our 'Ilda, but dunna forget as they'll axe questions. Hast thowt o' that?"

Hilda had thought of it but was not discouraged. It was all in *Chatterbox*—all the information and all the answers to any likely questions; and as soon as their Sunday supper of cold rice pudding and cocoa was over, she fetched the book from the front room and began to sketch out her Paper in pencil.

Joe, with an approving eye on *Chatterbox*—the only book besides the bible she was allowed to read on a Sunday—inquired what the Paper was to be about, and Hilda astonished them by her answer. "Spiders. There's plenty about spiders folks don't know. Look—all this is about them. How they catch their food and spin their webs and I don't know what."

Her mother and father gazed uncomprehending but admiring at the printed page, although Mrs Winstanley looked doubtful.

"Spiders," she repeated. "Reckon that's a rum thing to give a Paper about. What's to be had out o' knowing about spiders, our 'Ilda? Folks knows there's spiders, dunna they? What dost want to read a Paper about such things for? Folks'll only laugh at it, Ah reckon."

Hilda regarded her mother with affectionate scorn.

"It's a Mutual Improvement Society, isn't it? Folks want to be told something they don't know. And if you and Father could read what *Chatterbox* says about spiders you'd learn something you don't know too"; and with that she immersed herself in *Chatterbox* and was soon busy with her pencil while her mother bustled sharply about the kitchen, and her father, rocking slowly in his chair, watched every movement of her hand. He never ceased to wonder at her "gift" for putting words together and setting them down on paper. He did not share his wife's doubts about the subject of the Paper, and, looking at her still dis-approving face, remarked appeasingly: "Reckon it's aw reet, Mother. Happen our 'Ilda knows what she's about. It *mun* be aw reet if it's in *Chatterbox*, eh Hilda?"

Hilda nodded importantly, and after that was left in peace until it was time to get ready for bed.

Hilda worked at her Paper unceasingly, pruning it and polishing it until she had got it to her liking and was quite certain that not a single question could be asked to which she had not memorised the answer. Finally she copied it out neatly in a penny exercise book with ruled lines, and waited as patiently as she could till her turn arrived. At last the great night came, and Hilda, wearing her Sunday best, with her mother and father and Jim and Lily and John and Edie, entered the chapel vestry in a state of tense excitement. There was a good attendance, and chairs had been thoughtfully reserved in the front row for the members of the Lecturer's family.

Hilda, very red and very nervous, was led by Mr Headley to the table, on which she noticed with pride a glass jug of water and a tumbler. Mrs Gibbon, the President of the Society, gravely shook hands with her and motioned her to sit down while she made the announcement.

"Ladies and Gentlemen," she began, "it gives me very great pleasure to welcome as our lecturer tonight this young member of our Society, and I feel sure that what she has to say will be of great interest to us all. Ladies and Gentlemen, Miss Hilda Winstanley will now read to us a Paper entitled 'SPIDERS'."

There was a burst of surprised clapping, during which Hilda

nervously observed her audience. A good many farmers and their families were present, and of course Grandma Buckley was there, nodding encouragingly at her. She also saw the Superintendent of the Sunday School, and Elsie and Queenie Entwistle; while in the front row her own family were clapping as if they would never leave off. But the applause died down and, making a tremendous effort to control her shaking voice, Hilda began to read her Paper. After the first few sentences her confidence returned and she read on steadily to her wondering but by now thoroughly interested audience. She told them of how the spider first of all began to spin his web and how strong it was—so strong that even a big creature like a blue-bottle or a wasp could never, once in the mesh, extricate itself. And how the greedy and evil spider was always in hiding near the web watching for its victims. Of how, when the victim was thoroughly and hopelessly entangled, the spider pounced upon him and ate him up, head first. Of how there were many different sorts of spiders—from the little red money spider that it was so unlucky to shake off you ("Always let him go of his own free will or he will take your luck with him") to the big, crafty household spider for ever on the look-out for his next meal. She told them of the water-spiders that built complete homes for themselves in the banks of streams and brooks: homes with a front room and a back room and proper bedrooms and even a front door. And of strange, fierce spiders in foreign parts who would attack human beings and whose bite was poisonous. She gave them, cunningly adapted, the entire contents of the *Chatterbox* article on spiders of every kind, and ended up with an earnest appeal to her listeners to keep their eyes open on a sunny frosty morning and observe the delicacy of the hundreds and thousands of webs glistening in the hedges—some no bigger than a halfpenny; some as big as a saucer; some stretching right across the road on a single silken thread so fine that you could not see it with the naked eye, and only knew it was there when you felt it caress your face. She finished on a warning note.

"It is a complete fallacy to believe that a cobweb is a safe and certain cure for bleeding cuts. This is an old woman's tale and has in its time caused great suffering and even death. For the ordinary household cobweb is a dirty, germ-laden thing, and when applied to an open cut has been known to cause blood-poisoning."

There was an uneasy stir among the audience at this, but Hilda went on severely: "Yes—it has been proved beyond all question that people have actually died from blood-poisoning through putting cobwebs on their cuts." On this improving note she ended and stood there anxiously while the audience clapped. Every single answer to every possible question had gone completely out of her head, and she prayed fervently that nobody would get up and ask her anything. Mrs Gibbon, sensing her uneasiness, rose quickly and extended a warning hand.

"Ladies and Gentlemen, I do not think our speaker tonight has left us any questions to ask. I am sure we have all thoroughly enjoyed her most interesting talk, and I for one never knew that there was so much to learn about spiders. I shall never see a spider's web again without remembering the many interesting things I have heard tonight, and on behalf of our Mutual Improvement Society I vote that we now show our thanks in the usual way."

But Mrs Gibbon was too soon, for old Sarah Dumbell, who now hated the Winstanleys more than she had ever hated anyone in her mischief-making life, stood up defiantly and said in a tone heavy with malice: "Well, Ah for one dunna believe as a cobweb can do owt but good to a cut. Ah've dabbed one on meself and t'childer 'underds o' times. Better'n all the intment Ah've found them too. So what's got to say to that, Hilda *Winstanley*?"

She stressed the Winstanley malevolently, and waited viciously for Hilda's reply, which came with unexpected quickness and spirit.

"I can only tell you, Mrs Dumbell, that if you went to Doctor James and asked him he wouldn't hold with it at all. As I said in my Paper it's a proper old woman's tale and because no harm has come to you up to now that doesn't say it won't one day. For one day", she concluded darkly and magnificently, "you might get what they call septic poisoning, and if you get that you'll die sure as eggs is eggs. Because septic poisoning comes through dirt, and cobwebs in a house *are* dirt, as I'm sure everybody will agree."

There was a terrific burst of applause at this routing of the unlikeable Sarah, and whispers of "That's one for Sarah Dumbell, that is. That'll larn 'er. Interfering owd barm-pot trying to onsettle t'lass."

When the applause died down, Hilda joined her beaming family and although Mrs Winstanley still thought spiders a funny thing to talk about, and couldn't yet see that anybody was better off for knowing about them, both she and Joe were proud of Hilda and delighted that she had managed so neatly to put Sarah Dumbell in her place.

"Reckon Moss Ferry 'ud be a better place if she did get septic poisoning," observed Mrs Winstanley truculently. She did not rightly know what septic poisoning was, but felt that such a fearful and unknown end was no more than Sarah Dumbell deserved. "Trying to take it out of our 'Ilda that road." Joe warmly agreed by nodding his head, very slowly, several times, and, after a long reflective pause, made the authority on spiders glow with self-satisfaction by remarking: "Reckon it 'ud take a sight more than owd Sarah Dumbell to get the better of our 'Ilda —on spiders or owt else. Aye—reckon it would an' all."

CHAPTER VI
FOREIGNERS

Once every summer, during the school holidays, Moss Ferry fairly seethed with excitement, for any day the dancing bear would be coming to the village, and everybody, young and old, who had the time to spare, would drop whatever they were doing and go down to the big open green space behind *The Black Horse*, which was always leased for the Wakes and the dancing bear.

The owner of the bear was a very little man, and the big brown beast, when it reared on its hind legs, towered over him. But he was never in the least bit frightened of it, and the bear obeyed quietly every order he gave it in his queer, outlandish speech. Nobody ever found out what sort of a foreigner he was, for the only English he seemed to know was "Thank you". When he was satisfied that the news of the bear's arrival had thoroughly percolated into the mind of the village, he struck up a great capering performance on his own, while the bear sat up on its hind legs looking, as Mrs Winstanley remarked once, "fair mazed wi' his junketings". When the man had finished his own dance he bowed to the people and talked to the bear, who was fastened by a long heavy chain to an iron pole stuck deep into the ground. He talked at great speed and laughed a lot, and then prodded the bear with a little pointed stick. Then the bear would slowly raise itself on its hind paws, with its front paws swinging loosely and heavily, and very slowly, and very softly, would begin to dance. Round and round the pole it went, and all the time the man jabbered to it in his funny way and worked it up until it was circumambulating at a tremendous rate. At this point the children began to get frightened and their mothers would draw them farther away from the beast; there was an uneasy feeling that it might suddenly jerk the pole out of the ground and charge them. But it never did, for the man seemed to know just the right minute to start slowing it down. He would stop prodding with his sharp little stick and wave his hands instead, and he gave the impression that he was actually talking with his hands, for the bear seemed to understand every wave and gesture. He talked to it in words as well, and gradually the animal would slacken its pace and, at a final wave, plump down with its forepaws held out expectantly. The bear-man then took off his hat—a queer-looking soft hat made of a greyish green cloth—and placed it between the bear's outstretched paws. Then he bowed to the crowd and smiled and pointed to the hat. The mothers gave their pennies and halfpennies to the children who, very timidly, and one after the other, moved up and dropped them in. All this time the bear sat up perfectly still, its little deep brown eyes looking right through the children and away through their mothers as though they were not there at all. When everybody had given, the man dropped the coins into a rusty-looking black velvet bag, embroidered in red silk and with a thick red cord to fasten it. He then hung the bag round his neck and tucked it under his shirt, and, bowing and smiling and seeming to make a great effort, said "Thank you" so funnily that everybody laughed and some of the children clapped. He did not so much say it as throw it out of his mouth, as if it were a big stone he just had to be rid of somehow or other. He then always gave his bear a Garibaldi biscuit, and one never-to-be-forgotten summer he made the land-lady of *The Black Horse* understand by signs that his bear wanted a drink of water. She ran to the pump and fetched a bucketful, and the man indicated by more signs that she should give the bucket straight to the bear. Nervously she did so, and the bear raised it to its mouth and poured it all down at one go, and then quickly dropped the bucket as though it disgusted him. The man then rooted up the pole and put it over his shoulder, and he and his bear walked away in the direction of Daneshead, and everybody walked behind him, at a respectful distance, as far as the turn of the road. They all stood there, the children in front, watching him walking quickly along and sometimes breaking into a trot, for the bear took great soft strides and was sometimes in front of his owner, right at the end of the chain. Their eyes strained after the fascinating sight till the man looked no bigger than a rook and the bear not much larger than a shaggy farm dog, and by the doctor's house the road turned again and that was the end of them till next summer. But the excitement and wonder of the dancing bear lasted Moss Ferry for months, and because she had actually given the bear a bucket of water with her own hands, the landlady of *The Black Horse* became quite a figure in the neighbourhood, and was always ready to oblige when one or other of her husband's customers said coaxingly: "Come on, Missus, tell us on t'bear wi' his bucket o' water. Reckon tha felt feared on 'im that time, aw reet."

*　　　　*　　　　*

Even more exciting than the dancing bear was Wakes Week, which meant, not as it does now a general holiday, but a Fair, which lasted for a whole week, and for which every child and grown-up for miles around saved up halfpennies and pennies and whatever they could spare week by week from Christmas onwards.

The Wakes was held in April, so that although at night it was quite chilly and everybody would wrap up warmly, it was more romantic and beautiful than in warmer weather because the flares were lit, and the green space behind *The Black Horse* became a glowing circle of colour and light, with strange shadows dancing everywhere, and all the people looking so much more important and cheerful than they did in the daytime. Sometimes Mrs Winstanley would give Hilda and Lily a halfpenny apiece for the roundabouts after tea, but what they enjoyed best were Wednesday and Saturday nights, for then the entire family, except John, who never went to the Wakes till it got to Daneshead the following week and he could take Edie, gave themselves up to pure enjoyment. First they would wander all round the fairground, Hilda holding on to her father and Lily to her mother, both of whom were mortally afraid of what might be lurking in the caravans drawn up in the black circle behind the flare-lit ground and although no harm had ever been known to come from the fair-folk, they never let the two girls out of their sight. They'd heard queer tales of children being taken away by gypsies and fair-folk and never heard tell of again. Hilda had once read such a tale to them out of her *Chatterbox*. Jim, however, was allowed to go off and join his playmates, boys being able to look after themselves. They would come across friends and neighbours, and even Grandma Buckley would be there in her black bonnet and cape, with a long, mournful face, but thoroughly enjoying herself all the same. And every now and then Uncle Billy would come out of *The Black Horse*, each time looking a little wilder and jollier, and join their father in throwing for coconuts. Joe would spend quite large sums on this, making it a point of honour to get a coconut apiece for each member of his family, and one over for Grandma Buckley if Billy didn't manage it for her. He threw rings for hoopla too, but was no great shakes at this although he would continue stubbornly until his wife nudged him and said quietly, "That's enough, Father. Tha's only throwing good money after bad. Reckon t'childer would like a ride now." And then their father, giving them a halfpenny each, would hoist them on to a hobby-horse and stand there with their mother proudly watching their enjoyment as the music blared out and, slowly and heavily, the great roundabout began to revolve. The music went faster, and then they were riding madly round and round, up and down, clinging desperately to the wavy brass poles that rose so comfortingly out of the horses' backs. Past their father and mother they flashed, shrieking out to them un-intelligible words, and faster and still faster, so that Hilda, looking eagerly for her father, saw only a dim red blur of a face. Then came the dreaded moment when the music slowed down and the roundabout with it, until it stopped altogether, and there was their mother and father peering for them, and lifting them down. Now the man on the roundabout was calling gaily for more customers—"This way, this way please! Upsy-daisy," as he lifted a small boy on to a horse; and observing the look on the children's faces, Joe gave them another halfpenny apiece and again lifted them up, this time into the front seats of a racing chariot, and the mad, lovely ride began all over again. After the roundabout there were the swing-boats, but the two girls were not allowed in these by themselves—their mother would look round for a schoolmate for each, someone older and heavier and not likely to get up to any tricks such as swinging the boat so high that it would topple over and send its occupants hurtling to their deaths. Lily used to ask to go up with Elsie Entwistle, who was a big girl going on for fourteen and full of commonsense, and Hilda would nearly always manage to get hold of Alfie Hogben, with whom she had been close friends ever since she could remember. Alfie was tall and raw and always out-at-elbow because he grew so fast, but he had a knack of working the boat till it went nearly to the top, but not quite. Hilda would stand up in the boat as well as Alfie, and both worked their legs energetically to get it going faster. All this time Mr and Mrs Winstanley stood watching, and when the man motioned them to stop, time being up, Hilda called out to her father, begging for another go, and he always shouted back: "Aw reet, our 'Ilda. One more go, and our Lily too, and us'll pay for Alfie and Elsie as well."

After two rides on the roundabout and two in the swings, they began again walking round the fair ground, eating slabs of pink and white coconut ice or sucking toffee apples, watching the hoopla and the coconut shies, and talking to their friends; but on Saturday, the last night, there was the circus, and everybody deserted the fair ground for this. The big tent was packed to suffocation, and the great thrill of the evening came when the little brown horse, who could answer any and every question asked by his master, pranced knowingly into the ring. Everybody sat tense and expectant, wondering by what mysterious reasoning he arrived at the correct responses. He would come in, gaily decked out in shining harness and red, white and blue rosettes, and trot round and round the ring a few times to the music, and every year his master would ask him different questions and never once did he give the wrong answer.

There were three tiers of wooden benches rising one after the other in the tent, and one year Hilda and Lily, with their mother and father, and Grandma Buckley and Uncle Billy, were all sitting together in the first row, waiting for the horse to begin. And the first question the man asked it was: "Tell the ladies and gentlemen who can put away the biggest dollop o' beer in Moss Ferry."

All eyes immediately and tactlessly turned to poor Billy Buckley, sitting there red as a turkey-cock, and sure enough the little horse pranced round the ring and came to a dead stop right in front of him, stamping with its hoof and solemnly holding its head down. Everybody roared with laughter, and clapped the horse, and clapped Billy too, and Billy himself managed to laugh with them, though he would have liked to wring the horse's neck, and poor Grandma Buckley began to cry as usual and said it was a judgement on her son for his wicked behaviour at *The Black Horse* when even a dumb animal could find him out. But Billy's shame was soon eclipsed when the man put his second question. This time there was louder clapping and even louder laughter, and emphatic shouts of "That's reet enough, that is. By gum it is." For the question was: "Tell the ladies and gentlemen who can tell the biggest lie in Moss Ferry," and the little horse stopped dead in front of old Sarah Dumbell, sitting there all blowsy and dirty. Sarah scowled and struck viciously at the horse and its master remonstrated good-naturedly: "Now Missus, now Missus —it's only a bit o' fun. Can't you take a joke?" and off he went with the horse, round and round and round again, the whole audience holding its breath and waiting eagerly for the next question. This turned out the most popular of all: "Tell the ladies and gentlemen who's the biggest skinflint in Moss Ferry," and this time the little horse, throwing up its head as if enjoying the joke, stopped in front of a lean old man sitting in the top tier. This was James Shaw, who was a byword for meanness and miserliness and was known never to have given a halfpenny away throughout his entire life. Mrs Winstanley used to declare that James Shaw was that close-fisted and near he'd rob his own mother of her wedding ring if he could get at her coffin unbeknownst. He was the Winstanley's landlord, and the only landlord in Moss Ferry who at Christmas-time never gave the children of his tenants so much as an orange for their stockings. He lived by himself in the house next to the Winstanleys, and did for himself too. He even did his own washing and mending, and much speculation went on continually as to the probable length of James Shaw's private stocking, and what was the good of hoarding up, any road, when he had neither kith nor kin to leave it to. Mrs Amelia Starkey, from whom he bought his few groceries, once confided to Mrs Winstanley that she reckoned he lived half the week on sucking, over and over again, his bacon and cheese rinds, so small were the quantities he purchased of these commodities. He was a source of unending interest to Mrs Winstanley, she being his immediate neighbour as well as tenant, and many a night she would remark, apropos of nothing, "Wonder what old James Shaw's up to to-neet. Reckon 'e's sitting to table counting 'is money. Reckon 'e counts it up every neet just to mak' sure it 'asn't bin took. Eh…Ah'd give a lot to see 'im at it, that Ah would."

And as the little brown horse stood so cheekily in front of the old man, everybody in the tent wished the same thing—that one of these fine days the old scarecrow would be robbed, every penny took from him. He hadn't even paid to go into the circus. He owned the field behind *The Black Horse*, and the Wakes people had to pay him money down before a single caravan could get on to the ground, and of course he expected and received a free ticket for the circus. This time the people stamped and whistled to show their appreciation of the little horse's knowingness, and old James sat there vowing that he'd never let the circus folk hire his land again—though they knew he would, for he wasn't by a long chalk the only landlord in Moss Ferry with a field to let out.

After this wonderful and stimulating performance there was the lady who rode bare-backed on a beautiful milk-white horse, jumping on and off it like lightning, and never once missing her foothold. She was a fine, plump lady with bright yellow hair curled tightly all over her head; she wore tights and was, in the opinion of Mrs Winstanley and indeed all the other women in Moss Ferry, "no good", but all the same they enjoyed watching her every movement and applauded her generously when she stood there bowing and kissing her hands to them. Then came the lady and gentleman who swung perilously backwards and forwards right across the very top of the tent on a ring—holding on with one hand only. "Trapeze artists" it said on the programme, but nobody knew what that meant. Grandma Buckley remarked disapprovingly that these two were "over venturesome" and it was a wonder they hadn't broken their necks many a time. This was the last item, and when it was over they all stood up and sang "God Save the King", and then home, to talk of the Wakes and the circus until they came round again next year.

*　　　　　*　　　　　*

One winter, just before Christmas, two strange men with a caravan arrived at Moss Ferry and begged the loan of a small paddock on Ben Bartholomew's farm down School Lane. Here they erected a large tent, and then went from door to door telling the people that they had come to save them from eternal fire, and that a Revivalist Meeting would be held in the tent every night for a week, and admission was free though a collection would be taken after the service. They were very persuasive and the tent was packed night after night, people coming in from all the outlying houses and even from farms miles out on the Moss.

Hilda and Lily were taken one night with their mother and father, and all of them felt a solemn thrill as they entered the tent. There were rows of rough plank benches, and facing these a small white-scrubbed kitchen table, on which lay an immense bible and a hymn-book; and at the side of the table was a cottage harmonium at which one of the men was sitting. The Revivalist who did the preaching was a small dark-complexioned man, with jet-black hair and a jet-black moustache. He was not a Lancashire man, and afterwards Hilda heard somebody say he had come from Wales, from some place on the border between Cheshire and Flintshire—a town near Chester—and he was very well spoken and never at a loss for words.

The proceedings opened with everybody singing "Onward Christian Soldiers". Then the preacher said he would offer up a prayer to the Lord Jesus, and wrestle for the souls of the ungodly, but as there was no room between the benches for the congregation to kneel he asked them to show respect by standing up while he prayed for them. All stood up, but nobody closed his eyes except the Revivalist. He stood by the table jerking himself about and flinging his arms upwards and crying on the Lord Jesus to come down and save the ungodly. Hilda and Lily were very upset by his fervour, and Hilda looked at her mother and father. Her mother was all right, though looking very stiff, but her father was crying. She could hardly believe her eyes, for she had never seen him cry before, not even as they stood by Grandma Winstanley's coffin. The preacher was pleading with them all, each and every one, to stand forth in an upright fashion and confess their sins and be gathered safely into the waiting arms of the Lord Jesus. Hilda herself began to cry, and then and there made a solemn private vow that she would read the bible right through—every single word of it—beginning in bed the very next morning. Meantime the Revivalist had started to sway from side to side and rock backwards and forwards on his toes as though he were drunk, and then quite suddenly he stopped, opened his eyes as though awakening from a very long sleep and wondering where he was, and gave out another hymn. It was a Moody and Sankey hymn, with a rousing tune to it:

> I'll never run away till Jesus comes,
> Till Jesus comes, till Jesus comes.
> I'll never run away till Jesus comes
> And takes me safely home.

The other Revivalist played the harmonium and everybody sang loudly, while the preacher waved his hymn-book about as if conducting them. Grandma Buckley was there, crying as usual, and next to her, to everybody's surprise, her son Billy. When the hymn was over the Revivalist asked them all to be seated, and then began to preach.

"Dear brothers and sisters in God, Who gave His only begotten Son to save the World, is there one of you tonight who can stand forth and say he has not sinned? No, dear brothers and sisters, No, No, No! We are all sinners, but if we truly repent, if we stand forth unashamed and humbly confess our sins, then we shall be washed in the Blood of the Lamb, and our sins shall be made whiter than snow—yea, whiter than the driven snow. For the Lord Jesus is waiting, waiting for you, waiting for me, for every man, woman and child gathered here tonight, waiting to help us, to watch over us, to guide us, to lead us safely home. For, behold, the day cometh that shall burn as an oven; and all the proud, yea, and all that do wickedly, shall be stubble; and the day that cometh shall burn them up, saith the Lord of Hosts, it shall leave them neither root nor branch. But unto you that fear My name shall the Sun of righteousness arise with healing in his wings; and ye shall go forth, and grow up as calves of the stall. And ye shall tread down the wicked; for they shall be ashes under the soles of your feet in the day that I shall do this, saith the Lord of Hosts.

So, dear brothers and sisters, repent, repent while it is not yet too late! Stand forth, unashamed, and let the mercy of our Lord Jesus fall upon you—He will gather you safely in His arms. He will lead you safely home and your sins shall be washed whiter than snow, whiter than the driven snow. Yea, though your sins be as scarlet. Come, come to the Lord Jesus! For all that is in the world, the lust of the flesh, and the lust of the eye, and the pride of life, is not of the Father, but is of the world. And the world passeth away, and the lust thereof; but he that doeth the will of God abideth for ever. Abideth for ever. *Abideth for ever!* Think, brothers and sisters: *he that doeth the will of God abideth for ever!* And if we confess our sins, He is faithful and just to forgive us our sins, and to cleanse us from all unrighteousness. Therefore come, brothers and sisters, come and be saved—be cleansed from your sins, for the Lord is long-suffering towards us, not willing that any should perish, but that all should come to repentance. The Lord Jesus is waiting! Come!"

He held out his arms, the tears pouring down his cheeks, and Hilda watched with fearful eagerness, first one, and then another, walk slowly up to the table. Grandma Buckley was whispering to Billy and tugging at his coat sleeve. The miracle happened. Hilda saw her Uncle Billy give himself a sort of shake, and go with his mother to the table. The people were now very quiet, very tense, watching the scene at the little kitchen table. The preacher spoke to each penitent and shook hands, and then, raising his arms, cried passionately:

"Oh Lord Jesus, receive each of these children into Thy bosom, for they have truly repented and the Spirit of the Lord our God is in them! Guide them, oh Lord, comfort them, be with them always! Praise be to God, praise to the Lord God! Hallelujah, Hallelujah!"

They then sang "Jesu, Lover of my Soul", and the Revival was over for that night. Hilda could see that her mother was eager to get to Grandma Buckley and Billy, who, with the others that had been saved, were now talking and smiling with the preacher, so she and Lily hung on to their father. The Revivalist who had played the harmonium was standing at the opening of the tent, shaking hands with everyone and saying warmly "Goodnight, sister" or "Goodnight, brother," while everybody put something in the little bag he held in his other hand. Hilda, who had been very much moved by the preacher's eloquence, was astonished to find herself feeling in her pocket for the threepenny bit she had saved up to buy her father some of his favourite black twist for Christmas, and without really considering what she was doing, dropped it into the bag. The Revivalist gave her a specially grateful smile, and placed his hand on her shoulder for a second. She felt a great wave of virtue rush through her, particularly when her father remarked: "That's reet, our 'Ilda." He himself had given a sixpence he could ill afford, and indeed all the people had been so stirred by the address, and the sight of that great sinner, Billy Buckley, getting saved at last, that the two Revivalists were mostly rewarded by threepenny bits and sixpences, with here and there a shilling from a farmer and his wife.

The two girls, with their father, waited outside the tent for Grandma Buckley and Billy and their mother, who presently came out together, all crying quietly. The preacher had his arm round Billy's shoulders and was whispering to him, while Billy was looking very red and flustered, and Grandma was for once, in spite of her crying, looking pleased. They all said Goodnight, and Grandma and Billy went off arm in arm, an astonishing thing for relations to do in Moss Ferry, but Grandma was so proud of her Billy having been saved for Jesus that she wished it was full

93

daylight so that everybody could see them thus walking together. Joe and Lizzie and the two girls walked home without anybody saying a word, and it was not till they were all sitting round the table, while Mrs Winstanley made mugs of cocoa, that the silence was broken.

"Eh, but Ah never thowt Ah should live to see our Billy up and saved," she remarked as she handed round the steaming cocoa. "Reckon my mother'll go 'appy to her grave from this night on. Us mun write and tell our Susannah on it. Our 'Ilda can write her a letter tomorrow, eh, Hilda?"

Hilda assented eagerly. Very few letters ever went out from the Winstanley household because so few ever came into it, and whenever a letter did arrive it was a matter of tremendous importance. If it arrived when the girls were at school, Mrs Winstanley would prop it up against the Mazawattee tea caddy on the mantelpiece till dinner- or tea-time, and then give it to Hilda to open and read to her. She would ask for it to be read and re-read until she knew it almost word for word, and then it would go back on the mantelpiece till Joe came home to his tea, when Hilda once more read it out several times until he also knew it by heart. When John came back from work he would prop it up against the teapot and read it for himself; but Jim never bothered. His mother would tell him all about it, and if Hilda happened to be in would ask her to read it out again, which she was only too willing to do so as to impress her loutish brother with her own cleverness.

CHAPTER VII
ALL ARABIA

Although nearly all the social activities in Moss Ferry and Kiln-brook were arranged by the chapel for chapel-goers only, there was one important yearly treat organised by the Church of England for the schoolchildren and their parents. This Outing varied from year to year, covering Southport, St Anne's-on-Sea, Cleethorpes, Llandudno, New Brighton, Colwyn Bay and Rhyl. Hilda and Lily Winstanley used virtuously to save up all the year round in their post office moneyboxes for the trip. It was the one occasion of the year when they might lawfully spend as freely and heedlessly as they fancied, neither their mother nor father interfering or criticising. Mrs Winstanley too used to put by a bit week by week for this event, and in some miraculous way that they never fathomed, Joe always astonished his wife by giving her a sovereign for spending-money on the evening before the trip. Once at the seaside there was no stinting, and it was an unwritten law that nobody went home with anything but their return tickets and the presents they had bought for relations unable to be on the Outing too. The train journey from Kiln-brook was in itself an adventure and they enjoyed every minute of it. All the carriages were packed tight, and no sooner had the train started than they all began eating. Everybody had been up and stirring for hours, the farm workers having seen to their cattle and done all essential daily jobs before coming home to change into their Sunday clothes. Hilda liked it best when the trip was to Southport, which was such a clean, bright, pretty town even though the sea was a long way off. And next to Southport she liked Llandudno, because that too was so pretty and it was exciting to climb to Happy Valley and sit perilously, looking out to sea, on the steep sides of the Great Orme. Besides, Llandudno was as good as going to foreign parts, for on the way to the Great Orme they passed a cemetery and stared hard at the funny foreign names and verses on the tombstones, and the schoolmaster, Mr Woodville, made a joke about them and said he would give a sixpence to any child who could read Welsh.

During the train journey, the Vicar made a point of honouring as many compartments as possible with his presence, and for this purpose got out at every station. He would ask serious, puzzling questions, such as "If a herring and a half costs three halfpence, what would eleven herrings cost?" They would all solemnly and patiently try to work it out but nobody ever got the right answer. And then in one of the carriages somebody would start singing:

> When the fields are white with daisies,
> And the roses bloom again—
> Let the lovelight in your heart more brightly burn.
> For I'll love you, sweetheart, always,
> So remember when you're lonely—
> When the fields are white with daisies, I'll return!

And all the people in the other carriages would take it up, so that the men working on the line and in the fields would stop their work as the singing train rushed past them, to wave and shout friendly greetings.

And in a jiffy they were at their destination, and Mr Woodville and the Vicar were seeing that everybody got safely out of the train and shouting instructions where they were all to meet for tea and to be sure to be in good time, for it was going to be a knife-and-fork tea and therefore not to be hurried over.

When the Outing was to Southport, Hilda Winstanley always wanted first to walk down Lord Street, which was so wide and clean and had such grand shops on one side and big hotels and houses the other. And the first spending-money went on a bucket and spade and a shrimping net and a stick of Southport rock, and when properly furnished with these necessaries they made for the seaside itself. The sea was nearly always a long way out, but there were miles of shining sand and a big ornamental lake to paddle in. One year Hilda slipped on the sloping sides of this lake and her backside got soaked. Everybody thought it was a grand joke, and her mother made her lie flat on her stomach on the hot sand while the sun dried her. The beach was crowded with little stalls and shops where they sold necklaces and brooches, and cups and saucers with "A Present from Southport" written on them in gold letters; and Hilda, looking importantly into her purse and counting her money, was able to buy a shell-box pin-cushion for Grandma Buckley, a big moustache-cup for her father, and a beautiful purse, with a mother-of-pearl flap and a blue painting of the sea on it, for her mother. And when dinner-time came it was a real treat to go into one of the little wooden shanties and eat fish and chips off white american cloth covered tables and drink Kola or lemonade or ginger beer. The chips were gritty with sand, but nobody enjoyed them any the less for this. And there was ice-cream too, as much as they could eat. And at one end of the beach there was a big Wakes, with a Water Chute and a Haunted House and Caves. They all liked the Caves best for you went in a real boat through them and they were beautifully lit up with fairy lamps.

Once Hilda wandered off on her own and walked a long way over the sands towards the far-off sea. She was fascinated by the long line of shining blue-green water and wanted to get right up to it and touch it. Nobody seemed to have missed her, so she ran and as she came nearer to them was surprised to find that the waves were very big and looked quite dangerous. And then suddenly she heard her name being shouted, and turning round saw her father, his trousers rolled up to the knees, running after her and wildly waving for her to come back. But she stood there obstinately, and waited for him to come up with her. In his thick black clothes he was sweating and out of breath. He seized her arm and pulled her resentfully along with him towards the safety of the crowded shore. As they ran she looked round and saw the water was catching up with them, racing them. She began to feel scared, and she could see her father was scared too, and he ran faster till he was nearly dragging her along, her own feet just skimming the sand as he pulled. Presently, for lack of breath, he slowed down and they both looked back. The sea was still rushing after them and the waves now were high and fierce. They ran again and never stopped till Joe felt quite sure they were safe from the pursuing terror. Then he took out his white Sunday handkerchief and wiped his face and the inside of his stiffly-starched white Sunday collar, and the inside band of his bowler hat.

"Well, that was a near go, our 'Ilda. Tide's coming in and tha might 'a bin drowned. Thi mother's that moithered. Best go and play wi' our Lily a bit," he advised, knowing that his wife, seeing Hilda safe, would certainly give her a clouting to express her relief. "And keep away from t'water, do. Us dunna want no buryings i' Southport."

Hilda ran off to the lake, where Lily and the other children were paddling; and Joe rejoined his terrified wife, who, though thankful to have Hilda safely near her again, upbraided her husband for letting her go unpunished. "Tha's too soft wi' 'er, Joe Winstanley. She's that venturesome she'll come to a bad end if us lets 'er go 'er own road wi'out lifting a hand. Us'll 'ave to watch 'er", she concluded grimly, "day in, day out. Our own never gives us a minute's onrest, but our 'Ilda mun allus be up to summat or other. If us hadna missed 'er, she might be lying out yonder stiff and stark by this time. She's a proper nowt."

Joe sat sheepish and uncomfortable, but made no defence. When his wife got herself worked up he knew it was best to let her have her say out.

As the golden afternoon wore away, Hilda and Lily kept on asking their father the time, counting up how much longer yet before they had to leave this paradise of blue and gold. And of course there was still the knife-and-fork tea to look forward to before the Outing was over. This tea, which had all been properly arranged by Mr Woodville, was given free to the schoolchildren by the Vicar. The parents paid ninepence a head, but considered it good value. For there was ham and there was tongue, to say nothing of countless porkpies and jellies and scones and cakes. And it was held in a proper restaurant in Lord Street, where all sat down to long tables with white glossy cloths on them decorated with vases of flowers. The Reverend Black said grace, and when they had finished everybody stood up and gave thanks to God and the Vicar for their excellent tea, and Mr Woodville made a speech about the Reverend Black's kindness and thoughtfulness and asked them to show their appreciation in the usual way. They clapped and cheered willingly till Mr Black held up a hand and, turning towards the schoolmaster, said: "And now three cheers for your schoolmaster, who has so kindly arranged the Outing, and to whom all you children owe a debt you can never repay. If it wasn't for Mr Woodville here you would never become educated, and to become educated is the greatest blessing you can have. I want every one of you always to remember this." Mr Black looked for confirmation to the parents, who again clapped accommodatingly to show their understanding of what miracles education was doing for their offspring. Both the Vicar and the schoolmaster would have been astonished and horrified at the small percentage who really approved of it. But schooling was Government orders, otherwise Mr Woodville would have been hard put to it for pupils.

After this there was one more precious hour, counted minute by minute, on the shining sands, and then the wonderful day was over, and parents and children alike turned heavily towards the station and home.

*   *   *

The last real treat of the summer for both children and grown-ups was the Sunday School Outing on August Bank Holiday. James Turner, the Superintendent, somehow always managed that this should take place at a farm several miles from Kilnbrook and Moss Ferry. This ensured the excitement of riding there in wagonettes, for the ride counted as nearly the biggest part of the treat. Consequently, when Mr Holroyd, one of Kilnbrook's most prosperous farmers and a leading chapel-goer, sold his farm for an even bigger one on the outskirts of unknown and far-off Wigan, it was taken for granted that the August Bank Holiday treat should be held at his farm. This meant a long and interesting ride through hitherto unheard of villages and right through Wigan itself. There were six wagonettes full of singing children and their parents, rattling cheerfully along, and everybody waving and shouting to passers-by. The men, with magnificent reckless-ness, threw pennies and halfpennies to the staring children in the villages. And when the cavalcade was passing through Wigan the children in the streets did more than stare. They raced the galloping wagonettes and begged quite shamelessly, calling out hopefully: "Gi' us a penny, Mister, Gi' us a penny," and then burst into the Christmas-carol song:

If you haven't got a penny, a ha'penny will do,
If you haven't got a ha'penny, God bless you.

Touched and astonished by the cheekiness of this moving appeal, the pennies and ha'pennies fairly showered down, and when one adventurous lad suddenly turned a superb cartwheel almost under the wheels of the leading wagonette, Joe Winstanley, before his wife could stop him, had flung him a threepenny bit, for which loose spending he was severely nagged for weeks and even months afterwards. The ride through the town was over all too quickly and, whipping up their horses to shake off the procession of running, shrieking children, they were soon at Mr Holroyd's farm on the farther outskirts.

Mr and Mrs Holroyd, eager to welcome their old chapel friends and neighbours, were waiting for them at the gate, and gave a steadying hand to the children as they got down from the dangerously high steps of the wagonettes. There was a big marquee in one corner of the field, and when they were unloaded Mrs Holroyd invited all to help themselves to the ham sandwiches and buns and cups of tea which she had spent half the night and all the morning preparing. After this they formed up into little groups and wandered about the fields while the games were being organised.

None of the grown-ups envied Mr Holroyd for living so close to a town, for it all looked so grimy after the flat green fields of Kilnbrook and Moss Ferry. The tall black shafts of the coal mines dotted around frightened them, and Hilda, walking off by herself as she loved to do, discovered a great pit at the far end of the field and came tearing back to report that she had found a coal mine right in Mr Holroyd's own field. There was a stampede to see this amazing sight, and sure enough there was the coal. Little layers of it black and glistening between the brown soil. They stood on the edge, staring. It was the first time any of them had seen coal growing, and they were surprised to see how natural it looked against the earth and grass. Mr Holroyd seemed quite proud of it and explained that this pit was called a subsidence, and that there were several more like it in other of his fields, because the mines ran all underneath. The people looked at each other and then at the solid stone farm-house, and fears were expressed for its safety. But Mr Holroyd laughed and said it was nothing to worry about. The farm had been there longer than the mines and he reckoned it would stand up for his lifetime, any road. The mothers warned their children not to play too near the pit, and there was an unholy feeling of excitement that any minute the very ground they stood on might open and swallow them up—tent, wagonettes, farm-house and all. The Superintendent remarked warningly: "Prepare to meet thy God for in the midst of life we are in death," and immediately started to arrange the afternoon's entertainment as far from the gaping hole as possible. Mrs Winstanley kept an aggressive eye on Hilda and commanded Joe likewise not to let her out of his sight. "There's no knowing what she'll be up to next if us dunna watch 'er." She had a resentful feeling that Hilda, in unlawful collaboration with "t'Owd Lad", was directly responsible for the pit through her meddlesomeness in finding it. "Mun allus be a meddlesome Mattie," she grumbled to her husband. "Reckon it's all this book-reading does her no good. Other folks' childer dunnot go finding coal mines. Our 'Ilda's got no gumption—sometimes," she qualified grudgingly. She grumbled herself cheerful, and with her husband sat down happily to watch the "thread a

needle while you run" race. Both Hilda and Lily entered for
this, but the prize fell to Elsie Entwistle, and there was friendly
applause for Elsie when the Superintendent presented her with a
little round box of Fry's Chocolate Drops, tied up with a length
of pink satin ribbon.

For the egg-and-spoon race Hilda and Lily again entered, their
feet and legs in potato sacks, and Lily Winstanley, usually so
clumsy, astounded Hilda and everybody else by winning it.
Hilda fell and dropped her egg only a few yards from the starting
point, but got herself upright again and struggled along greedily
with her eyes fixed enviously on Lily's stolid back several yards
ahead of them all. Lily, showing great commonsense, made no
sensational attempts at speed. She just plodded cautiously, never
once turning round to see what was happening behind, and
reached the winning post without having suffered a single fall.
There was the same generous applause as they had given to Elsie,
and the Superintendent smilingly handed Lily a book. Her face
fell, and she came back to her family sullenly, holding out the
prize for them to inspect. It was a pretty, dark red book, and
Lily slowly read out the title—*The Lady of the Forest*. She was
bitterly disappointed, and looked sourly over at Mrs Entwistle,
sitting with Elsie's chocolate drops on her lap. Hilda came running
up and reached out for the book, but Lily kept tight hold of it.

"No, our 'Ilda. I won it. But you can buy it if you like. Threepence. Only you'll have to give it me *now*," Lily stipulated
malevolently, well knowing that her sister hadn't got threepence
and wouldn't have till Saturday came and Jack paid her for
cleaning his boots.

Mrs Winstanley was both pleased and shocked at this piece of
astuteness on Lily's part, but Hilda's face darkened and she
jeered at her sister: "Mardy, mardy, tell-tale, sausage fingers!

Fancy the Superintendent giving *you* a book. He might ha'
known you couldn't read it properly. Let me have it. *Give* it
me. I'll pay you Saturday. See!"—and she wet a forefinger and
drew it dramatically across her throat,—"Cut my throat and
pierce my heart if I don't!"

But Lily stood firm, unmoved by this solemn and traditional
promise, her podgy hands holding tightly the unwanted prize,
her small brown eyes fixed cunningly on her sister's face.

Hilda's face worked ominously, and she turned to her father.

"Lend it me, Father. I'll pay back Saturday. And you gave
that cartwheel boy threepence for nothing," she added unjustly.

Joe, uneasily remembering the recklessly flung threepenny bit,
and not daring to look at his wife, gave Hilda three pennies.

"Here, our Lily. *Now* give it me!" Lily's eyes shone greedily
as Hilda handed over the pennies and received in exchange *The
Lady of the Forest.* But her joy was cut short, for Mrs Winstanley took the book firmly from her. "Nay, our 'Ilda. This is
Sunday School Treat and no time for book-reading. Plenty o'
time for such idleness any day o' the week. Ah'll keep it. And
give over crying, do. A great girl o' your age crying o'er a book.
'Tisn't natural. And folks looking at us—whatever next!"

Joe sat there looking soft and unhappy. He couldn't see any
harm in letting Hilda have the book now she had paid for it, but
a glance at his wife's face warned him to keep quiet.

The Superintendent was now calling for competitors to enter
the tug-of-war and, seeing that neither crying nor sulking would
move her mother, Hilda prepared with Lily to go and join in.
But before going a thought struck her.

"If I can't have the book our Lily's no right to my threepence,"
she argued reasonably. "Give it me back," she ordered the
crestfallen Lily.

Lily looked at her mother, and her mother looked at Joe.

"Reckon that's reet enough, Mother. You keep t'book and t'money till us gets 'ome. That's nobbut reet and proper." So, sulkily, Lily gave her mother the threepence and the two girls went off to the tug-of-war. As soon as they were out of hearing, Mrs Winstanley turned sharply on her husband.

"Allus letting 'er 'ave 'er own road. Give our Lily a book and it does 'er no 'arm, but our 'Ilda's allus at book-reading and no good'll come of it, Joe Winstanley. Ah'm pleased wi' our Lily, though, 'aving t'gumption to sell it."

She stroked the book and turned over a few leaves admiringly. "It's a nice looking book. Us mun get 'Ilda to read it us. And see she pays back Saturday. Tha's too soft wi' 'er. Allus giving way. She's that 'eadstrong. Us mun watch 'er." And with this Mrs Winstanley regained her natural cheerfulness and sat contentedly watching the tug-of-war.

When all the races had been run there was tea in the marquee, and after tea the Superintendent, with several big paper bags in his arms, called all the children round him in the field. First he threw handfuls of mixed nuts, for which they scrambled eagerly, and then handfuls of wrapped sweets. And when these had all gone each child filed past him and received an apple and an orange and a shining new penny.

When it was time to start for home and all were in the farmyard by the wagonettes, the Superintendent called for silence. With a sense of what was proper and fitting he led them gravely into the hymn:

> Abide with me, fast falls the eventide,
> The darkness deepens, Lord with me abide....

He then asked for three cheers for Mr and Mrs Holroyd, which were given so gratefully and heartily that Mrs Holroyd was seen to wipe her eyes. Both of them stood at the gate till the procession disappeared into the growing darkness. Jolting home through the hay-scented countryside they sang their favourite hymns to the accompaniment of accomplished performers on the mouth-organ, and when they grew tired of hymns a powerful voice in the leading wagonette launched them into "The Holy City"—

> Jerusalem, Jerusalem,
> Lift up your gates and sing
> Hosannah; Ho-oh-ho-sannah!
> Hosannah to the King!

The entire company took it up with bursting hearts for the wonderful Bank Holiday which was now drawing to a close and, as the deep Hosannahs rolled out into the quiet night, doors were opened and strange voices called friendly greetings after them.

Everybody was dead tired but there was a warm feeling of neighbourliness and companionableness all round. Mrs Winstanley, now that it was too dark to read, gave Hilda *The Lady of the Forest* to hold, and Lily her threepence. The men pulled out thick wads of honey-smelling black twist and smoked their pipes with a leisurely air. The children sucked and crunched the few toffees which they had, by a great effort of will-power, managed to save for the ride home. As they drew near their two villages the cavalcade stopped every now and then to set down families at their own front doors. It was a point of honour for all to thank the drivers, as well as the Lord Jesus, for bringing them safely back through the perils of the night. Nor were the horses forgotten. Knobs of sugar were brought out, the drivers waiting as a matter of course while these well-earned dues were given to their animals. After each halt the "good-neets" rang out loudly, and then, with an affectionate "gee-up, gee-up" from the drivers, the procession again moved off into the night.

CHAPTER VIII

EARLY DAYS

The Winstanleys did not move to the house in School Lane until Hilda was nearly ten, and John was already working at the foundry in Daneshead and Jim at Morgan's farm up in Mad Lane. Before that they lived in the first of three cottages at the corner of Mad Lane and the high road to Daneshead. The cottages were known simply as The Dip because they were built in a hollow, with deep stone steps down to their front doors, and their back gardens rising steeply to the Lovers' Field behind. Across the high road was an old stone bridge over a noisy little brook—the Mad Brook—which, though narrow, was fairly deep and rushed between high banks to the wide Mersey only two fields away.

Hilda and Lily and the other children of The Dip spent many hours in summer exploring the Mad Brook, and once Hilda, peering very closely at the bright pebbly bed, saw a shining halfpenny wedged firmly between the stones, and was much worried as to the best way to dig it out. For narrow though it was, the brook was too wide for her to straddle, and there was nothing for it but to take off her boots and stockings and stand knee-deep in the rushing water. It was a fearful thing to do for she knew she would get into trouble if her mother heard she had been up to her knees in the water. There was only one legitimate place for the Moss Ferry children to go barefooted, and that was the seaside. But a halfpenny was a halfpenny and she would have risked her life in the dark waters of the Mersey itself for such a treasure. Hilda looked round cautiously. There was nobody about, though any minute she feared the tell-tale Lily might turn up. If that happened she would have to share the fruits of the halfpenny as the price of silence, and even so she couldn't trust Lily. She quickly unlaced her heavy boots and took off her black elastic garters and black woollen stockings and then, holding her frock and petticoat well above her middle with one hand, slipped down into the water. But she had reckoned without her sleeves. They were long and gathered tightly at the wrists and wouldn't roll up above an inch or two. She'd have to take her frock right off, and though she had never in her life done such a dreadful thing out of doors, the halfpenny was worth it. She pulled the frock over her head and threw it on to the bank, standing there in her red flannel weekday petticoat and white calico chemise buttoned up to her throat. At the first try she secured the halfpenny and wiped it dry on her petticoat. Visions of Mrs Wright's American gums rose before her eyes. Four ounces a penny. Two ounces for a halfpenny. Or she could buy eight aniseed balls or a long strip of "Spanish" liquorice or some pink and white coconut chips. While she stood there, enjoying the feel of the cool water round her legs and greedily anticipating these pleasing alternatives, she heard her mother calling, and before she could move saw her coming round the bend with Lucy Stringer, and Lily trotting behind.

Her face went as red as her petticoat. Lucy Stringer to see her like that! And wouldn't she catch it now from her mother! Her grip tightened on the halfpenny, now hot and damp in her feverish palm, but it gave her no comfort and she wished it was still at the bottom of the Mad Brook.

Mrs Winstanley could scarcely believe her eyes. Hilda, standing practically naked in the Mad Brook in the middle of the afternoon, and Lucy Stringer to see her so. Her face reddened, and it was Lucy who spoke first.

"Come out of that, Hilda Winstanley! You'll catch your death." She held out a hand and pulled her up the bank and hustled her into her frock, her arms all wet as they were. "Now wipe your legs and feet. Use your stockings, child. They'll dry. Put your boots on and come in."

Hilda, afraid to look at her mother, did as she was told and they went back to The Dip, Lily walking virtuously ahead. Lucy Stringer kept on looking at Hilda and made her feel very uncomfortable. She was so tall and stiff. Walked straight like a poker, and her expression was such that Hilda lost all desire to explain the discovery of the halfpenny. When they got indoors, Mrs Winstanley took Hilda's stockings and put them in the oven to dry, ordering her to sit still meanwhile. She turned ingratiatingly to Lucy. "T'kettle's just on t'boil. You'll stop for a cup o' tea. Ah don't know what's come over our 'Ilda showing 'erself naked. After t'way us 'as brought 'er up, too. Reckon Joe'll 'ave summat to say when 'e 'ears on it."

She turned reproachfully on the unfortunate girl. "Shame on you, 'Ilda Winstanley, standing ondressed in t'middle of t'afternoon. *Anybody* might 'a seen you from t'bridge. Nice talk there'll be if it gets heard on. Did anybody see you? Tell me no lies, now. Did they?"

Hilda shook her head and, looking apprehensively at Lucy Stringer, revealed the halfpenny and explained the reason for her unusual behaviour. Mrs Winstanley, when she had heard the full story, softened and even Lucy's iron jaws relaxed as she drank her tea.

"Well, reckon childer's allus up to summat," she remarked reasonably. "If it isn't one thing then it's another," and, now quite mellowed by the tea and cake, she took out her purse and surprisingly presented Hilda with yet another halfpenny.

"Now you've got a whole penny to spend, and here's a penny ıor Lily too. But don't you go standing i' cold water again. Enough to give you your death and no mistake."

When Mrs Winstanley related the shameful episode to her husband that night he only laughed.

"Reckon Ah'd 'a done same at 'Ilda's age, danged if Ah' wouldna. Nobbut sense to pick up a halfpenny, any age. Lucky too."

*   *   *

Though all the children of The Dip were strictly forbidden to go near the Mersey, it was more than some of them could bear not to explore along the Mad Brook till it poured into the big river. For in summer its banks were bright with clumps of marsh marigolds and tangles of purple mallow and meadowsweet, and tadpoles no thicker than darning needles darted in their thousands at the bottom. And there were hundreds of frogs, and occasionally a terrifying toad would hop out resentfully and, believing it capable of spitting black poison at them and so shrivelling them to a horrible, inescapable death, they would leave it respectfully alone, not even daring to poke at it with a stick. Sometimes a more venturesome child would throw little stones and twigs to make it jump, and then run screaming till a safe distance away from the swollen brown horror.

Once safely out of sight of the bridge, the children followed the brook to the river, on the other side of which was the Haunted House. None of the children in Moss Ferry knew the story of the house, though they felt that more than one old woman in the village could say a thing or two if only she would. It was a very big house, in a sort of Victorian Italian renaissance style, covered with dark grey stucco that was peeling off in great dank patches, and nearly all the tall windows were broken and cobwebbed and the whole place was in a wretched, desolate condition. It stood in a thick shrubbery of elms, so that in the summer you could only see it in the gaps between the foliage. But in the winter the entire front of the house and the outbuildings were visible, and even part of the neglected, grass-covered drive to the front door. Hilda was continually sneaking off along the brook to have a look at the Haunted House, and even on the hottest day it made her feel cold just to sit on the river bank and look over at it. For though the country surrounding it might be trembling in summer haze, the Haunted House never seemed to get the smallest ray of sunlight, and the cold issuing from it flowed right over the river, enveloping all who passed on the opposite bank. Nobody had lived there for years. Indeed nobody in Moss Ferry could remember who had last lived there. Hilda had only once mentioned it to her mother and father, and both had turned on her in fear and told her to ask no questions and they would tell her no lies. The Haunted House over in Cheshire! They held their breaths at the words. "You leave it be Hilda Winstanley. There's no call for childer to be knowing of such things. Like as not t'Owd Lad 'isself lives there. And boggarts, too."

It never occurred to any of the children to get close up to the house, although it could have been reached by the Wilverton Bridge farther up the river, or by the ferry at the top of the village. Hilda, by long observation, had discovered that no matter how fiercely the sun was shining on the ships coming down from Manchester, as soon as they sailed the stretch of river in front of the house the light was struck from them, and did not return till they were safely past and heading for the Wilverton Bridge. It was this astonishing sight which fascinated her and

made her sit patiently for hours waiting for a boat to come up.
She watched closely as it drew nearer and nearer, and immediately it entered the evil stretch of water it was enshrouded in its
own shadow, emerging, as from a black caul, only when past the
Haunted House and cutting again through clean water.

*   *   *

One momentous event of Hilda's first years at the cottage in
The Dip was the Christmas when Lucy and Grandma Stringer
arrived with a glorious doll for her—the first big, expensive doll
she had ever owned. Every Christmas, along with other presents,
she had had a little doll, dressed only in a fragile chemise and a
shady straw hat, but this beauty was the size of a new-born baby,
and Lucy had made a complete set of clothes for it: a chemise of
white calico edged with real torchon lace, with drawers to match;
a cream flannel scalloped petticoat, and a lovely frock of bright
pink cashmere, with a bonnet of the same material as the frock
framing its golden curls and pink and white face. And as though
the clothes were not wonder enough, it talked when its stomach
was pressed, shrilling out "Mama" and "Papa". It was the only
talking doll ever seen in Moss Ferry, and Hilda used to take it
out for special walks just to show it off.

Being a rather solemn religious child, Hilda felt that her new
doll also must find grace and be properly and legally baptised, so
one day, with Lily holding it tenderly, Hilda took the part of the
minister and, marking with a pin a small cross in the centre of
the doll's waxen forehead, and sprinkling water on its rosy cheeks,
she gave it officially the high-sounding name of Agnes Mary.
Mrs Winstanley was shocked when she saw the cross, and
smacked Hilda for being both heathenish and destructive. She
said the cross was Roman Catholic and no thing for good chapel-

going folks to be mixed up with. And whatever would Lucy Stringer say when she saw the doll again after all the money it must have cost! But the cross remained and the name remained and not till she was a big girl of twelve did Hilda cease openly to make much of Agnes Mary.

One day, as she was nursing her on the bridge over the Mad Brook, a passing tramp spoke to her and admired the beautiful doll and said what a lucky girl she was to own it. Then, taking his hand from his pocket, he placed it swiftly right under Agnes Mary's clothes, looking round to see if anybody was about. Hilda was too surprised and too frightened to say a word or to call out for her mother, and not till the tramp had moved off did she look to see what he had put there. She was astonished to find three halfpennies! Immediately she ran in, excitedly showing the halfpennies to her mother, chattering about the tramp and how funny of him to put them under Agnes Mary's clothes instead of giving them to her properly. At this information her mother's face darkened and she ran out into the road to get a look at the tramp. But he was a good way up the road, nearly at *The Black Horse*, and Mrs Winstanley returned to question Hilda.

"Did 'e say owt else except about you being a lucky girl? Did 'e lay a finger on you? Dunna be feared to say. Us mun tell your father on this. It winna do to 'ave tramps traipsing round interfering wi' childer. And dunna you ever talk to any on 'em, our 'Ilda. 'Tisna safe. 'E might 'a carried you off happen you hadna bin reet outside. Never 'eard tell o' such a thing afore."

Her mother's alarm infected Hilda, for though the tramp had spoken to her pleasantly enough, she now began to see herself as one who had escaped from fearful and unknown perils. The tramp might have taken her off like the gypsies took the little boy in *Chatterbox*. From that day, in spite of the three halfpennies, she was afraid of every tramp who passed, ready to run madly for home if he should so much as look at her.

*　　　　*　　　　*

Mick, the Winstanley's thirteen-year-old ginger and white cat, had lived all his life in The Dip and was justly famed throughout the neighbourhood for his handsome appearance and his superior intelligence. He was acknowledged by all to be the best ratter for miles, and when his blood was up even water had no terrors for him. Mrs Winstanley was never tired of relating his epic victory over the rats that infested the Mersey. Whenever "company" stooped to stroke and admire him she would pause for attention and say: "Aye! He's a rare 'un is our Mick. Ah call to mind when Mr Maudsley, t'postman from Daneshead, popped in for a drink o' tea one morning and asked who owned t'ginger and white cat as was allus laying up by t'Mersey.

"'Sounds like our Mick, Mr Maudsley,' Ah said.

"'Well, Missus, reckon you've got a goldmine then. Ah've watched him many a time dive into t'river and nip out a rat quicker than any dog could 'a done it. Ah've seen 'im lay as many as six deaders neat as a pod o' peas on t'bank.'"

So it was a very dark day in the cottage when Mick was suddenly taken poorly. None of them ever found out the reason, and when Grandma Buckley, miserable as ever, said she reckoned it was just old age, Mrs Winstanley turned on her quite savagely and said, No—he'd never ailed in his life, and she for one reckoned it was poison; like as not put down for him in Sarah Dumbell's orchard. For Mrs Dumbell had no love for man or beast and more than once her neighbour, Mrs Wright of the parlour-shop, had seen her throw things at Mick when he'd walked through her orchard.

The whole family was terribly upset when, in spite of all that Mrs Winstanley could do, Mick died; and Hilda and Lily asked if they might wear a black hair-ribbon for him. He was older by years than either of them, and they cried loudly when their mother, her own face working, said dramatically when they came home from school at dinner-time: "He's gone! He knowed everything, our Mick did. Like one of us 'e was and us'll give 'im a proper burying. When your father's 'ad 'is tea 'e'll dig 'im a proper tidy grave and us'll all be there. Our Jack and Jim too. And step in to Grandma Buckley when you loose from school and ask 'er to come down. She was allus one for our Mick, so reckon she'd not like 'im put away wi'out a last look."

When the menfolk had finished their tea, Joe heavily took his spade and they all followed him into the back garden, looking for a suitable place for Mick's last home. After much debate they settled on a spot at the very end of the garden, beyond the potato patch, and Joe began to dig while the family stood miserably around. He dug quite deep—nearly three feet.

"Us dunna want 'im to be scratched up again," he explained, and when the grave was ready Mrs Winstanley, the tears rolling down, went into the shed to fetch the body. Jack meanwhile had lined the grave with big rhubarb leaves, and on these Mick was laid reverently, with a covering of rhubarb leaves and a bunch of white and purple asters on top. They stood there in the lovely August evening. Joe in his corduroys and working shirt. Jim likewise. Jack too in his foundry overalls. Mrs Winstanley had put on a clean white apron and Grandma was wearing her Sunday bonnet and black beaded cape, while the two girls, to show their sense of occasion, wore their white muslin frocks. No one spoke, but before Joe filled in the grave each stooped to pick up a handful of earth, which they dropped solemnly on the rhubarb leaves.

Then Joe, with a gulping "Best get it ower", shovelled in the earth and smoothed it down, leaving a neat little mound. And for many weeks both Hilda and Lily placed flowers in a stone jam-jar on the mound, and Hilda made a little wooden cross to put at the head of poor Mick's grave and printed on it in red mapping ink:

In Loving Memory of Mick.
Died August 14th 1905.
Aged thirteen years.

REST IN PEACE

CHAPTER IX
SCHOOL

Every child in Moss Ferry went to school at the first opportunity. Some, with an older brother or sister to take them, began as early as three if they were what Mrs Winstanley described as "clean in their 'abits". Hilda was one of these and she had a dim recollection of trotting along to St Margaret's, the National Church School, holding on to Jack at first, and then, when he left school to work in the foundry, she was looked after, grudgingly, by the loutish Jim. By the time she was five, responsibility fell easily upon her, and in her turn she took charge of the three-year-old Lily, whose personal habits were also, thanks to the rigours of Mrs Winstanley's upbringing, beyond suspicion.

St Margaret's was a small, stone-built school, very solid, very ugly, and surprisingly warm in the heavy winters, for in each of its classrooms was an ordinary hob-fire, with a guard in front of it, kept plentifully supplied with coal. The headmaster was Mr Woodville, a tall, lean, dark, unhappy-looking man who lived with his wife and four daughters in the schoolhouse adjoining the school itself.

There were only two rooms, in one of which were the Infants, taught by Mrs Pretty, a kind-hearted woman who came every day by train from Warrington. The other room was divided by a glass partition, in one section of which Mr Woodville taught the children who had somehow achieved the higher Standards. In the other section were Standards I and II, in charge of Miss Fanny Askew, a young, uncertificated teacher, and III and IV, taught by Miss Maudie Holroyd, dark, beautiful, young and clever. Maudie Holroyd, although her father, Tom Holroyd, was only the village cobbler and had a wooden leg at that, had passed all her examinations brilliantly and was a properly accredited teacher, admired and envied by her fellow teacher, Fanny Askew, and greatly respected by Mrs Pretty and Mr Woodville. She had a quick temper and used her cane freely, but in spite of this all her scholars loved her, and none more passionately than Hilda Winstanley. Each child, as soon as it emerged from the Infants, paid twopence a week for its education. The children had to buy their own pencils and indiarubbers as well, and it was Mrs Winstanley's proud boast that she had never owed a penny for her children's schooling. Sometimes, when they filed past their teacher's desk on a Monday morning to pay, a child would hang back miserably, muttering that he hadn't got the money today, but would bring it next Monday for sure. The teacher was always very nice, and said it didn't matter for once, but they must tell their mothers not to make a habit of it.

Hilda's first years in the Infants passed happily, and she learnt to count with big coloured wooden beads in a frame, and to draw her first letters in wet sand on a wooden tray. And then came pothooks in ruled copybooks, and then spelling the first simple words, and by the time she was five she could read little stories and recite verses. And at six she was promoted to Miss Askew's Standard I, and learnt scripture and geography and button-holing and her first sums. But it was not till she reached Standard III and had the beautiful Maudie Holroyd for teacher that her education proper began. For Miss Holroyd, perceiving her natural quickness at all lessons but arithmetic, made much of her and took extra pains to get her forward with her sums. And Hilda, because she loved Miss Holroyd and to show her love wanted to be the best scholar in the class, worked painstakingly at these. But it was no good. She arrived at the stage when she could certainly, by the given rules, get them, after much labour, to come out right, but at mental arithmetic—the severest test—she was so slow that after a time Miss Holroyd gave up worrying her, and instead encouraged her in all the other subjects. She usually came out top in spelling, and was good at history and geography and English composition. More than once, when the class had been set an essay to write, Miss Holroyd had taken Hilda's effort in to Mr Woodville. And Mr Woodville had come in with it and smiled at Hilda and said: "Now children. I want you to listen to Hilda Winstanley's essay on 'The Trip to Llandudno', and next time try to do as well. Hilda uses her imagination. And that's what Miss Holroyd wants all of you to do. Now pay attention while I read it."

Miss Askew, who had to stop her own lesson while Mr Woodville was reading, would smile too at Hilda, proud of the fact that she had been in her class and was sure to go far—perhaps become a pupil teacher like herself, or even a properly certificated one like Maudie Holroyd.

As soon as the school was loosed Hilda flew home, calling out to her mother directly she entered the kitchen: "Mr Woodville read my English composition out loud to the class." And her mother, who had no idea what an English composition was, showed that she was pleased but nevertheless admonished Hilda not to go getting above herself. And when her husband came home, and both Hilda and Lily were out playing, she would relate to him how Maudie Holroyd and Mr Woodville thought a lot of their Hilda at her schooling. And Joe, relishing his tea of bacon and toasted cheese, would nod slowly and say: "Aye. Reckon she's got it in her. There's nowt like being a good scholard when all's said and done."

*   *   *

St Margaret's being a Church of England school, all the pupils were well grounded in the Scriptures, and scripture was the first lesson of the day. Only the poor, dirty, Roman Catholic Doyles were exempted from this lesson, and even so Mr Woodville insisted on their being in the playground when the bell rang at nine o'clock. After that they had to wait in the lobby where the hats and coats were hung, till the scripture lesson was over. There were a great number of them, all boys save the eldest, Mary Doyle, and they lived in a rotting and miserable two-roomed wooden shack away up on the Moss. Their father, Patrick Doyle, was a farm labourer, and they were the sole congregation of the little Roman Catholic Chapel in Moss Ferry. All the school-teachers, from Mr Woodville down, disliked them because of their unwashed faces and hands and dirty clothes, and the other children used to jeer at their funny, foreign-sounding speech, and resented their shiftlessness in having been born out of the proper Christian faith. This heathenish religion of theirs set them apart, and all their poverty and misfortunes were put down to its sinister and unnatural hold over them. Mr Woodville especially made no effort to hide his dislike of them, and once when Mary Doyle, in the depth of winter, was discovered to be wearing no stockings under her unblacked clogs, he made her sit away from the other children as a punishment for coming to school so indecently dressed. Mary Doyle sat there, blue and green with cold, her frozen fingers stumbling with her pen, and her frozen wits trying desperately to take in the lesson. But she couldn't learn a thing, and when Mr Woodville began to question one child after another on the lesson, only Mary Doyle couldn't utter a sound. She looked more like an old woman than a girl of twelve, and when the schoolmaster, enraged by her silence, ordered her savagely to collect her stupid wits or it would be the worse for her, she startled them all by crying shrilly: "I can't. I can't. I'm hungry," and laying her head on her arms wept noisily and hopelessly.

There was an awful stillness. Hungry! The word shot through the room like a bullet. Mary Doyle hungry! It had a shameful sound and the frightened children waited breathlessly for Mr Woodville to say something. For a second he only glared at her and then, commanding the class to keep silent, went out. When he returned, his peevish face looking very grave, they were astonished to see that he had a cup of steaming cocoa and a thick slice of bread and treacle, which he handed to the crying girl.

"Drink up," he said roughly. "You'll feel better for it. And Mrs Woodville thinks she can find you some of Florrie's old stockings. Bring it up to the fire, and stop crying, there's a good girl."

Mary looked at the food timidly and then, realising that it was really meant for her, ate and drank shamefacedly. The rest of the class, sharply called to attention, went on with the lesson, their eyes continually slewing over to Mary Doyle. Hilda thought of her own good breakfast that morning. A big bowl of Quaker Oats with golden syrup and a mug of cocoa and as much bread and jam as she could eat. She had never seen anybody go hungry before. What a tale to tell her mother at dinner-time!

When the news got around the village that the Doyles, dirty and heathenish though they were, were so put to it that they sent their children clemmed to school, there was a general feeling that something must be done. And it became an unwritten law on baking days to put in an extra loaf or a few more tea-cakes for the children to take to the Doyles.

"Us'll never miss it," said Mrs Winstanley, wrapping up a big currant loaf. "It's not reet for childer to go clemmed—heathen or not. Reckon Parish'll 'ave to do summat now. What's a man to do wi' all them childer to fend for and nobbut eighteen shilling a week coming in. And", turning accusingly to Hilda and Lily, "you be thankful for your own good home. There's bin no empty bellies i' this house, though Ah've been fair moithered many a time to make do on your father's wage, and what Lucy Stringer brings for our 'Ilda, afore Jack and Jim started to earn."

           *   *   *

Examination time at St Margaret's, which came only once a year, took place just before the school broke up for the summer holidays at the end of July. For weeks before the Inspector was due, the entire school from Standard I to Standard VII was in a state of tremendous agitation. Mr Woodville, looking more worried and peevish than ever, used his cane freely and threatened horrible beatings to any child who was not given a reasonable number of marks by the Inspector. Maudie Holroyd and Fanny Askew urged their respective classes to do their utmost, and Miss Holroyd paid special attention to the one bright hope of Standard IV, Hilda Winstanley, while Mr Woodville paid an equal attention to his eldest daughter, Florrie, and Peter Pettener, the only two pupils from whom he had anything to expect when the Examination was held. If the main body of children just scraped through he was satisfied, but through Peter Pettener, Florrie, and Hilda Winstanley he prayed for glory in the form of warm praise from the Inspector, of whom he was just as frightened as the children. Peter Pettener, big, gawky, and always several inches beyond his clothes, was the son of a farm labourer. But Peter had ambition. No farm work for him. His hopes on leaving school were set on getting into the tiny booking-office of the Cheshire Lines at Kilnbrook. A gentleman's job which might eventually lead to higher things, such as work for the Company in Warrington, or, higher still, in Manchester. Both his mother and father, anxious for his betterment, encouraged him to this end. Florrie Woodville, whose long, thick, golden hair was the wonder of the district, was her father's best pupil at arithmetic, and fairly good as well at most other subjects; and out of his class of some thirty children, Mr Woodville relied on these two to save him from ignominy with the School Authorities.

Maudie Holroyd, with her Standards III and IV, had only Hilda Winstanley to see her through, and black horror descended on her when, only a week from Examination Day, Lily Winstanley brought the terrible news that their Hilda had got the influenza and Doctor James said she was not to come back to school before it broke up.

Meanwhile Hilda, kept safely in bed, was fretting that if she didn't get better in time for the Examination, things would never be the same again between herself and Miss Holroyd. Miss Holroyd came to see her frequently, bringing egg custards to strengthen her, and urging her to get well enough to be in school when the Inspector came. The day before he was due she came again and spoke earnestly with Mrs Winstanley. Hilda, now able to sit downstairs, was still very weak and obviously in no state to go to school next day. But Miss Holroyd was desperate and herself went to see Doctor James, begging his permission for Hilda Winstanley to attend school for a short time next day. In the end, realising the seriousness of the situation, he agreed that Hilda could attend for the Examination, provided she was well wrapped up and remained in school only while Miss Holroyd's class was being examined. Though her bones still ached and her heavy boots felt like lead on her shaking legs, Hilda was in her appointed place when the Inspector arrived, covered up in her mother's grey woollen shawl, and an object of intense interest to her classmates, and to herself. For she was proud of being thus acknowledged the best scholar in Miss Holroyd's class, and was thoroughly enjoying her glorious martyrdom.

Mr Woodville, wearing his Sunday clothes, came in and told her not to get frightened. Miss Holroyd would explain to the Inspector about the influenza, and he would no doubt take this into account when examining.

"But do your best, Hilda, for your own sake as well as Miss Holroyd's. You'll be in Standard V if you pass today, and it's a high standard for a girl of your age."

The children were all fidgety and restless, waiting for the Inspector's arrival, and when he was seen to be actually shaking hands with Mr Woodville there was complete quiet in the two classrooms. Mr Woodville introduced him to Miss Holroyd and Miss Askew, both of whom were, like Mr Woodville, wearing their Sunday clothes. The Inspector, a tall, fair man with glasses and a pleasant smile, started first with Miss Askew's class, setting them easy sums and taking them in history and geography, while Miss Askew looked nervously on. When he had finished the Inspector said something to her in a very low voice, and the children were embarrassed when they saw her eyes fill with tears. The Inspector too looked embarrassed, and with a friendly smile turned hastily to Miss Holroyd and her class. Hilda observed Miss Holroyd, after a few words with the Inspector, point at her, and the Inspector nodded. Then he began to examine, and soon they were all busy with their exercise books writing down sums. Miss Holroyd, watching anxiously, saw Hilda pause uncertainly in the middle of a multiplication sum, and gave her an encouraging smile. Hilda, her heart thumping, made a stupendous effort and managed to get it right. She finished in time and then, the written sums being over, set herself to face the agony of mental arithmetic. She watched the Inspector waiting significantly for the answers to his questions, trembling lest he should suddenly pounce upon her. She tried desperately to keep calm and again saw Miss Holroyd smiling at her. She need not have worried, for the stabbing forefinger passed her by completely. Mental arithmetic was over and done with, and Hilda, once more at ease, waited confidently for the spelling and history and geography, the answers to which she was fairly certain to get right. The Examination ended by the children having to write a short essay on "The Royal Family", and when they had finished the Inspector collected half a dozen at random, beginning with Hilda's. While he was reading her essay, which she had written easily and quickly and finished long before anybody else, she saw him pause, frown, and turn accusingly to Miss Holroyd. Miss Holroyd looked at the essay and flushed. The Inspector then beckoned Hilda to the blackboard and told her to write "The Prince of Wales". Hilda, puzzled, and with Miss Holroyd looking beseechingly at her, took up the chalk and wrote boldly:

"The Prince of Whales."

The Inspector again looked at Miss Holroyd, and then asked Hilda to look at what she had written carefully, and to write underneath it "The Princess of Wales", and Hilda, now shaking with apprehension, again wrote, but less boldly:

"The Princess of Whales."

Miss Holroyd, her face burning, was in tears, and turning crossly to Hilda the Inspector asked: "In what country is Caernarvon situated?"

"In the country of Wales," stammered Hilda.

"Right," said the Inspector. "Now write on the blackboard—Caernarvon is in the country of Wales."

Hilda, her fingers shaking so that she could scarcely guide the chalk, wrote:

"Caernarvon is in the country of Wales."

The Inspector's face lightened, and so did Miss Holroyd's.

"Now, child, tell me what made you write the first Wales with an 'h'?"

Hilda, red with shame, and instantly perceiving the stupid mistake, answered miserably: "I don't know, Sir. I've never written it that road before. I don't know what made me do it." She began to cry, but the Inspector patted her shoulder kindly and laughed.

"Well—it's a funny mistake I must say, but I shan't give you a bad mark for it. Your teacher tells me you've been very poorly so I shall make allowance. But for that your essay is very good, very good indeed. You can go back to your place, and don't worry."

Hilda, crying now with relief, sat down self-consciously, and as soon as the Inspector went out to examine Mr Woodville's class, Miss Holroyd let her go home, after giving her the little bag of boiled sweets which she always presented to each of her pupils on the day before school broke up.

On returning to school after the holidays, Hilda found herself passed with top marks to Standard V. She was now ten years old and beginning on the last stage of her school life.

*　　　　　*　　　　　*

Although pleased and proud to have attained Mr Woodville's class, Hilda, like all his other pupils, was nervous lest she should make any mistake to bring down his wrath. For Mr Woodville, not an ill-natured man in himself, had the unhappiest home life of anyone in either Moss Ferry or Kilnbrook. Everybody felt sorry for him, for it was common talk that his wife, with her white, bad-tempered face, led him what Mrs Winstanley described as "a proper dance". Whenever there had been a scene between the pair of them, and such scenes were frequent, Mr Woodville took it out of his class, as if only in this way could he obtain relief from the nagging misery of his home. Mrs Clark, who lived in the end cottage in School Lane and often came in to have a cup of tea and a gossip with Mrs Winstanley, told how, one morning when she had been helping the Woodville's little servant with the heavy weekly washing, Mr Woodville had come into the house for a minute during playtime. Mrs Woodville was in the kitchen, criss-crossing with a fork the mashed-potato top of a large meat and potato pie for the family dinner. Mr Woodville had said something to her quite pleasantly—what the words were Mrs Clark had been unable to catch—but something to do with Doris, their third daughter, and Mrs Woodville's favourite.

"And without a word of a lie", related Mrs Clark impressively, "she took up that meat and potato pie and smashed it on the floor in her temper. I'd never have believed it if I hadn't seen it with my own eyes. And it was a lovely pie too—as big round as that," and Mrs Clark held her hands apart to stress the tragedy of the ruined dinner.

The Woodvilles had four daughters. Florrie, the eldest, nearly fourteen, and after her May, Doris and Margery. Doris, who had her mother's evil temper, was a continual cause for excitement with her tantrums, and no matter what she did her mother always, in the face of all reason, took her part. One playtime, while most of the girls were playing hopscotch, they gaped to see Doris Woodville run screaming out of the house and across the playground, pursued by her father, who held a cane in his hand. As he caught up with Doris she fell on her back, screaming at the top of her voice and kicking out at her father while he, beside himself with rage, whipped savagely at her legs and arms with the cane. Mrs Woodville, her black hair falling down, her face livid with anger, rushed up and, tearing the cane from her husband and shouting foul abuse at him, struck him wildly across the face, picked up the now hysterical Doris and ran with her into the house. Embarrassed and terrified, the girls had all stopped their games and stood staring at their schoolmaster, not daring to move. For a second or two he stood stock still, unconscious of the staring faces, and then, without even looking at them, turned and went into the school. Lessons for the rest of the day were a nightmare. He caned savagely right and left for the smallest fault, and Hilda, failing to get one of her sums right, was unjustly caned on both hands and went crying back to her place, emptied of all desire for further education at St Margaret's, and wishing passionately that she could afford to go to a proper school like Manchester High School, a hopeless, lovely dream that was always with her. Mr Woodville even caned Florrie, of whom he was fonder than any of his children, for not answering a question quickly enough, and the final misery came when Alfie Hogben, a big stupid boy of twelve, was discovered enjoying a mixture of oatmeal and sugar which he acquired by dipping a wet finger into a paper bag he held between his knees. Mr Woodville, his eyes fairly bulging, seized the trembling Alfie and laid him over a desk. The oatmeal scattered and made an awful mess on the floor. Alfie screamed and kicked, but the schoolmaster, holding him down firmly by digging a knee into his back, caned him unmercifully, and Alfie's sister, Polly, shouted out boldly that if he didn't leave off she would tell her father at dinner-time. Whereupon Mr Woodville, leaving the now whimpering Alfie, made Polly hold out her hands, and caned her hard for her impertinence in daring to question his authority.

Dinner-time came at last, and the children, like so many prisoners, raced home to relate what had happened that morning. Hilda, holding out her swollen, stinging palms for sympathy, was given a halfpenny to spend on sweets before going back to school, but in the Hogben's cottage by the church, Alfie Hogben, standing in his shirt, sick and crying, was being examined by his father. As Tom Hogben looked at the red weals on his legs and buttocks, and listened to Polly's account of Mr Woodville's savage attack, his cheerful, round red face hardened and, turning to his wife, who was looking as sick as the two children, ordered: "Keep them both at home this afternoon. Ah'll larn that bugger to knock my childer about. Let 'im take it out of 'is own flesh and blood if 'e's a mind to, but 'e shanna lift 'is 'and to one o' mine again."

Waiting apprehensively for the first lesson of the afternoon to begin, the class was startled by a loud knock on the door and immediately afterwards in walked Alfie Hogben's father. He walked confidently towards the schoolmaster, for Tom Hogben was no mere labourer, but a man in charge of men, being a ganger on the roads under the Council. In his rough cloth cap and loosely-knotted red choker and corduroy trousers, tied under the knees with straw bindings, he had a terrible dignity—like some great bull about to savage. Mr Woodville, surprised and uneasy, asked him civilly what his business was. Tom made no answer. The two men were now facing each other, the schoolmaster, for all his gentlemanly clothes and stiff white collar, looking seedy and useless against the solid working-class Tom who, suddenly closing his enormous hands round the schoolmaster's neck, said briefly: "Sithee, Mister, if tha lays a finger on my lad again, or on t'wench either, Ah'll choke thee."

Mr Woodville's face was now a purplish-green and he began to mutter something about his discipline and authority having to be maintained. Slowly, not even troubling to take in what the schoolmaster was saying, Tom Hogben, his blue saucer-eyes fixed steadily on Mr Woodville's neck, as if wondering whether it would not be best to squeeze the life out of him there and then, let go his strangling grip and without a word walked heavily out of the classroom.

The schoolmaster, the green receding from his face, looked at his frightened pupils, then picked up his chalk and began the lesson.

It was lucky for Alfie Hogben that he was so near the end of his schooling, for, though he was never caned after that terrible scene, Mr Woodville managed to make him wretched in a hundred different ways.

CHAPTER X

MR WINSTANLEY BETTERS HIMSELF

Soon after Hilda's promotion to the higher standard at school, a problem of absorbing interest and gravity arose in the Winstanley cottage. For Tom Hogben, the road ganger and an old friend of Joe's, told him that very soon he would be taking on another man in his gang, and wouldn't Joe like to have the job.

"Money's good," explained Tom. "Twenty-one shilling a week and regular hours, and no standing off i' bad weather. Think on it, Joe. There's no 'urry for a week or two."

Mrs Winstanley was immediately and whole-heartedly in favour of it. Not so much because of the extra three shillings a week, which, when set against her husband's harvest money and the Christmas Box and odd presents Mrs Gibbon was always sending them, in the long run came to no more. She was attracted, rather, by the improved social status a job on the roads would confer upon her husband and family. Working for the Council was a step above farm labouring and, as she impressively pointed out to the wavering Joe, he could reckon on being home to his tea regular and not for ever at Mr Gibbon's beck and call when anything went wrong at the farm with the animals.

But Joe, though flattered by Tom's interest, took a lot of persuading. He'd worked for Mr Gibbon for fifteen years, and all his life had been spent at farm work.

"Reckon Ah'm used to 'im and 'is ways, Mother. He'll find it none so easy to work wi' a stranger," he argued, hoping faintly that Lizzie would soften and counsel him to remain loyally with Mr Gibbon.

"Reckon you're a barm-pot then, Joe Winstanley. Us 'as got to look out for oursen and 'tisn't every chap as gets t'chance o' working for t'Council, as tha knows very well. Ah've no patience wi' your gormless ways. Look at t'road Tom Hogben stood up to Mr Woodville over their Alfie. That's what comes of 'aving good work under t'Council. And Mr Gibbon's not one to stand i' your road, that Ah do know."

Joe, realising that his wife had made up her mind and that there was no further hope, gave in his notice to Mr Gibbon, standing alongside him red and shamefaced and apologetic. Mr Gibbon could not believe that he had heard aright. Joe Winstanley, the steadiest man who had ever worked with him, throwing up good farm work for a la-di-da job on the roads. Sweeping up muck instead of ploughing the living land, sowing the living seed and reaping the living grain. Working like a machine along of other machines. Taking his orders from Tom Hogben instead of giving his own orders to honest beasts like the farm horses. Mr Gibbon regarded him sorrowfully.

"Well, Joe, I never thought I should live to see this day. You and me have worked together a good many years, and if it's only a matter of a shilling or two, reckon I can manage it all right. Tell you what, I'll raise your wage to a pound a week, and there's not another farm labourer in Lancashire or anywhere else getting that, I do know. Let's say no more about it. A pound a week, eh?"

And thinking the matter quite settled he went on with his hoeing, but Joe, still standing miserably, gulped: "Reckon tha's got to take my notice, Mester. Lizzie's set on my working for t'Council, and there's no shifting her."

Mr Gibbon, realising that he was beaten, looked sadly at Joe and then, with a quiet "All right. Reckon there's no more to be said," went indoors to break the bad news to his wife.

Joe's last week on the farm was the most miserable ever passed in the Winstanley household. Always quiet, he was now quieter than ever, and Lizzie seeing how he was taking it to heart, was tempted more than once to weaken and consent to him letting the road work go. Also she remembered uneasily the many kindnesses shown them by Mrs Gibbon, and what a friend Mr Gibbon had been when her brother Billy was up before the Bench at Warrington. But hardening herself she pointed out to her husband that he wasn't the first man in Moss Ferry to better himself, though he might very well be the last if he missed this chance. She emphasised dramatically that Council jobs didn't grow on gooseberry bushes, and not again in his lifetime could he hope for such advancement to come his way. The terrible week dragged heavily along, and on Saturday evening Joe came home a bit later than usual. He explained that he had been invited to stop for a sup of tea with Mr and Mrs Gibbon, both of whom had hoped, up to the very last minute, that he would change his mind and stay on with them.

*   *   *

Directly her husband started to work for the Council, Mrs Winstanley, feeling that their improved social status demanded something better than the old cottage in The Dip, began to look out for a house in the village, and settled on the end house of three which stood in School Lane. It was a bigger rent than they paid in The Dip, but it had a fine orchard and a big vegetable garden, and plenty of room for fowls, and a shed in the garden where she could do her washing without cluttering up the kitchen every Monday. And it had, too, a proper front room where she could entertain her company in state, and a little bedroom for Hilda and Lily. At the cottage they had slept in the same back

11   133

room as their brothers, with a curtain the length of the room to ensure privacy. It was also very near the school, and she would now have the pleasant company of quite a few neighbours. For Mrs Winstanley liked a bit of gossip, and the only time Hilda remembered her father being so angry that he raised his hand as though to strike her, but restrained himself with a great effort, was one evening when he came home from work to find only Hilda and Lily in the kitchen and no tea ready for him.

"Where's your mother," he inquired mildly.

"Up at Mrs Clark's," answered Hilda pertly. "She's been there gossiping ever since we had our tea. She's always out gossiping somewhere or another. She...." She stopped, frightened by her father's face, which had turned a dark red.

"Don't let me hear you talk of your mother that road again, or Ah'll give you a belting, big as you are. If your mother likes to 'ave a bit of a talk it's not for you, or anyone else, to say no. You mind that, our 'Ilda," he ended severely, and proceeded to fill the kettle from the big bucket of drinking water which stood by the copper.

There was a pump outside which served the three cottages with water, but it was not considered fit for drinking, and the drinking water had to be fetched daily from the well in Mrs Pettener's orchard, a little way up the lane. Hilda never minded being sent to fetch the well water. She enjoyed peering down into the awful black cavern, dropping the bucket with a splash and manoeuvring to draw it up full. And Mrs Pettener was never tired of relating how, when her Peter was nobbut three, she had one day found him trying to push his year-old sister down the hole so that he could hear her splash.

In the cottage immediately facing the Winstanley's lived Jim and Fanny Entwistle, with their two girls, Elsie, Hilda's special friend, and Queenie, her sister. Jim Entwistle worked on the railway at Kilnbrook, and his wife, for six shillings a week, tramped a round of eight miles, winter and summer, delivering the post. In winter she used to wear one of her husband's old cloth caps and a pair of men's heavy working boots, and it was well known throughout Moss Ferry that they were a very saving couple and had a tidy bit put by.

"Ah knows for a fact", said Mrs Winstanley impressively, "that Fanny Entwistle has never drawn her divi from t'Co-op. since day it opened. Reckon she's got 'underds o' pounds to come."

Hilda ingratiated herself as hard as she could with Mrs Entwistle, who was a great reader and supplied her regularly, week by week, with *Home Chat* and other entrancing literature, eyed unfavourably by Mrs Winstanley as book-reading of an advanced and dangerous nature and likely to do their Hilda no good. But she welcomed these journals, all the same, when Hilda had devoured them, for use in the closet, and it was Hilda's special job when fresh supplies were needed to cut the pages neatly in half, thread a string through them, and hang them up there. Sometimes, when Mr and Mrs Entwistle were out for the evening, Hilda was asked in to keep Elsie and Queenie company. This was a very special treat for Hilda, and she and Elsie sat in friendly silence reading their novelettes, while Queenie, who never read at all, did her crochet.

*   *   *

Now that her father worked on the roads, Hilda was able, during the school holidays, to take his dinner to him, for dinner-time was short—a half-hour only—and not to be squandered by walking to and from his home. She liked this daily trip and

135

generally managed to stuff a *Home Chat* under her frock for leisurely consumption on the way back, for although her mother could not stop her from reading at home after tea, she kept a sharp look-out for such idleness during the daytime, and Hilda was put to all sorts of shifts to indulge her passion for the printed word, even making frequent unnecessary visits to the closet at the far end of the garden, to sit there solemnly reading in the dim light which came through the top of the door. She never dared leave the door open for fear the sneaking Lily should come along and catch her.

Mrs Winstanley usually made her husband a meat and potato pie in a brown earthenware dish, and she tied this, smoking hot from the oven, in a red handkerchief and, together with a knife and fork and a bottle of tea, packed them in a wicker basket with a lid to it and a good firm handle. Hilda found it very pleasant going in search of the road gang. Sometimes they were up Mad Lane; sometimes nearly in Daneshead on the main road; sometimes near the big Wilverton Bridge. It was pleasant, too, sitting alongside her father and his mates while they ate. All the others had their dinners with them as well, except Tom Hogben, the ganger. He got the biggest wage—twenty-five shillings a week—and was able to afford the luxury of a bicycle on which to go home to his meal. The men knocked off from half-past twelve to one o'clock, and the time flew. Hilda sat contentedly by her father, who occasionally offered her a forkful of the savoury pie and a drink of his tea. They talked gravely, their discourse ranging from politics to the artful and fearsome habits of rats. When they talked of politics it was chiefly about a gentleman called Joynson-Hicks, who was standing for Parliament for their division, and was greatly admired and looked up to by them all. Mr Joynson-Hicks had promised to do all sorts of things for the working man, and especially for the working man of Moss Ferry and Kilnbrook. They were going to vote solid for him when the election took place, to show how they appreciated his special interest in them. Hilda never properly understood what it was Mr Joynson-Hicks was going to do for her father and his friends, and any road they all seemed quite happy and satisfied on their wage of twenty-one shillings a week. But feeling ran high for Mr Joynson-Hicks, and one or two among them who could read would relate bits they had seen in the Sunday papers from his speeches in the Free Trade Hall at Manchester. And they would nod approvingly about Mr Joynson-Hicks's plans for bettering their lives, saying: "Aye. Joynson-Hicks is t'chap for my money. Reckon 'e knows what 'e's about. There's no denying 'e's a clever chap." Hilda, listening attentively, would begin herself to have feelings of passionate loyalty towards Mr Joynson-Hicks, though she did not quite understand what "standing for Parliament"—a phrase they used frequently and impressively—meant.

But her interest in Mr Joynson-Hicks, deep though it was, never equalled her interest in the evil ways of the Moss Ferry and Kilnbrook rats. Nearly all the men had fox terriers and they used these regularly for ratting, going from one farm to another at night. They used to compare the number of rats which their respective terriers had killed, and chaff one another cheerfully when they knew the other was telling a downright lie. Hilda had heard her father tell the story of Will Stringer, her grandfather at Bridge Farm, over and over again, but she never tired of hearing it. It had happened one August evening. Her grandfather was taking a side of home-cured bacon over to a customer, and had it slung in a sack over his shoulder. He was going by a short cut across the fields, and as he neared the end of one field he noticed that in the next Ben Bartholomew had cut down his hayrick, and, proceeding from the place where the rick had formerly stood, in a neat, perfectly formed four-square company, were the rats who had lately lived in it. They were coming straight at him, silently, stealthily, and with a paralysing, concentrated attention. They stopped, sniffed, and again moved forward. Will Stringer did not hesitate. He flung the sack from him as far as he could and ran backwards for his life, not stopping till he had put a respectable distance between himself and the advancing brown army. When he looked round they were tearing at the sack; and when, next morning, he went out of curiosity to the place where he had flung the bacon, all that remained were a few splinters of bone.

"And that was a near go for Will Stringer, Ah reckon," said her father. "He said he felt in his bones if he hadna given them the bacon they'd 'a took it, and 'im wi' it."

The dinner-time was over all too soon, and Hilda, taking up the basket, walked slowly back to her own dinner, devouring *Home Chat* till she came in sight of home.

She liked it best of all when the gang was in the neighbourhood of the Wilverton Bridge, and she could stand on the bridge and watch the ships sailing up towards Warrington from Manchester. And from the middle of the bridge there was a splendid view of the Haunted House, at which she never tired of staring. Sometimes she stuck her head through the iron balustrade of the bridge as a ship was about to pass under. She shouted and waved to the sailors and, just as the boat was disappearing, gave a great spit, hoping to see it land on the ship. But it never did because she was so high up that it was always blown into nothingness before it reached the water.

Once her head got firmly wedged in the ironwork, and though she nearly wrenched it off she couldn't free herself. Her screams brought her father and his mates running up, and they shoved and pushed and nearly broke her neck in their efforts to release her. Finally there was grave talk of a file having to be used, and at this Hilda, crying loudly with self-pity at the shameful prospect of having to be sawn out of the Wilverton Bridge, made one last desperate effort to free herself. It nearly tore off her ears, but it succeeded and she stood feeling her injured head, which seemed to have swollen to twice its normal size, while they all laughed and said it would be a lesson to her. Her father, in his relief, gave her a halfpenny, and Jim Hogben, Tom's brother, said he reckoned she wouldn't go getting swelled head again—not by a long chalk she wouldn't.

CHAPTER XI

"LUTES, LOBSTERS, SEAS OF MILK AND SHIPS OF AMBER"

A good many tramps passed up and down on the high road between Manchester and Warrington, and some of them, as they became familiar with the district, found short cuts and, in the summer, used them, often asking a farmer's permission to pass a night in his barn. Such permission was never refused, the farmer only exacting in return a solemn promise from the tramp that he would not smoke. The farmer, too, would see that the tramp had a good supper of bread and cheese and nettle beer, and always sent him away in the morning with his belly full. But there had been times when a tramp had spent the night in a farmer's barn uninvited, and it was these that were most dreaded; for spent matches had been found more than once, and the farmer, with no fire-fighting machinery nearer than Warrington, feared an outbreak of fire more than he feared anything. The cottagers, too, never turned a tramp from their door without giving him food. Money, being scarce, was never offered. Once, helping her mother to wash up the dinner things, Hilda heard a hurried gulping sound outside the kitchen door, and both she and her mother were horrified to see a tramp ravenously eating the dog's dinner—a big plateful of scraps and potatoes and gravy placed there for when Prince, their fox terrier, should return from his excursions in the surrounding fields.

Mrs Winstanley sharply reproved the tramp for not asking properly for food, saying there was no call for him to go hungry in Moss Ferry and still less call for him to eat like a dog. She invited him to sit on the doorstep while she cut him a "buttey" and made him a brew of tea.

"Reckon tha must 'a bin fair clemmed to eat t'dog's dinner," she remarked sympathetically. When he had gone and they had resumed the washing-up, she talked to Hilda for a long time about the hardships of folk poorer than themselves, and ended up by thanking the Lord for their own good home and the many blessings He had bestowed upon them. A good husband and father in good work, and two good sons like John and Jim, and Lily anxious for the time when she could leave school and begin to earn too. But on Hilda, fidgeting to be done with the washing-up so that she could go out and play with Elsie Entwistle, she turned a reproving eye and muttered darkly about "too much book-reading", inferring that this would be Hilda's downfall—a snare set by t'Owd Lad for her ultimate damnation. For she was con-vinced that if Hilda did not soon begin to realise that there were other things in life more serious than "larning", she alone out of their household would burn for ever in the Lake of Fire, while Joe and herself, John and Jim and Lily, when their appointed hour came, would take their reserved seats among the other angels, wearing crowns of gold and robes of spotless white.

On the evening of the day when the tramp had eaten Prince's dinner, Hilda, lying in bed with a corner of the window curtain pushed aside to enable her to read as long as possible, Lily fast asleep beside her, heard unusual movements and shoutings coming up the lane. She jumped to the window and leaned out. Some-body was running fast, shouting: "Fire at Bartholomew's! Fire at Bartholomew's!"

The owner of the voice raced past the house, followed by others, and Hilda, not waiting to hear whether her father and mother had been wakened, hammered on their door, shrilling the same cry. "Fire at Bartholomew's! Everybody's going there. They're all running in the lane. I'm going too. I'll go and tell our Lily and our Jim."

She knocked on the door of Jim's room. "Fire at Bartholomew's, our Jim! We're all going." She prodded the still sleeping Lily and quickly dressed herself. By now she could hear her mother and father moving about, and, from the back room, sounds of Jim getting up. Jack was not yet home from Daneshead, where he was seeing Edie.

Her mother called out: "Come on, our 'Ilda and Lily! Let's away." There was no question of either Hilda or Lily stopping at home, for, except once when a hayrick in a field on Mr Gibbon's farm had been burnt out, there had never been a fire in Moss Ferry, and none but the old and children-in-arms would have missed for anything the chance of seeing this one.

Being mid-August there was still a faint light in the sky, though it was past ten o'clock, and against this, in dreadful silhouette, the outbuildings of Ben Bartholomew's farm were burning fiercely, and her father, saying something about Ben's horses, ran faster than she had ever seen him run—even faster than that afternoon in Southport when the sea was chasing them and they only just got away in time.

Mrs Winstanley, shouting after her husband to mind himself, ran too, Hilda and Lily alongside and Jim clomping behind. When they got to the farm gates they joined the crowd of women and children already there, and listened eagerly for any news that was going as to how the fire had started. All the men had joined Ben Bartholomew and his two sons and were working desperately to get the horses and cows and pigs safely out before the fire spread from the big barn to the stables and shippens. Mrs Bartholomew, her grey hair hanging down in a plait and with a coat

142

buttoned over her nightdress, came running to the women at the gate.

"Water. Come and help at t'pond. It munna get to the house." Instantly they followed her to the duckpond, filling buckets and milk cans and jugs, and passing them from hand to hand to other women who dashed them hopelessly against the flames. Hilda, working alongside her mother and Lily, heard men calling out orders and horses whinnying and plunging. Looking up for a second she saw her father, sweat pouring off him, walking steadily between two terrified, kicking horses, holding them firmly and speaking to them as though they were frightened children: "Whoa back, Bess! Steady, steady, lass," and handing them over to Jim while he turned to go back to the stables.

The cows were the most difficult, for, on being driven from their shippen, they blundered pathetically all over the yard, some making straight for the burning barn, and though headed off time after time always stampeding back again in that direction, so that they finally had to be driven to safety in the meadow.

Presently Mr Bartholomew, his voice shaking, could be heard saying that his cattle were safe, but the fowls could not be got at. Many of them roosted in the barn and must have been suffocated before the doors were got open. The great task now was to stop the fire from spreading to the house, and to save if possible the two big hayricks in the field adjoining the blazing barn. For though both the house and the ricks were at a fairly safe distance from the barn, there was the danger from flying sparks, particularly on the ricks. The farm-house itself had a slate roof and was less likely to catch in spite of Mrs Bartholomew's fears. But the ricks were dry as tinder in the August heat.

Ben Bartholomew, seeing that there was no hope of saving his barn, warned the people to get further back as any minute the roof might go, and they backed nearly to the gates, waiting fearfully for the crash. Hilda, holding on to her mother, looked at the crowd. Everybody seemed to be there, not only from Moss Ferry but from Kilnbrook as well, and all the time other farmers from up on the Moss were driving in. Even Isaac Hodson was there, and his farm was a couple of miles away at least. There was no explaining the mystery of how they could have known about the fire at Bartholomew's, but there they all were. Mr Woodville, the schoolmaster, was there, and the Reverend Black. Also Grandma Buckley and Billy, who had done a good job by helping Jim and Mr Bartholomew's sons to drive out the squealing pigs. They all stood waiting, till at last, with a grinding, tearing roar, the roof crashed down and the four walls of the barn, jagged where the timbers had torn away, stood up like a gigantic empty egg-shell. The stables and shippens, smaller and made almost entirely of wood, were already nearly burnt out. It was a windless night and the flames burnt skywards, and Mr Bartholomew, now that his cattle were safe, thanked the women for their help and urged them to go home. He assured the men too that, with the help of his sons, he would be all right now, but not a man made to go. "Us'll see you right, Ben," said first one and then another.

Hilda and Lily, dropping with sleep, went home with their mother, who kept on recalling the tramp and wondering if it had been he who had started the fire. That it was tramp's work nobody had the smallest doubt, although Mr Bartholomew had seen nobody about. Hilda said hopefully that maybe he had been roasted alive like the fowls, and her mother, looking back to where the buildings still burned against the darkness, said that if it was the tramp it would be no more than he deserved if he had met his end so horribly. It was a judgement on him for sleeping in Mr Bartholomew's barn without first asking leave, and causing such wicked damage with his shiftless ways.

But, when the ruined building was cool enough to be searched, there was no sign of him. Only burnt fowls and the blackened carcases of two pigs which, when they were being driven to safety from their sty, had blundered madly into the raging barn and whose screams, Mrs Winstanley said, would interfere for evermore with her enjoyment of roast pork, every mouthful of which, she reflected sadly, would from this day forth fair rise up and choke her.

*　　　　*　　　　*

Only four or five daily newspapers came to Moss Ferry, since few of its inhabitants could afford one, and many could not even read. But news from the outside world reached them fast enough, for the Vicar took *The Times*, so did the Farnhams at Pleasant Farm; while the schoolmaster favoured *The Manchester Guardian*. And it was from the latter, many years earlier, when Hilda was still in the Infants' class, that the most memorable of all those echoes from the great world came to them. One morning before lessons began Mr Woodville startled the assembled children by announcing that Queen Victoria was dead and that there would now be both a King *and* a Queen—the Prince and Princess of Wales. The children received the news solemnly, for they all knew about the wonderful old Queen who had reigned so long and so gloriously. Indeed in nearly every cottage hung a magnificent almanac portrait of Queen Victoria, wearing a white lace cap and a white lace fichu and a lot of jewels and a wide blue watered silk sash across her bodice with numerous medals pinned on to it and a big blazing diamond in the middle of her fichu.

When he had told them of the Queen's death, Mr Woodville said they would now sing the National Anthem, but from now on they must always remember to sing "God Save Our Gracious King" instead of "God Save Our Gracious Queen"; and he cheered them up considerably by announcing that the day of the funeral would be a school holiday. And he instructed them all to wear a rosette of black ribbon until after the funeral as a mark of respect, and the next Sunday everybody at chapel wore something black, and the Minister said a special prayer for the new King and Queen. When the excitement of the funeral was over, there was the coronation of King Edward VII and Queen Alexandra to look forward to, and for this great event both Church and Chapel made a great stir. The school was given another holiday on Coronation Day, and the Church and Chapel Sunday Schools, forgetting their social differences in a wave of heart-felt patriotism, united in providing a grand Coronation Tea, at which every child was presented with a Coronation Mug and a very pretty medal with portraits of Their Majesties on it in profile.

The Winstanley household received four Coronation Mugs, and Mrs Winstanley arranged them all in a neat row on the kitchen mantelpiece, till John pointed out that it was a waste to have four in one place, whereupon his mother put one either side of the mantelpiece in the front room.

When, a few years later, it became known that King Edward and his lovely Queen were going to pay a visit to Lord Derby at Knowsley, and were actually going to stop for a few minutes in Daneshead on their way, the whole neighbourhood was beside itself with pride. All the schoolchildren for miles around were commanded to be present at Daneshead, dressed in their Sunday clothes, for there were to be magnificent stands erected at the spot where the King and Queen would halt, and at a given signal from the Reverend James Black everybody was to stand up and not sit down again until their Majesties had left.

For weeks before the visit Hilda rummaged through her pile of *Chatterboxes* reading up all she could find about Their Majesties. In one volume there was a whole article about Queen Alexandra, with photographs showing her as a baby, and then as a little girl, and then as a schoolgirl, and finally in her wedding dress being married in Westminster Abbey, London, to Edward, Prince of Wales. She read out to her mother and father how the Queen had been brought up to be both good and useful. She could make her own clothes, and before she was married she only had a very small amount of pocket money every week, out of which she saved up to buy Christmas and birthday presents for her many relations. And there was a picture of her with her first baby on her lap, and her husband, the Prince of Wales, standing beside her. And there were some pretty verses adapted from Alfred, Lord Tennyson, which Hilda recited fervently:

> Sea-Kings' daughter from over the sea,
> Saxon and Norman and Dane are we,
> But all of us one in our welcome of thee,
> Alexandra!

The day at last arrived—a hot, sunny day in July—and the Moss Ferry children assembled in the school playground and were formed into a procession. Each child was given a small Union Jack to wave, and the procession started on its way to the stands. There were crowds of folk already ahead of them on the road to Daneshead; everybody, even the farm labourers, had been given a few hours off to see the wonderful sight. For this was the first time within living memory that the Sovereign had honoured Lancashire with his presence, and Lancashire meant to show how it loved and respected him and his Queen. The stands were reserved entirely for the children and the old people; the rest were arranged in orderly fashion on either side of the road.

Their Majesties were to be formally welcomed by Councillor Bridges of Daneshead, who was an awe-inspiring figure in a frock coat and a silk hat. All were in their places at least two hours before the Royalties were due, but nobody even noticed the long wait. The children chattered and fluttered their flags, and all eyes were strained continuously in the direction They would come. At last there was an excited buzzing and the Reverend James Black, his face shining with loyalty, shouted: "Now children, all together," and they stood up and burst into the National Anthem. And there, in a big, black, open motor-car, was King Edward, and beside him, in a parma-violet coloured frock and a toque to match, smiling and bowing, was Queen Alexandra. Nobody in Daneshead had ever seen anybody so beautiful as Queen Alexandra, and Hilda Winstanley, who was an undoubted authority on that great lady, indignantly reflected that her photographs in *Chatterbox* had failed to do her justice. Hilda was so full of admiration and love for her that the tears rolled down her cheeks, and when the Vicar called for "Three cheers for Their Majesties", she nearly burst her frock in her eagerness to show her loyalty.

The tall, well-set-up man with the jolly red face was Lord Derby, and he stood by the door of the car, silk hat in hand, and helped the King to get out. And standing respectfully a little way off was Councillor Bridges. Lord Derby beckoned to him to move forward, and then whispered something to His Majesty, who smiled at the Councillor and shook hands with him. Then the King presented him to Queen Alexandra, who also smiled at him and spoke a few words. Then Councillor Bridges backed slowly away, and Lord Derby helped the King back into his car. And very slowly, to the cheers and the flag-waving, the royal procession moved off. All eyes followed until the cars looked no bigger than black beetles, and then, talking excitedly, the people slowly and reluctantly dispersed. All were agreed that it was the grandest thing that had ever happened to any of them, and that King Edward and his Missus were champion—a real gradely couple and no mistake.

*   *   *

Because of his own humble status, Joe Winstanley was tremendously proud of his one well-to-do relation, his mother's youngest sister, Keziah, married to Matthew Turnbull, who kept *The White Swan* in Market Place, Ashton-under-Lyne. Aunt Keziah came, at long intervals, to spend the day with the Winstanleys in Moss Ferry, and Mrs Winstanley fairly shone with importance whenever these visits were expected, polishing and cleaning and cooking as though the Reverend Vane himself was to be her guest. Aunt Keziah was so well off that she wore black satin, as a matter of course, on *weekdays*. Mrs Winstanley, discussing with Grandma Buckley Aunt Keziah's distinguished appearance, never failed to stress that Joe's rich relation at Ashton-under-Lyne didn't know what it was to have Sunday best. Everything she had was Sunday best any road, and not even the gentry could go one properer than that!

Aunt Keziah was tall and stout and had a very red, cheerful, shining face—so red and so shiny that it cast quite a warm glow over the black satin of her bodice. And her purse, said Mrs Winstanley, must be as deep as the bottomless pit, for she never went away without giving Hilda and Lily a shilling apiece. Whenever she came to see them she always urged Joe and Lizzie to spend a day with herself and Mat, but it was not till her two sons were at work that Mrs Winstanley felt she had earned the luxury of a day at Aunt Keziah's. The longed-for day came, however, when Mr and Mrs Winstanley, Hilda and Lily set off for Ashton-under-Lyne.

It was a Saturday, and Joe, by losing half-a-day's money, had got the morning free. Dressed in their Sunday clothes, they were at Kilnbrook station by nine o'clock, waiting for the 9.30 train that would take them to Ashton-under-Lyne. Hilda, who held in her hand Uncle Mat's written instructions as to how they were to get to *The White Swan* from the station (for Aunt Keziah, like the Winstanleys, could neither read nor write), was thoroughly enjoying her status as guide to the expedition. Her mother and father, terrified of getting lost, deferred to her as though they were a couple of children younger than herself. In due course they arrived at the door of *The White Swan* and, not noticing the private door, went timidly through the main door into the bar. Hilda and Lily, who had never been inside a public-house before, and had been brought up strictly to believe that no self-respecting female ever did go into one, gazed fearfully round the room and at the men standing up at the counter drinking out of blue and pink mugs. Uncle Mat was behind the counter, and though he had never before set eyes on either Mrs Winstanley or the two girls, he welcomed them loudly and warmly. Instantly he asked Joe what he would take and, without waiting for his answer, drew him a pint of beer.

"And reckon tha'll take a drop o' port, Lizzie, and these two" —with an affectionate smile at Hilda and Lily—"'ll not say no to a ginger beer, I'm thinking. And dunna be afraid o' these," and he pushed towards them a big glass cake stand piled high with Eccles cakes.

Uncle Mat, his hospitable instincts satisfied, called out for his wife. Aunt Keziah, in her shining rich black satin, came bustling in, and she too had a glass of port to keep Lizzie company, and then took the two girls and their mother through into the house.

Mrs Winstanley, flushed by the port, expressed great uneasiness at Joe being left behind with Mat and, dropping her voice so that the girls should not hear, hoped Mat wouldn't press him to take too much. Aunt Keziah laughed and said Joe would be all right. Mat was never one to overstep the mark, and any road it would do Joe no harm if he did take a drop more than usual on such a special occasion. "It's not every day you come to see us, Lizzie," she ended cheerfully.

In the big comfortable kitchen a girl of about fifteen was setting out the knives and forks, and Mrs Winstanley felt prouder than ever of her husband's relations. It was plain to see that they had money to burn, having a servant and all.

There was a hot baked dinner just as if it was Sunday and, calling Joe, they sat down to it. Mat would have his afterwards while Aunt Keziah attended to the customers. Aunt Keziah pressed Lizzie to take something with her dinner, and after a great deal of persuasion she agreed to a glass of stout. Aunt Keziah kept her company, and Joe, looking very soft and red after his drinks with Uncle Mat, had another half-pint. Hilda and Lily were given more ginger beer and decided they had never enjoyed a dinner so much in their lives.

When Uncle Mat had had his meal, Aunt Keziah asked if they would like to go to the moving pictures, which had only just come to Ashton-under-Lyne. Hilda's heart began to thump. She had read about the moving pictures in Jack's Sunday newspaper. It would be wonderful. Like going to the theatre. Aunt Keziah, delighted at their excited interest, hustled them out and astonished them by taking a tramcar, although the picture house was not above ten minutes walk from Market Place. It was the first time any of the Winstanleys had been on a tramcar, and the swaying, jolting, clanging ride was an adventure in itself. This reckless expenditure on Aunt Keziah's part so impressed Mrs Winstanley that she talked of it for months afterwards, pointing out to Grandma Buckley and other relations that it was proof positive that Aunt Keziah and Uncle Mat wanted for nothing. Aunt Keziah bought the very best seats, and, fidgety with excitement, they settled down. The picture-house was very big and not quite dark, with only a few people in it. A young lady was playing a piano and went on playing it for a very long time until the man working the pictures got his machine right. He kept on flashing things on the big white sheet—sometimes upside down, sometimes dazzling and flickering—but at last he got it to work properly. Then the young lady stopped playing and the picture began.

It looked like a tremendous magic-lantern slide except that the people actually moved. Hilda, craning forward, could scarcely believe her eyes, and she heard her mother give a gasp and an astonished "Eh—I never!" as a lady and gentleman walked right across the sheet. The story was all about love, but, with the exception of Aunt Keziah, they were all so amazed at seeing photos moving and breathing, life-like and life-size, that they gave up trying to understand the story. They just sat and watched intently every least movement of the lady and gentleman, expecting any minute that they would walk right off the sheet and into the picture-house itself. The picture flickered quite often, and sometimes was nearly blotted out, but they watched till their eyes ached, and only rose, reluctantly, when the story ended with the lady and gentleman kissing each other.

When they were in the street Aunt Keziah surveyed them, waiting eagerly for their comments.

Mrs Winstanley was the first to speak. "Well, Aunt Keziah,

reckon us winna think owt o' t'magic lantern after this do. Ah'd never 'ave believed it if Ah hadna seen it wi' my own eyes. Fancy a likeness walking as if it was flesh and blood. Whatever will folks be up to next!"

Aunt Keziah laughed and Hilda, anxious to show off her knowledge, said emphatically: "But they *are* flesh and blood. Same as us. I've read about them in our Jack's Sunday newspaper. They come from America, like Amelia Starkey's cousin. It said in the newspaper how the moving pictures have come to stop. They have proper actors and actresses in them from the theatre. And it said how they are only just beginning, but before many months are up there won't be a town in the whole of the world without them. They've got them all over America now. It said so."

They all gazed at Hilda admiringly and, turning to Aunt Keziah, Mrs Winstanley said proudly: "Just fancy our 'Ilda getting all that out of the newspaper! Reckon they put in about everything in the newspaper. Well, it's bin a rare do for us, Aunt Keziah, thanks to you. Reckon us'll never get over it, eh Father?"

Joe nodded a slow agreement and, delighted at their pleasure, Aunt Keziah, in spite of Mrs Winstanley's shocked protest that it was nobbut a step to Market Place, shepherded them all on to a tramcar again, explaining that her legs were not what they used to be, and, with her weight and all, she had to be careful not to overdo herself traipsing about.

"Mat never lets me put foot to the ground if he knows it. And you can get anywhere in Ashton on a penny tram. 'Tisna like Moss Ferry. That traipse up from Kilnbrook fair takes it out o' me. But reckon living in a town makes you soft—wi' everything to your 'and, so to speak."

After a big tea of pork pies and tinned salmon and jellies and cakes, and a final glass of port for Lizzie while Joe had a pint with Mat, the grand outing was over and Aunt Keziah saw them again on to a tramcar for the station, telling the conductor just where to put them down.

Mrs Winstanley, terrified at finding herself and her family on the swaying perilous tramcar without Aunt Keziah's heartening presence, handed her purse to Hilda and told her to take the fares. Both she and Joe would have preferred to walk to the station, but there was no gainsaying Aunt Keziah. And, any road, Hilda and Lily were enjoying the ride.

"Well," said Mrs Winstanley when they were safely in the train for Kilnbrook, "Ah mun say as Keziah Turnbull's not one to stint. Pity they've 'ad no childer to spend on.... And moving pictures too! Reckon us'll 'ave summat to tell Moss Ferry on this time. Pity 'er legs is bad. All them tramcar rides must mount up. A penny 'ere and a penny there. And she thinks nowt on it, either," she concluded admiringly, and with an approving look at her husband for his great good sense in being allied to such well-to-do relations.

CHAPTER XII

"SEE AFAR THE LIGHTS OF LONDON!"

At the cottage in The Dip, Hilda had been too young to sense
more than vaguely that there was some mystery about her
parentage, and that the gaunt, forbidding Lucy Stringer's regular
monthly visits were somehow connected with this fact. But when
they moved to the house in School Lane and were in the village
proper she began to ask questions, and to listen eagerly to the
whispering that sometimes went on among the grown-ups about
her being a "love child".

Since her promotion to Standard V she had become very
friendly with both Florrie and May Woodville, the schoolmaster's
children, and several times had been home to tea with them. She
was surprised to find that there was really very little difference
between the Woodville's tea-table and her own at home, except
that May Woodville assured her that they always had a white
tablecloth, whereas Mrs Winstanley only spread out her best
damask cloth when they had company to tea in the front room.
But she was flattered at being considered good enough to mix in-
timately and on terms of social equality with the Woodville family,
and Mrs Winstanley, when Hilda was once boasting to Lily of
this new friendship, accused her angrily of getting above herself.

"No use to give yoursen airs, our 'Ilda. You've got to earn
when you finish your schooling same as our Lily and same as
everybody else. Lucy Stringer won't bring the money for you
once you've turned thirteen, that Ah do know. And Mr Woodville's childer'll 'ave to earn too, so dunna go getting ideas, and
give over axing me questions, do. Axe me no questions and Ah'll
tell you no lies."

Ever since Mrs Dumbell had told her that her father was a "gentleman born", Hilda had secretly romanced about herself, for she dared not discuss the matter openly. She sensed, however, that folks knew there was something about her different from her sister Lily, and thrilled with pleasure when Florrie Woodville confirmed this by confiding: "Father says it'll be a shame if you have to go into service, Hilda. He was telling my mother you ought to have your chance of something better. Maybe the dressmaking, like I'm going into; or perhaps", she added somewhat doubtfully, remembering Hilda's well-known agonies over arithmetic, "pupil teaching like Miss Askew. Our May wants to go into the post office at Manchester. But you have to be good at figures for that, same as for teaching."

Hilda proudly reported at home Mr Woodville's ideas for her future, but her mother instantly threw cold water over them.

"You don't earn at the dressmaking for two year, and Ah dunna think they'll pay the money till you're that age. Why, you'll be fifteen. And if your Grandma canna pay she canna, and us winna be able to keep you for nowt. Our Lily'll 'ave to earn soon as she leaves school and reckon you'll 'ave to do t'same, so give over moithering. You're no age yet, so plenty o' time afore you leave off your schooling."

And with this, for the time, Hilda had to be satisfied. But she made up her mind that she would *not* go into service whatever happened. The dressmaking held no special attractions for her, but, any road, it was work she could do without shame. And Mrs Dumbell, deliberately and maliciously doing her utmost to unsettle her and cause her to be continually worrying at home with questions about her parentage, had told her that she even had relations at London. Who they were and what they were, Mrs Dumbell, for the very good reason that she did not know,

could not tell her. But London! Her mind, unconsciously, began
to work that way. Somehow, some time, she would get to
London. She felt quite certain of it, although she dared not
mention the awful name to her mother and father. For to them,
and especially to her mother, even Manchester, only fourteen
miles away, was the very embodiment of wickedness. People in
Manchester went to theatres, and it was only the godless and
ignorant who did that. Nobody in Moss Ferry had ever been
inside a theatre, not even Fanny Entwistle, who had been to
Manchester several times, and was acknowledged to be very go-
ahead in all her ways.

With the magic name firmly fixed in her mind, Hilda set herself to learn all that Mr Woodville could teach her; and life at
school, in spite of his frequent outbursts of bad temper, went on
agreeably enough. He was so pleased with the progress made by
herself and his daughter Florrie, and Peter Pettener, that they
became the envy of the entire school, and many parents grumbled
that Mr Woodville favoured some above others and that such
favouritism was not seemly in a schoolmaster.

*   *   *

As St Margaret's was a Church of England school, the Vicar,
every now and again when he found the time hanging too heavily
on his hands, would make his entry unannounced during the
scripture lesson and examine them spiritually. Whenever his
black figure appeared, the entire class stood up, as a mark of
respect, and looking very pleased at this deference he bade them
a cheerful "Good morning, children." Mr Woodville was always
a little nervous of Mr Black's visits, and it was then that he hoped
for, and received, the most solid support from the chapel-going
children. For the heretic chapel-goers were nourished on the

bible. It was the only book to be found in most of their homes, and their knowledge of it was deep. Hilda, who for years had nurtured a passion for the Reverend Vane, the Minister at her own chapel in Kilnbrook, felt an equal passion for the Reverend Black, though he was far from being as sweet natured as the Reverend Vane. Mr Vane preached with great earnestness and sincerity and held his entire congregation, children as well as grown-ups, in a state of breathless interest. Whenever she heard him, Hilda always felt that Mr Vane was preaching specially to her, and she never took her eyes from his face. Even when they were singing the hymns she gazed at him, her heart filled with love.

Her passion for the Reverend Black, although equal in its intensity, was different. It was a snobbish passion, for between the Church of England Vicar and the Nonconformist Minister was an impassable social gulf. The Reverend Black gabbled his sermons in a cold, tired, uninspiring voice, as though for some reason it was desirable to get it over and done with as quickly as he could. But he was the Vicar, high and fashionable, and Hilda passionately desired that he should notice her, approve of her, praise her for her wide knowledge of the Scriptures, thus lessening the social ignominy of her position as a chapel-goer who had nevertheless been honourably baptised into the Church of England and thereby secured, for all time, a distinction which no amount of chapel-going could take from her.

And the Reverend Black, one morning, did notice her, standing up with her hand out, wriggling it urgently to show that she alone, out of the whole class, could tell him that it was Ahasuerus who so cruelly cast off Vashti and took Esther for his queen. Mr Black took a good look at her, and asked Mr Woodville what Standard she was in.

"Standard V," answered Mr Woodville.

Hilda, for weeks and even months afterwards, savoured the sweetness of the Vicar's answering remark, said out loud for all to hear: "I shouldn't have thought it. She ought to be in Standard VI or even VII. It's a pleasure to examine such an intelligent child."

And her intellectual passion for the Reverend Black increased, so that she blushed whenever he came into the schoolroom, or she passed him in the lane. And Mr Woodville, gratified that one of his scholars had been so singled out for notice, marked her down for special favours and, instead of caning her if she had been unusually backward with her sums, made her stay in during playtime instead.

*   *   *

Sometimes Mrs Pretty, the Infants' teacher, would ask for the help of one of the big girls if she was not feeling very well, and Mr Woodville, pointing out what a great honour he was conferring, would allow his daughter Florrie or Hilda Winstanley to go in to help with the Infants, so letting them take it fairly in turn.

Hilda loved helping Mrs Pretty, for she was so pleasant and made her feel so important, and it was lovely standing in front of the class and keeping order among the children. Helping them with their sand trays, teaching them to count on their wooden beads, telling them stories from her *Chatterbox* and hearing them recite their "pieces". And all the time keeping on the alert for certain wrigglings, and taking them out to the closets before disaster flooded over them. Sometimes Mrs Pretty, anxious to have the children right out of her sight and hearing for a bit, would, if it was a bright, warm day, let Hilda take them for a walk down School Lane as far as Ben Bartholomew's farm, and she would form them into a little "tail", walking proudly alongside and hoping everybody would notice them as they went past. Once Mrs Pretty had such a sick headache that Mr Woodville kindly urged her to go home at dinner-time, and complete and glorious responsibility for the well-being of the Infants fell upon Hilda for the whole afternoon, and much as she liked and admired Mrs Pretty, she found herself praying that the headache would keep her away from school the next day as well, so exciting was it to be alone in the Infants' classroom, taking entire charge, and having one of Miss Holroyd's scholars bring her a cup of tea at three o'clock as if she was a grown-up, certificated teacher. And Mrs Pretty, whenever Florrie or Hilda helped her, always brought them a little present the next day from Warrington—a handkerchief, or a length of silk hair-ribbon, or a bag of extra good sweets.

*　　　　*　　　　*

During her whole school life, Hilda experienced nothing quite so terrible as the black week when Eddie Tubbs, one of Mr Woodville's scholars, and the same age as herself, lay dying of diphtheria. Eddie's father, Roger Tubbs, was, in the eyes of Moss Ferry, a gentleman, for he worked in an office in Manchester. Mrs Tubbs kept herself very aloof from the villagers, and although Eddie and Olive Tubbs came to the village school they were always dressed differently from the other pupils, wearing good plain clothes like the Woodville children. And because of their clothes, and their father working in an office and not with his hands, they had a certain glamour and importance, although at their lessons they were stupid, and Olive Tubbs was even described by her teachers as backward. But Hilda used to regard Olive's untrimmed navy sailor frock enviously, and fought many a losing battle with her mother on the desirability of being dressed herself in this elegant fashion. Mrs Winstanley remained adamant.

In her opinion a frock that had no trimming on it—"nowt but plain serge"—was a poor thing indeed, and Lucy Stringer backed her up in this unreasonable attitude.

Olive and her brother had few friends at school. Because of their father's professional status they were accused of giving themselves airs, and were encouraged in this by their mother, a heavy-featured woman disliked by all Moss Ferry because of her stand-offish ways. But when her son lay fighting for his life the whole village fought with him, and prayers were said for him not only in church, but in all the chapels as well. Every morning at school during that last terrible week, the Reverend Black came in during scripture and at the end of the lesson stood by Mr Woodville's desk and, while the children knelt, prayed that Eddie's life might be spared. And every child in Moss Ferry and Kilnbrook included a special plea for Eddie Tubbs in his nightly prayers. But one morning Mr Woodville, wearing a black tie, announced gravely that Eddie Tubbs was dead and that, to show respect, they must each wear some little sign of mourning till after his funeral. Mr Woodville also announced that, with the exception of the Infants, the entire school was to attend the funeral, walking in a procession behind the coffin from Eddie's home to the church, and from the church across to the cemetery. A subscription was opened for a wreath, every child bringing the utmost its parents could afford. Mrs Pretty bought the wreath in Warrington, and, before sending it to Eddie's house, the schoolmaster had it on his desk and the children filed past to look at it. It was a beautiful cross of lilies and roses and maidenhair fern, with an inscription written by Mr Woodville:

> In loving memory of Eddie, from the
> scholars and teachers of St Margaret's,

and the honour of taking it fell to Peter Pettener.

On the day of the funeral the teachers assembled the children in the playground. Most of the girls were in their white muslin frocks with black sashes and wearing their winter coats. The boys wore their Sunday best with black ties—some bought specially for the occasion, some borrowed, some, on the very poorest children, merely lengths of broad black tape.

The church was already decorated with flowers for Easter, and Eddie's coffin looked beautiful resting before the altar, smothered with wreaths and the big cross from St Margaret's in the very centre. The Reverend Black preached about the love God had for little children, and when they had nearly finished the last hymn and were singing:

> On that happy Easter morning
> All the graves their dead restore;
> Father, sister, child, and mother,
> meet once more,

Mrs Tubbs could be heard crying even above the singing.

When the coffin had been lowered into the grave, and everybody, even the children, had dropped a handful of earth on to it, and the Vicar, after shaking hands with Mr and Mrs Tubbs and Olive, was moving away, Mrs Tubbs, sobbing loudly, made as if to jump on to the coffin, crying out: "Let me go with him! I can't leave him there by himself. Let me go too!"

There was a desperate struggle on the very edge of the grave, and Maudie Holroyd and Miss Askew ran round to Mrs Tubbs and helped her husband to restrain her. The children stood stock still, not daring to move, until Mr Woodville told them sharply that they could go home. Looking back hopefully, Hilda was disappointed to see Mr and Mrs Tubbs, arm in arm, with Olive holding her father's hand, walking slowly and heavily out of the cemetery. What if Mrs Tubbs, before anybody could stop her, had jumped into Eddie's grave! What a story to go home and tell her mother. As it was, when her father was having his tea, she enjoyed relating dramatically that dreadful scene on the brink of the grave, and when she casually remarked that any road Mrs Tubbs still had Olive and nearly another, there was an embarrassed silence. Her mother and father looked first at each other, then at her, neither knowing how to deal with this unexpected display of knowledge on Hilda's part.

Mrs Winstanley acted first by boxing her ears smartly and asking suspiciously: "How dost know? Who's bin talking to you? 'Ave you bin hearkening to Sarah Dumbell? Tell me no lies, now."

Hilda, recalling Mrs Tubbs's heavy, black-clothed figure with the high, protruding stomach, stammered: "I don't know, really. But anybody can see Mrs Tubbs is going to have a baby. Any road, I do know Doctor James doesn't bring them in his bag," she ended defiantly.

"Shame on you," shouted her mother. "And don't let's hear such talk again. There's no call for childer to know such things. Ah'll lay somebody's said summat. You go off now and play, and don't go talking such idleness to our Lily or Ah'll give you summat as you winna forget."

Mrs Winstanley was deeply shocked and worried by Hilda's revelation. Previously, whenever she had shown interest at the arrival of a baby in the village, and had inquired how it came, she had always been satisfied with her mother's explanation that Doctor James had brought it in the black kit-bag he always carried. But she discussed the matter gravely with Joe, and they decided it was best to leave it alone. "Reckon she's 'eard somebody say summat," Joe concluded. "Best let 'er be."

Meanwhile Hilda, frightened at her mother's anger, thought it wiser to keep quiet as to how she had acquired her astonishing information. At school the big girls were always getting together in little groups during playtime and whispering about the arrival of somebody's new baby, and it was Florrie Woodville who, walking with Hilda to Daneshead one day, had talked impressively, Hilda hanging on to every word, about the way a baby came into the world.

"Fancy! Out of its mother's stomach and nowhere else," she explained seriously. But in spite of her knowing air, even Florrie could not explain how a baby got into anybody's stomach. She only knew for certain that that was where it came from, and not, as every Moss Ferry child was given to understand, out of Doctor James's bag in the middle of the night.

CHAPTER XIII

SPLENDOURS AND MISERIES

Apart from the School Outing to the seaside, and the Sunday School Treat for the chapel-goers on August Bank holiday, most of the Moss Ferry children spent their summer holidays cheerfully at home. Only the gentry and the very wealthiest of the farmers went to the seaside to stay, and when Susie and Maggie Hodson, daughters of Isaac Hodson who farmed up on the Moss, were taken one year for a whole week to Southport, they immediately became the focus of interest for all the other children.

They always had plenty of spending-money too, more in a month than any other child of the village in a year. Susie, the eldest, was a fat, happy, red-faced girl, the same age as Hilda, for whom she unaccountably developed a devouring passion, giving her bags of sweets and continually inviting her to tea during the holidays. Hilda, who felt no answering passion for Susie, was nevertheless pleased with the sweets and flattered by the invitations to tea. She also enjoyed the long, solitary walk to the Hodson's farm, and thoroughly relished the splendid set-out which she always got there. A tea which, as she impressively informed her mother, the Hodsons had every day of their lives and not just when there was company. Mrs Winstanley, though flattered too at Hilda's intimacy with the well-off Hodsons, did not like her going such a distance by herself, for the lane leading up to and over the Moss was lonely, and ever since the queer incident of the tramp who had pushed three halfpennies under Agnes Mary's frock, she was afraid for both Hilda and Lily if they ventured too far from the village.

But though Hilda went every week during the holidays to tea with Susie, she only once had company on her journey. This was old Granfer Hodson, Susie's grandfather, who lived at the farm and was known to be a bit soft in the head. Hilda walked sedately along with the old man, who kept on talking of Jesus in a very familiar way which Hilda, in spite of her own happy religious upbringing, felt was not quite respectful. Granfer Hodson talked about Him as though He actually lived at the farm too: indeed as though He was just one of the Hodson family, keeping an eye on things for them at lambing time and when the cows had their calves. Granfer stressed emphatically that everything the Hodsons had they owed to Jesus, and every few hundred yards, his weak old voice rising to a trembling screech, he fell on his knees right in the road, the tears running down his seamy cheeks, as he testified to his great love for the Lord Jesus. There was such yearning in his attitude that Hilda expected any minute to see an angel fly down from the sky, take Granfer by the hand and soar with him to Heaven. And as Granfer went on praying she even found herself hoping that the angel would appear, for she was terrified lest somebody should come up the lane and find her in such embarrassing company. But at last, after one of these outbursts, Granfer, observing her detached attitude and feeling it to be inadequate, stared fiercely at her, seized her by the shoulders and shouted: "Do *you* believe in Jesus?"

Hilda, half paralysed with fear, stammered "Yes—I do," which pleased the old man so much that he gave her a penny and asked her to kneel down with him there and then to testify. But Hilda, in spite of the penny, was so frightened that she ran madly towards the farm, turning round only once to see if Granfer was pursuing her. But she was quite safe for he was still kneeling and gesticulating in the middle of the road.

Mrs Hodson and Susie were very upset when Hilda, breathless and crying, managed to gasp out what had happened, and Isaac Hodson looked very uncomfortable. Mrs Hodson, to whom her father-in-law had been a sore trial for years, turned on her husband and said angrily that Granfer ought to be put away, going about that road scaring childer to death.

*   *   *

Although the Winstanleys had a fine large orchard which was full of apple and damson and plum trees, they had not a single pear tree, so every autumn Hilda, longing for pears, would make it her business to go blackberrying round the field which adjoined the big orchard at Pleasant Farm, where the Farnhams lived. For there, over-hanging the field, was the most famous pear tree in Moss Ferry and Kilnbrook. Plenty of other orchards had trees that yielded pears as big as a fist, but there was nothing to touch the little round pears on Mr Farnham's knotty old tree. They were no bigger round than a penny and so sweet and juicy that you could eat them at one go, pips as well. Mr Farnham was very proud of his pear tree and had made it known that it would be the worse for any child caught raiding it. He did not mind the children picking up the windfalls so long as they ate them on the spot; but no pears were to be taken away. The children outwitted him easily by cramming their pockets full, the girls stuffing them down their long black stockings so that they looked as though they had mumps in the wrong place, all the while keeping a sharp lookout for Miss Nellie or Miss Alice Farnham.

On one of her blackberrying expeditions Hilda had the bright idea of first half-filling her basket with the little pears, and then covering them over with blackberries. It was a great success and, full of admiration for her own cleverness, she sauntered unconcernedly along the path that led past the farm. She stopped to peer into the steamy glasshouse—a wonderful place full of bright strange plants and ferns, and was found gaping there by Miss Alice. Miss Farnham spoke very kindly to her and asked if she would like to go inside. Hilda eagerly accepted, holding tightly to her basket, fearful lest the pears should be discovered. She had never been inside a glasshouse before, and this was the only really big one in Moss Ferry. She was astonished at the variety of flowers and ferns and cactus which Miss Farnham pointed out to her, telling her their names, which all sounded queer and foreign. Miss Farnham, pleased at her visitor's interest and admiration, admired in her turn the big basketful of blackberries, and Hilda, her conscience very uneasy, explained that her mother was going to make wine and jelly from them. When they came out of the glasshouse, Miss Farnham, smiling at her, told her to wait by the yard entrance and she would fetch her something nice—a surprise. She came back with a paper bag which she laid on top of the blackberries.

"There, Hilda. Three for you and three for your sister. Sugar plums," she added impressively. "See if you like them."

Hilda, quite overcome by this unexpected graciousness, felt a strong desire to tell Miss Farnham about the pears, but, fearing that Miss Farnham would then take away not only the pears but also the sugar plums, repressed this virtuous impulse and, gulping out her thanks, bit into a plum. She had never seen, or even heard of, sugar plums before and ate it slowly, savouring the damp crystallised sugar that covered it and thinking how rich the Farnhams must be to afford such dainties. Miss Farnham watched her, smiling all the time, and seeming to enjoy herself nearly as much as Hilda.

When she had eaten it, Miss Farnham patted her shoulder and

said: "You'd better be getting along home now, child. And if you go back round the orchard maybe you'll find a few pears in the grass. There was a big wind last night so there's sure to be some windfalls. And you can take them home, just this once."

She turned towards the house and Hilda, her conscience by now as heavy as her basket, sneaked past the pear tree and went wretchedly home, the whole sky flaming with the words of the text that was the sole adornment of her bedroom walls:

THOU GOD SEEST ME

*　　　　　*　　　　　*

In addition to her visits to Susie Hodson, and the long hours she spent with her great friend Elsie Entwistle, Hilda occasionally during the holidays went on expeditions with May Woodville, the schoolmaster's second daughter. She was very proud of this friendship with a girl socially above her. May, unlike Florrie her elder sister, was small and plain, but she was a great talker and, like Hilda, loved doing something a little different from the ordinary. She and Hilda used to take long walks, each provided with a bottle of cold tea and a thick slab of buttered currant cake. Sometimes, if funds permitted, these excursions were enriched by a bottle of Kola between them and a bag of Mrs Wright's famous American gums, great favourites on account of their lasting properties. They could be sucked enjoyably till no bigger than a pinhead, keeping their gummy flavour right to the end. Four ounces, a pennyworth, lasted the pair of them for an entire afternoon. Although both May and Hilda were forbidden to go very far, and on no account to go near the river, they walked great distances over the Moss, and, if sure that nobody had seen them, nearly always ended up by going to their own private bit of beach by the Mersey, nearly opposite the Haunted House, sucking their American gums contentedly and eating their tea hours before tea-time, so that they arrived home famished, May asking genteely for bread and butter and Hilda demanding a "sugar buttey".

It was May who proposed the exciting trip to Daneshead and tea in a shop, the first time either of them had done such a tremendous thing on their own. There were several problems to be tackled before this scheme could be carried out, and the greatest of these was that of money. May confided that she had got a whole shilling of her own, but Hilda was faced with the ticklish job of extracting this huge sum from her post office money-box without attracting the notice of either her mother or the tell-tale Lily, and this, she explained, would necessarily take some days, probably a week. So they fixed a day a week ahead for their adventure. Meanwhile Hilda watched craftily for her opportunity, extracting skilfully a penny or two pennies every time her mother went to the closet or the wash-shed or popped in to have a talk with Mrs Clark. It was a long job, for if Mrs Winstanley was out of the house Lily was almost sure to be there, and vice versa. By the end of the week, however, Hilda had managed to extract one shilling in pennies and halfpennies, which she tied up in a piece of rag and hid in the shed. When Saturday arrived, no suspicions were aroused when she announced that May Woodville wanted her to go that afternoon to Daneshead, for Mrs Woodville got all her groceries at the Co-op. there, and Mrs Winstanley asked Hilda to write down a list of the groceries she also wanted. The only thing that troubled Hilda was her clothes. She would have liked to wear her Sunday frock for this great occasion, but knew that her mother would never hear of it. Sunday clothes were for funerals and weddings and

Sundays; for the Sunday School Treat and the School Outing; not for a Saturday afternoon in Daneshead.

May called for Hilda and they set off, each with a string bag apiece for the shopping, and Hilda with her bag of her own stolen money concealed in the top of her stocking and held in place by her elastic garter. It was a hot lovely day and they walked along happily. It was an excitement just to go into Daneshead anyway, for not only was there the big bright Co-op. but several boot shops much bigger than the one in Moss Ferry, before each of which they stood for minutes at a time admiring the ladies' button boots and the smart black and brown kid shoes and the felt slippers. And there were two drapers' shops, with hats and blouses and bib-aprons and stockings, and quite a variety of sweet and cake shops. And at last was the cake shop where they were to have their tea. May walked in boldly, Hilda following in wonder. The tinkling of the bell brought a pleasant-faced woman to the counter, and May, with complete assurance, asked for tea and cakes and walked unconcernedly to the one small table by the window. It had a clean white cloth and a vase of red paper roses, and through the long lace curtains they could, themselves unobserved, see the busy Saturday afternoon life of Daneshead going past.

The woman showed no surprise at this unusual request for tea in the middle of the afternoon by two ten-year-old girls. May, in her neat navy sailor frock and hat with H.M.S. Eurydice in gold letters across the band, was evidently a gentleman's child with plenty of spending-money, probably treating the one in the blue and white gingham and rather dirty white straw hat. While she was getting the tea, Hilda, uneasy lest they had not enough money to pay for this illicit grandeur, suggested to May that before beginning they should ask what it was going to cost, and May, also uneasy, agreed that it would be a good idea, but pointed out that as she had ordered the tea it was only fair and reasonable that Hilda should put the awkward question.

They waited eagerly, thrilling with pride when the woman set in front of them a big enamelled teapot, white china cups and saucers, and a glass stand holding a great variety of little buns and iced cakes. As the final plate was placed in front of her, Hilda, making a tremendous effort to appear at ease, asked what it would all come to. The woman smiled at her pleasantly: "Fourpence for the tea, and the cakes are a halfpenny each."

Hilda and May both smiled back with relief. They had a whole shilling apiece to spend and, as soon as they were alone, gave themselves up to pure enjoyment. Hilda, slowly licking round the pink icing of her last cake, reflected that this was nearly as big a treat as going to Southport, and only wished she could go home and boast about it to Lily. Every now and then, when a customer came into the shop, her heart gave a jump lest it should be somebody who knew her: Aunt Emma or some of the chapel folk, who would be sure to mention this amazing sight when next meeting her mother. But she got through her tea safely, listening earnestly to what May was telling her about Florrie and Dick Pettener, Peter's eldest brother.

"You're not to tell anybody, Hilda Winstanley. Cut your throat and pierce your heart if you do, but our Florrie and Dick Pettener have been seen walking out. Isaac Hodson told my father he had seen them on the Moss. Our Florrie's only just turned fourteen you know, and Dick Pettener's only sixteen. My father gave her a good hiding and she's not to go out now at night unless my mother's with her. My father went to see Mr Pettener too, and he said he'd give Dick a good talking to, carrying on with our Florrie at his age. Any road Dick Pettener

172

only works on a farm," May ended superciliously, "and my father says he's got nothing in front of him. And our Florrie's going into the dressmaking, you know."

When they had been there so long that they could not, for shame, stay longer, they paid—the combined bill coming to tenpence. They each expended a further penny on a bar of Fry's Chocolate Cream—a big bar—and set out to do their lawful shopping. Hilda, now that the treat was over, felt oppressed by her sin in having taken so much from her moneybox. Feeling the sixpence she still had left, she argued that if she put it back into her moneybox it would not be so bad, for she would then only have stolen sixpence, a crime she had committed before without undue remorse.

And reassured by this specious argument, reassured even further by her as yet unconsumed bar of Fry's Chocolate Cream, she made her way with May into the splendour of the Daneshead Co-op. shop.

*　　　*　　　*

It was only during the holidays that Hilda got a chance of seeing spread out the wonders of the tallyman's pack, from which Mrs Winstanley did a good deal of her buying. He came to Moss Ferry and the surrounding villages regularly every month. He would spread out his huge shiny black american cloth pack by the kitchen door, Mrs Winstanley protesting, every time he called, that she wouldn't be wanting anything this month. But the tallyman, talking all the time, quickly and brightly, would make clucking noises and say never mind, he'd just like her to take a look at the new bib-aprons now so fashionable, or the new patterned zephyrs. And while he was talking away he was un-fastening his pack, and when it was spread out flat he would wave his hands over it triumphantly as though casting a spell upon it, and invite her confidently to inspect the contents and not be feared of handling anything that took her fancy. He sold frocks and pinafores; stays and drawers, chemises and petticoats; men's working shirts and Sunday shirts and collars; ladies' and children's black woollen stockings; reels of cotton and hanks of mending wool; coarse roller towels; pins and needles; tablecloths and collar studs and combs; rolls of red flannel for weekday, and cream flannel for Sunday, petticoats; sheets and pillow cases; prints and serges and even pearl bead necklaces. It was an unending wonder to his customers how he got them all in without creasing and crushing them to pulp.

Hilda and Lily watched, fascinated, as he held up garment after garment for their mother's closer inspection. He dangled the beautiful shining pearl bead necklaces, invited her to test the quality of his flannel and the strength of the coarse union shirts which, he assured her solemnly and untruthfully, would stand any amount of sweat and never, never wear out. Mrs Winstanley, her will-power slowly drawn from her by the tallyman's dreadful charm, and tempted beyond all human limits by the dazzling display, would protest feebly that she was a bit short this week. Whereupon the tallyman, shrinking back as though she had hit him, would regard her sorrowfully and ask gently how she could, for one moment, think that it was her money he was after. Nothing, he assured her gravely, was further from his thoughts. It would, he added vigorously, be a pleasure and a privilege to serve her needs for nothing. She could maybe manage to pay a shilling or two now and the rest month by month as convenient. He always contrived to convey the flattering impression that, out of his vast multitude of customers, she alone was possessed of such honesty that he could trust her even if he had to wait until Doomsday for his money. Thus beguiled and encouraged,

Mrs Winstanley, appraising with a critical eye the wearing qualities of various articles, admitted that her husband could do with a couple of working shirts, and herself with some new aprons, or Lily with a new Sunday pinafore. Hilda, to her great disappointment, never had any of her clothes bought from the tallyman, since all her wants were supplied by Grandma Stringer. But on one occasion, her mother having bought a specially fancy white pinny for Lily to wear on Sundays, and moved by Hilda's envious look, bought them a pearl bead necklace apiece, impressing on them that these treasures were to be worn on Sundays only and must be taken the greatest care of lest they lose their shining lustre. Hilda, touched and grateful, determined that when her mother's birthday came round she would buy her something really breath-taking, and virtuously began to save up her weekly pennies and halfpennies for this purpose.

The tallyman, satisfied with his sales, entered them carefully into an exercise book, rolled up his depleted pack, and in a general atmosphere of mutual esteem and friendliness, walked jauntily on his way.

*　　　　*　　　　*

Hilda, proud of her pearl bead necklace, did not forget her resolve to buy her mother a memorable birthday present, and saved up until she had acquired a whole sixpence. Lily, dull and unenterprising, had purchased a plain white linen handkerchief for her mother's special use on Sundays, but Hilda's present was to be much more impressive, and for several weeks before the birthday was due she teased her mother, and aggravated her sister, by boasting about it as the nicest thing obtainable in Mrs Starkey's shop. In earnest consultation with Mrs Starkey she was a very long time deciding on the gift, her choice wavering between a sensible but attractive leather purse and a far from sensible but altogether lovely jewelled back comb. Mrs Starkey, perceiving that Hilda was hankering more after the flashing comb than the useful purse, and anxious to get back to her housework, counselled her gravely to buy the comb, pointing out how brightly it would shine in her mother's black hair, and knowing too that Lizzie Winstanley had always been one for a bit of show. And so the momentous choice was made and Mrs Starkey thoughtfully rummaged round till she found a small scented-soap box in which to pack it.

When the birthday morning arrived, Hilda cunningly allowed Lily to give her present first and then, with a boastful flourish, produced the soap box, stoutly wrapped in brown paper, and waited eagerly for her mother's delighted expression when her eyes fell on the ruby- and emerald- and diamond-studded comb. Mrs Winstanley, as the "jewels" shone up at her, was unwise enough to give a little gasp of pleasure, and Lily shot a malevolent look at her sister, hating her for giving their mother a present that made the white handkerchief look so dull and ordinary.

Hilda, delighted, hovered round her mother, urging that she should immediately begin to wear the comb, but Mrs Winstanley, glancing at Lily's sullen face, said: "Nay. Reckon it's too good for weekdays, same as our Lily's handkerchief. They're both for best," and she carefully folded the handkerchief and laid it ceremoniously in the box with the jewelled comb.

"Ah'll keep t'box downstairs till your father comes home. Reckon 'e'll want to see what you've both got me. And us'll 'ave a sponge wi' our tea."

The sponge cake was her way of thanking them and showed

how pleased and touched she was by their presents, for she never made a sponge cake unless they were having company, and was justly proud of her fame in Moss Ferry as having a rare light hand with a sponge.

*   *   *

Not least of the many exciting things in the weekly journals which Mrs Entwistle so generously passed over to Hilda were the word-picture competitions, although she warned Hilda that there was always a catch in them somewhere and that it would be foolish of her to spend her money on a single one of them. Hilda, however, used to work them out for her own private satisfaction, and for the pleasure of demonstrating to her stupid sister and to her mother and father how clever she was. She argued, too, with her mother that maybe Mrs Entwistle was mistaken and that there was not a catch in them at all, the glittering prizes being awarded purely for merit and that any road it was worth risking even so large a sum as sixpence—the amount to be sent in stamps together with the solutions—to receive in return such prizes as a rolled gold bracelet with locket attached, or a "Mizpah" brooch or, in the case of one journal, a genuine rolled gold watch with a lovers' knot brooch to secure it. Mrs Winstanley, nevertheless, remained dubious and expressed the opinion that Fanny Entwistle knew what she was about and undoubtedly had the right of it. For no stranger, she declared emphatically, ever sent to another stranger "summat for nowt". It would, she contended, be against nature. Did not the sixpence they asked for in stamps conclusively prove this? Hilda, only half-convinced by her mother's commonsense, remained proof against the allurements of the rolled gold bracelet complete with locket, and the "Mizpah" brooch, but when the rolled gold watch, with rolled gold lovers' knot brooch attached, was cunningly illustrated in a full-page

177

advertisement, and she knew how easily she could fill in the word picture that should bring her this treasure, she worried her mother for permission to extract sixpence from her moneybox and try her luck. Ever since the wedding of Aunt Emma, who had worn pinned to the bodice of her bridal frock the beautiful gold watch Uncle Fred had given her, Hilda had yearned for a gold watch of her own. And here was an unrepeatable chance to obtain one, and all for a solitary sixpence.

The competition which should bring her this coveted treasure was simple. First there was a word, and then a picture suggesting a word, the completed puzzle making a well-known proverb, thus: The (picture of the sun rising over a hill-top) (picture of a blackbird) catches the (picture of a long, sinuous, unmistakable worm).

Triumphantly Hilda filled it in and read it out impressively to her mother and father: THE EARLY BIRD CATCHES THE WORM!

There could be no possible mistake about it. Nothing could go wrong, and the genuine rolled gold watch with lovers' knot brooch attached was as good as hers already. Though agreeing that the pictures undoubtedly made up this well-known adage, Mrs Winstanley still remarked uneasily that she knew there was a catch in it somewhere, but finally gave in and Hilda excitedly posted it off, complete with six penny stamps, to the queer-sounding address in London given at the bottom of the picture. Eagerly she waited for the watch to arrive, and her excitement when the postwoman one morning handed her a small hard packet was fever-high. She tore off the wrappings, her mother and Lily watching expectantly, and opened the neat cardboard box. It contained a wretchedly thin lovers' knot brooch and a flimsy piece

178

of printed paper, but no rolled gold watch. Hilda, in a trembling voice, read out:

Dear Madam,

We have great pleasure in advising you that your solution of our puzzle—THE EARLY BIRD CATCHES THE WORM— is quite correct, and we therefore send you herewith a genuine rolled gold lovers' knot brooch. On receipt from you of the sum of three shillings, sent in the form of a postal order, we shall have great pleasure in sending you also a genuine rolled gold watch as stated in our advertisement. Thus, for the almost negligible out-lay of three shillings and sixpence, you will acquire a genuine gold watch and pin that will be a pleasure for you to wear, and the envy and admiration of all your friends. In asking you to give your earnest consideration to this generous and unrepeatable offer, we beg respectfully to point out that a watch of this quality cannot be obtained elsewhere for less than ten shillings. We feel sure, therefore, that in your own interests you will undoubtedly avail yourself of this remarkable bargain, and we await your esteemed reply.

Hilda, when she came to the end of this document, burst into tears. Three shillings! It was a fortune. She had not got anything like it in her moneybox, already depleted by sixpence for the lovers' knot brooch, and had no possible means of acquiring it. The golden vision faded and she wept now for the sixpence so foolishly paid for the miserable and quite useless brooch. For nobody ever wore a lovers' knot brooch without a watch to keep it company. Her mother, fingering the brooch indignantly, and upset herself by Hilda's bitter disappointment, comforted her with the assurance that she would undoubtedly have a gold watch some day.

"Come you're twenty-one, our 'Ilda, and us'll give you a gold watch, and a proper thick brooch with it too. And our Lily when it's her twenty-first. Wish you'd hearkened to Fanny Entwistle. Reckon she knew for sartain there was a catch in it. T'world's full o' robbers, and let this be a proper warning not to go wasting your money on such idleness. You're no match for them strangers at London. Ah've 'eard tell o' such goings-on afore. A ten shilling gold watch for three shilling! It dusna make sense any road."

CHAPTER XIV

SUNDAY

Everybody in the Winstanley household had an extra lie-in on Sunday morning, and Mr Winstanley, who from the age of about seven had risen at five o'clock, had the luxury of a cup of tea in bed. On weekdays he was always the first to be up, and made tea not only for himself but for John and Jim as well, taking up a cup to his wife before he left for his work. On Sunday, Hilda and Lily got up first, Hilda lighting the fire and making tea in the big blue enamel family pot, taking a cup each to her mother and father, and also to her brothers. She used to take the tea right into her brothers' room, but always left the cups for her mother and father outside their door, modesty forbidding that either herself or Lily or indeed anyone should see them in bed. Lily meanwhile set out the table and cut bread and butter. After the two girls, Mrs Winstanley was the first to come down, washing herself at the sink and twisting up her thick black hair in front of the little looking-glass. While she was getting the special Sunday breakfast of a boiled egg apiece, the rest of the family made their appearance, each washing in cold water at the sink; and it was a crowded cheerful table when all were seated.

As soon as breakfast was over, Hilda and Lily and their brothers set out for Sunday School at Kilnbrook. Hilda used to walk along happily with Jack, while Lily fell behind with Jim. Neither Lily nor Jim spoke much, but Jack and Hilda talked freely, mostly about Edie, his sweetheart at Daneshead, and Edie's family, and Hilda looked forward eagerly to going there to tea one day. Jack spent nearly all his evenings at Edie's home, dressing himself up in his second-best suit, and Mrs Winstanley, bitterly jealous, frequent^lv and ungenerously remarked that he might just as well live there for all his own mother and father saw of him of a night-time. Sunday was the only day he was really seen much at home and even then, after dinner, he set off for Daneshead, going with Edie to her Congregational both after-noon and evening and not getting back till past ten o'clock.

They all liked Sunday School, and only illness ever kept them away. Indeed both Hilda and Lily went nearly as regularly as Jack, who had got his silver medal for going twelve years without once missing. Jim was the least regular, and often had to stay away in the winter because of his bronchitis.

James Turner, the Superintendent, opened with a hymn, then they all knelt while he prayed, remembering by name any who were away through sickness and asking the Lord to give them His special protection. After this the teaching began. To be a Sunday School teacher was considered the greatest honour at-tainable in the chapel, and Hilda earnestly looked forward to the time when she too would sit on a Windsor chair with her scholars ranged cosily round three sides of her, expounding to them the teachings of the Gospel, and explaining the Parables in plain, simple language. She felt quite sure of her ability to teach better than Nellie Mort, who was always pulling out her gold watch and obviously longing for Mr Turner to announce the closing hymn. And Nellie Mort couldn't explain the Parables properly either, and often came to a full stop over quite simple words in them. Both Jack and Jim were in the Bible Class, which was taken by the Superintendent himself, and all the classes were conducted very quietly, the teachers leaning forward and giving their instruction in low voices so as not to disturb the other groups.

Both going and coming, the United Methodists had to pass the

Primitive Methodists; and just as the proud church-goers looked down on the chapel-goers, so the United Methodists looked down on the Primitive Methodists. For the United Methodists worshipped in a handsome building of red brick and yellow stone, with a proper chapel upstairs and a fine large Sunday School room beneath, whereas the Primitive Methodists had a poor corrugated iron building, with no separate Sunday School at all. In years past there had been only one chapel in Kilnbrook, the original United Methodist, but, over a grave question of policy, severing old friendships and causing life-long feuds even among close relations, part of the congregation had seceded and defiantly erected the miserable tin building where, as Primitive Methodists, they now worshipped. Later, after many years of saving, they were able to build a magnificent new chapel of even redder brick and yellower stone than the United Methodists. By contrast, the old chapel of the Uniteds acquired a sad, shabby dignity, and though at the annual Whitsun Walk the bitter feud between the two chapels was ignored for just one day, it was, generally speaking, firmly believed by the Uniteds that the Word, as preached in the showy new building of the Primitives, was not the true Word at all; and the faithful Uniteds looked down more than ever on the Primitives, regarding them as no better than heathen who had evolved some outlandish faith of their own in order to justify their wicked expenditure on the new chapel. A faith which, though it might sustain their stubborn pride adequately enough in this world, was none the less a poor earthly thing that would never gain them admittance through the shining pearly gates into the Life Everlasting.

Sunday dinner at the Winstanleys, as indeed in every other cottage, was the big event of the week, and Mrs Winstanley, aware of its importance, spared neither time nor trouble to make it enjoyable. It was the only dinner meal of the week at which they all sat down together, and it was the only day on which they had a piece of hot roast butcher's meat. It was pleasant walking home from Sunday School to anticipate the roast beef and Yorkshire pudding, with a big rice pudding or apple pie to follow, and a strong cup of sweet tea to wash it all down with before setting out again for afternoon Sunday School. Hilda, who always enjoyed going with her mother and Lily on a Saturday night to do the shopping in Daneshead, used to get impatient at the time her mother took over buying the Sunday joint. The butcher would show her various joints, pointing out the undoubted merits of each as he weighed them, and waiting respectfully while Mrs Winstanley made up her mind. She used to press the meat between her thumb and forefinger, asking various searching questions, and always differing about the price. When she had examined them all, the butcher, having known all along exactly which joint had taken her fancy, wrapped it up in a piece of newspaper and put it in her string shopping bag; then, leaning confidentially over his chopping block while she felt for her purse, would remark engagingly: "I wouldn't do it for everybody, Missus, but I'll knock threepence off for a customer like you as knows a good bit o' meat when you see it."

And her mother, handing over the money, would leave the shop contented, remarking triumphantly when out of the butcher's hearing: "Threepence saved is threepence gained. It'll buy a relish to pack up for your father's dinner Monday."

During the remainder of the week they had odd scraps of meat from Mr Raike, the butcher in Moss Ferry, or sometimes Jim brought home a rabbit from the farm where he worked; sometimes they even ate chicken, which Mrs Winstanley regarded as tasteless insubstantial meat fit only for the very poorly and in no sense to be compared for taste and nourishment with good red butcher's meat.

Afternoon Sunday School was different from morning. There was no actual class teaching, but the Superintendent read the bible out loud and then expounded the Word. This proceeding lasted for a half-hour only, after which the entire Sunday School went up into the chapel for afternoon service.

Sometimes in the winter, when the snow lay very thick, Mrs Winstanley would let Hilda and Lily take their tea to chapel, giving them tea and sugar mixed in a screw of paper, milk in a medicine bottle, bread and butter and jam sandwiches and a piece of cake. They thoroughly enjoyed staying to tea at chapel, for quite a few grown-ups, who had to come long distances, stayed too in order to attend evening service. There were cups and saucers and teapots in plenty and a big fire in the vestry on which to boil the kettle. Staying to tea at chapel was nearly as exciting, in fact, as an Outing. Some of the grown-ups used to share their cake around among the children, and they all sat at the trestle table eating their different teas in an atmosphere of great good humour and friendliness. Some people even had a boiled egg to their tea, and always gave the sliced-off top to one or other of the children.

Mr and Mrs Winstanley never missed evening chapel, and sometimes, when they were invited to tea by Aunt Annie, who lived close by the chapel, came for the afternoon service as well. They always sat on the same bench, Hilda finding the hymns and sharing the hymn-book with her father, while Lily did the same with her mother. Hilda did this out of pride, for her father knew every hymn by heart and would not have needed a hymn-book even had he been able to read it.

With her mother's approval she sometimes sat on the bench

immediately in front with old Mr and Mrs Sankey, who came from a long way out on Chat Moss. They couldn't read either, and Hilda pleased them by sitting between them and holding up the hymn-book as if they could read as well as herself. They were a childless couple, and loved to have her sit with them, and, when the Reverend Vane began his sermon, Mrs Sankey always produced a bag of threepenny-bit peppermints and passed them first to her husband and then to Hilda to share with her. The three sat contentedly, sucking quietly at their peppermints, while the Reverend Vane thundered at the evil-doers and laid continual emphasis on the burning horrors of the Lake of Fire.

Mrs Sankey, who was tall and very bony, had an extremely red, lined face and always dressed in black. Her hands were the knottiest Hilda had ever seen. They were so seamed with hard work that no scrubbing brush would ever get them clean, and Hilda was thankful that she handed her the bag of peppermints to help herself instead of doling out one at a time.

After chapel, various friends and relations stood outside in little groups, exchanging the week's news and waiting so that they could bid goodnight to the Reverend Vane. They were all very proud of their minister who, though little, was, they all stressed loudly, *good*, and, in his shining silk hat and neat frock coat, a minister any chapel, or church either, could be justly proud of.

When he had bid the various groups a pleasant goodnight, they broke up and went cheerfully home. Sunday, the happiest, pleasantest day of the week was over, and not one of them but looked forward to Sunday again; and so on from week to week.

*　　　*　　　*

To those members of the chapel who lived within reasonable distance of it fell the honour and privilege of having the minister to tea on Sundays, for he did not live in the neighbourhood but came from several miles away. This coveted pleasure was taken in rotation, no distinction being made between the poorest cottager and the wealthiest farmer. Some of the farmers' wives would have been only too glad to have the Reverend Vane to tea every Sunday, but it was an unwritten law that no favouritism should be shown.

Mrs Winstanley's turn came once a year only, and so important was the occasion that she turned out the entire house for it, even washing specially all the window curtains. Hilda, in return for "book-reading" concessions, was always willing to help her mother with the housework, and particularly when they were going to have such distinguished company as the Minister for Sunday tea. On the Saturday preceding the visit she scrubbed and polished with extra vigour, burnishing the steel fittings of the big oven grate in the front room till they glittered like old silver, while she polished the massive mahogany cheffonier with linseed oil till the entire room was reflected in its dark panels. She took down the pictures and washed them, and washed also the various china ornaments on the mantelpiece. She dusted all the Sunday School prize books that were stacked impressively either side of the cheffonier looking-glass, moving various knick-knacks which obscured them, so that the Minister could admire the books. Mrs Winstanley meanwhile baked bread and cakes and fruit pies; and except for Joe, who was nervous, they all looked forward to the visitor. Lily and Hilda brought him home from afternoon chapel, Lily, tongue-tied, answering his questions awkwardly, while Hilda, once over her shyness, talked freely of her prowess at school and her passionate desire for further, more comprehensive, education. The Reverend Vane was very pleasant, and impressed upon her the virtues of always remaining contented with one's lot; but he showed great interest in her reading and advised her earnestly to get the novels of Mrs Henry Wood out of the Co-op. library. He recommended warmly *East Lynne* and urged her also to read *The Pilgrim's Progress* by John Bunyan. Hilda drank in every word and resolved that over tea she would ask him again to give her the names of these books for her mother's benefit. For Mrs Winstanley remained firmly and deeply suspicious of every book, apart from *Chatterbox* and her other prizes, that Hilda read, but even she could hardly find fault with books recommended by the Reverend Vane.

The tea was a great success, the Minister making himself at home just as easily as he had done at Aunt Emma's wedding tea; and Hilda, cunningly watching her opportunity, asked him to repeat the names of the books he had already mentioned so that she might write them down. The Reverend Vane, sensing Mrs Winstanley's unlettered antagonism to book-reading in general, and pleased by Hilda's eager desire for knowledge, talked for quite a long time about books and what a comfort they were and how nobody was ever the worse off for having read a good, well-written book, provided always of course that they never neglected to read first and foremost the Book of books. Hilda, watching her mother closely, noted triumphantly that she was impressed; and when the Minister, equally observant, ended up with friendly advice to his young listener to read all she could get from the library, her love for him filled her whole being, and she knew that from now on she was safe to bring home any book she fancied from the Co-op. library in Daneshead.

*   *   *

Until the unforgettable opening of this little library, Hilda had been dependent for her serious reading on her own Sunday

School and day school prizes, and those of her brothers and sister, while Mrs Entwistle kept her generously supplied with various weekly journals and twopenny novelettes. Among her prize books, *Chatterbox*, which was given to her annually at Sunday School from her fourth to her ninth year, remained first favourite, and she read it carefully and happily, right through, several times a year. Her mother and father never tired either of hearing her read out any stories it contained about the Royal Family, and Mrs Winstanley knew everything there was to know about every new Royal baby, and never failed to comment, when a little Prince or Princess was christened, that it was a shame to burden it so heavily with such a long string of useless and high-falutin' names.

Another favourite they also loved to hear over and over again was the terrible story of the great earthquake which destroyed a place in foreign parts called Martinique. The story was about the wonderful escape of Tomas, a planter on Martinique, who, with big stones and great rocks falling like hail over the island, and clouds of sulphurous burning smoke nearly choking him, ran for his life to a cave he alone knew of, holding over his head and shoulders a large tin bath. There was a picture of Tomas lurching blindly along under the bath. His house was destroyed to its foundations and his plantation ruined, and he lived for many weeks in the cave, venturing out only a little way to dig in the blackened earth for yams, on which he lived. Out of all the village, Tomas, because of his thoughtfulness over the bath, was the only person left alive, and the tale of his daily life in the cave fascinated the Winstanleys. Mrs Winstanley, obstinately ignoring his ingenuity over the bath, was firmly convinced that the earthquake was a Judgement on the wicked people of Martinique, and that the Lord had specially intervened to save Tomas because of his upright and God-fearing life, although there was no mention in the story of any outstanding virtue on the part of Tomas. No matter how often Hilda read them the story, her mother and father listened breathlessly, and at the conclusion Mrs Winstanley always made the same remark—that Tomas had been spared a-purpose, it being the Lord's will, plain for all to see, that not a hair of his head should be harmed—tin bath or no tin bath.

While *Chatterbox*, because of its wide and exciting variety of stories and anecdotes and pictures, never lost first place, Hilda became deeply attached to all her prize books, and particularly to *The Basket of Flowers*, a harrowing story of a thieving magpie who stole a costly diamond ring from a fashionable lady. For this theft a virtuously brought-up little girl called Mary was cruelly imprisoned and whipped, and then, with James, her saintly old father, banished for life from her native village, not all the tears and pleadings of the Countess and her daughter, Amelia, availing to save her from this terrible fate. Mary and James endured great hardships in their wanderings and, as Hilda read out the moving scene when old James died, leaving Mary to face the world alone, Mrs Winstanley cried unashamedly and her husband looked very solemn, and neither brightened up till Hilda came to the exciting chapter where, many years afterwards, the ring was found in the magpie's nest high up a tall fir tree, and Mary, poor and friendless, discovered sobbing over her father's grave by the Countess and her daughter, was taken home to live with them, like a lady, in their castle.

But, when the Co-op. library opened, Hilda's reading became a serious matter, causing many scenes between herself and her mother. And it was not till the Reverend Vane spoke up so stoutly for book-reading in general that she was allowed to spend twopence every week on getting a fresh book to read. Mrs Winstanley did not give in without a struggle, being unable to see any sense in this wanton spending of twopence a week.

"What dost want to go and give t'Co-op. tuppence a week for wi' all them prizes in t'house?" she asked resentfully. "It ud be different if you got a divi on it—but to go and give tuppence every week just for the lend of a book seems downright idleness, and no good'll come of it."

If she could have counted on support from her husband she would have forbidden this weekly extravagance, being firmly convinced, in spite of the Reverend Vane, that by reading a different book every single week Hilda was doing herself serious harm—onsettling herself as she put it. Of the Co-op. books she had the darkest suspicions, for with only a week in which to get through them Hilda could not always spare the time to read them out aloud, and this fact, Mrs Winstanley asserted, was proof beyond all doubt that they were not fit reading at all for a girl of her age. But Hilda, after virtuously doing the small household jobs expected of her after tea—such as drying the dishes, cleaning the few knives by working them up and down in the earth till they shone clean, helping on washing-day to turn the mangle and fold up the sheets, fetching the daily supply of drinking water from Mrs Pettener's well—would settle down obstinately to her book. In summer she sat at the table under the front-room window, and gave herself up to pure enjoyment. Occasionally her mother came in to fetch something from the cupboard and eyed the offending book unfavourably, always, as she went out, saying: "Satan allus finds work for idle hands to do." When Hilda, irritated by the interruption and the unjustness of the criticism, pointed out in an aggrieved tone that she was *not* idle, having faithfully performed all that had been asked of her, her mother grudgingly admitted that this was so but all the same it

would do her more good to be out in the lane playing hopscotch
with Lily than sitting indoors cooped up over a book. Hilda,
her hatred of the smug and self-righteous Lily boiling over, was
once unwise enough to shout out that hopscotch was all Lily
Winstanley was fit for, and very properly and promptly received
in exchange a smart box on the ear.

In winter, there being no fire in the front room except on
Sundays, she sat in her own corner of the horse-hair sofa in the
kitchen, oblivious to everything that went on around, not disturbed at all by the talk flowing about her. Her father would
come in from work and wash himself and then settle down
comfortably to his tea. Then Jim, always smelling of manure and
slopping down his tea noisily and dirtily, and occasionally taking
the trouble to jeer at his sister and her book-reading. Lily,
laboriously sewing and, sitting next to Hilda, every now and
then spitefully jabbing an elbow into her. Mrs Winstanley, always
busy making the different teas. Hilda, deep in *Robinson Crusoe*
or *East Lynne* or *Tess of the D'Urbervilles* heard nothing and saw
nothing. Even Lily's vicious pokes never really broke through
the magic circle that the book made for her. Only when it was
bedtime and Lily had again jabbed her, virtuously and legally
this time, and Mrs Winstanley, impatient and angry, had snatched
the book smartly from her, did she find herself in the kitchen
again to hear her mother saying: "Ah do believe you'd sit there
if t'ouse was a-fire. You and your book-reading. It's gone nine
and time for bed. Reckon you've read enough for one night.
And dunna forget your prayers."

The two girls went up to bed, undressing in the dark for their
mother never allowed them to have a candle. If it was very cold
they said their prayers in bed, an unspoken understanding existing
between them to keep this unorthodox practice entirely to them-

selves, though with a guilty feeling that prayers said in comfort were worse than no prayers at all and would certainly not be answered. The bed was warm through and through, their mother having put a hot brick wrapped in flannel in the middle of it an hour before. Only when they desired something very urgently, or it was Sunday and they were feeling particularly good, did they kneel down on the cold linoleum, shivering in their flannelette nightdresses, and pray in the approved, traditional fashion. They always said goodnight to each other, and Lily, her mind completely empty, was soon asleep, while Hilda lay awake for a time going over and over again the chapters she had been reading, till she fell asleep in happy recollection.

*　　　　　*　　　　　*

Although she had no ear whatsoever for music, Hilda longed passionately to be able to play on the piano, an accomplishment which would set a social seal upon her and mark her out for distinction in whatever society she might find herself. There were very few pianos in Moss Ferry, and among her schoolfellows not more than two or three who could play. Florrie and May Woodville had lessons from their father, and the proud Holroyd girls were taught by their aunt, Maudie Holroyd, Hilda's old schoolteacher. Miss Askew could play a little too, and even the stupid Susie Hodson had contrived to get as far as "Snowdrop Waltz", also under Miss Holroyd's tuition. But there was no possible hope that Mrs Winstanley would ever be able to afford the luxury of a piano, although she admitted that a piano would look well in the front room if only Grandma Stringer would pay for Hilda to learn, and she herself could afford to pay for Lily. Mrs Winstanley, in spite of her deep-seated hostility to "book-larnin'", was all for bettering her social status, and gave the question of the piano long and earnest consideration. She and Joe talked it over night after night for many weeks, but finally decided that there was no getting round it. To buy a piano, paying for it by weekly instalments, would take them a lifetime, to say nothing of the expense of the lessons. Hilda, for a wonder, accepted the disappointment philosophically, but made up her mind resolutely to acquire at least one high social accomplishment that would astonish Moss Ferry—she would learn French!

When she announced this amazing ambition her mother stared at her unbelieving.

"Learn *French*, our 'Ilda! Reckon you've gone clean daft. What do you want to do a thing like that for?"

"Oh—just so I can speak French, and read French too," Hilda explained seriously. "Mildred Holroyd can speak French. She learnt it before they came to live here. She says everybody who's properly educated can speak French. If I went to Manchester High School I should learn it. Mildred Holroyd says they teach it at all high-class schools same as if it was English. Her father knows it, and her mother too. I can learn it myself," added Hilda earnestly. "There's books about it, you know."

Mrs Winstanley shook her head.

"Nay—Ah never 'eard anything like it. What's to be gained by it, any road? Tell me that! Learning French! And where'll you get t'books to learn it with? Out of t'Co-op.?"

"No. They don't have them there. I've asked. I'm going to ask the Superintendent to give me a French book for my next Sunday School prize. Now I can get proper books out of the Co-op., I don't want any more story books for prizes. Reckon he'll give me a French book if I tell him I'm going to learn French."

Her mother regarded Hilda sadly.

"Reckon James Turner'll think it's funny. No good'll come of it, mark my words. Nobody knows French, any road. If you learn it what'll you do wi' it? Answer me that!"

Hilda sighed.

"If I learn French I'll be educated," she replied, "and I've told you what Mildred Holroyd said. And any road I'm going to learn it. There's no harm to it, and you leave me be, Mother."

Mrs Winstanley, to relieve her outraged feelings, boxed Hilda's ears.

"Don't you talk that road to your mother, 'Ilda Winstanley. It's all that book-reading. Day in, day out, when other childer's out playing and behaving natural. And now learning French. Reckon your father'll 'ave summat to say to this. And your Grandma Stringer too. Idling your time away learning foreigners' talk."

In spite of her mother's continued opposition, Hilda, as Christmas drew near, timidly approached the Sunday School Superintendent and made her astonishing request for a French book to be given her out of which she could teach herself the French language. The Superintendent was surprised and perturbed, and asked gravely if she was quite sure she would not prefer a nice story book. Hilda remained firm. She wanted to learn French and she would learn French and, seeing that her mind was made up, Mr Turner agreed and said he would make inquiries about the best sort of book to get for her.

When the prize-giving night came round, Hilda, sitting with her family in the chapel, rose self-consciously when her name was called out. All the prize books were stacked up on a big table and were handed out by the Superintendent. First of all he called the name of the prize-winner and then the name of the book, and as each prize was handed over everybody clapped.

When Hilda, blushing, reached the table her heart thumped as she saw a fat black and red book taken from the pile. Mr Turner looked at it solemnly, and then read out, slowly and impressively: "To Hilda Winstanley, for early attendance and good conduct, Cassell's New French-English English-French Dictionary."

As he handed it over he said gravely, and, she fancied, with slight disapproval: "I hope it will make you a good scholar, Hilda."

As Hilda, firmly holding her coveted prize, walked quickly back to her family, she could feel the surprise which ran through the audience, and only the Superintendent and the teachers remembered to clap.

Her mother, looking red and uncomfortable and feeling that everybody in the chapel was thinking what a funny taste Hilda Winstanley had in prizes and that she could not, in consequence, have been brought up properly, turned a hostile face when Hilda proudly showed her the book. She softened, however, when Hilda, noticing that the pencilled price had not been properly rubbed out, whispered excitedly that it had cost three shillings and sixpence! It was the most expensive book the Sunday School had ever awarded, and Mrs Winstanley reflected consolingly that they must think a lot of Hilda to have gone and paid all that. And that maybe there was summat to be said for French after all. A foreign tongue that cost three shillings and sixpence to learn was evidently not to be despised, though for the life of her she couldn't make head or tail of Hilda's passionate desire to talk it.

CHAPTER XV

EARNING

Ever since the time when the Vicar had taken notice of her during the scripture lesson, Hilda had nursed an earnest social desire to see more of him, although she still did not really like him and continued to compare him unfavourably with the chapel Minister, the Reverend Vane. But she was immensely flattered when, meeting him near the Vicarage one afternoon after school, he asked kindly whether she had ever thought of beginning to earn a little money for herself now that she was getting to be a big girl, and if so would she care to have a word with his house-keeper, Miss Minnie Brown. Hilda, thrilled at the prospect, and not waiting to consult with her mother, turned into the Vicarage with him, and was left in the kitchen with Miss Brown, who explained that she could do with a little extra help, as the whole work of the Vicarage, which was very large, was becoming too much for her. Hilda, anxious to establish her independence by earning real money for herself, was nevertheless surprised and disappointed when Miss Brown, gradually coming to the question of wages, suggested that, for an hour's work every morning before school, and all day Saturday until four o'clock, ninepence would be a just reward. Hilda, having no idea of what her services were worth, and too shy to ask for more, agreed. Nine-pence a week seemed quite a big sum after all. It never occurred to her that Miss Brown, knowing that in a very few months she would be leaving school, had it in mind that she should work there altogether.

Hilda, eager to earn even ninepence by her own efforts, saw no shame in helping Miss Brown of her own free will, but she had no intention of earning her living as a servant. This fact she had established quite firmly for herself, although she did not yet know what plans Grandma Stringer had in mind for her. That she would have to do something as soon as she left school was, however, quite clear, her mother having repeatedly impressed upon her that at thirteen the money for her keep would stop and she would have to supply it from her own earnings.

When, having agreed to Miss Brown's terms, she ran home to inform her mother, Mrs Winstanley was doubtful and, when she heard of the ninepence a week, definitely disapproving.

"It's not a wage," she pointed out angrily. "Nobbut a few pence. Reckon twice as much wouldna hurt them. Going every morning and all Saturday. But you mun please yourself. Ah'll not say one way or t'other. Any road, no harm trying it for a bit. Lucy Stringer was saying only last month it's time for us to be thinking of what you're to be put to. You'll be turned thirteen come June."

And so, for the last few months of her school days, Hilda worked at the Vicarage; and although she found the work hard, she was proud to receive her ninepence, which she generously offered, the first week, to her mother, who refused it, giving her good advice instead about saving some of it and warning her not to go spending more than her usual twopence a week at the Co-op. library.

Hilda quite enjoyed working at the Vicarage, for Miss Brown, though she gave her all the dirty jobs to do, was kind in her way and talked to her freely and almost as though she were a grown-up. Several times, when the Vicar was away for the night, she slept with Miss Brown for company and was thrilled at being able to wash herself, next morning, luxuriously in the hand-basin in the bathroom, where, guiltily, she squeezed out some of Miss Brown's toothpaste on to her handkerchief and rubbed her teeth vigorously with it. There were no toothbrushes at home. Very occasionally the different members of the family cleaned their teeth with salt, rubbing it on with a piece of flannel and swilling their mouths out afterwards. And nobody ever thought of going to a dentist, although one came regularly every month to Daneshead. If they had a toothache they tied a woollen stocking round their heads, and if the tooth ached and jumped very badly applied a scalding bread poultice under the stocking. When the ache became so violent and persistent that more drastic measures were necessary, they tied a piece of string round the offending tooth, secured the other end of the string to a door knob, and pulled and wriggled till the tooth came out, a procedure which sometimes took several days. Doctor James was always willing to pull out a tooth with his forceps, but hurt them more than if they did it themselves.

Hilda had not worked very long at the Vicarage before, out of her weekly ninepence, she purchased herself a toothbrush and a tube of clean-smelling paste, which brought accusations from her mother that she was getting too lady-like and above herself.

Surveying the toothpaste resentfully, Mrs Winstanley admonished: "That's no road to be spending your earnings! There's nowt like salt for cleaning, whether it's teeth or t'kitchen table. Ah've nowt to say against brush, but dunna go spending again on new-fangled stuff like this"; and she sniffed disapprovingly at the bulging tube.

Hilda, however, once having enjoyed the clean sweet feel of her mouth after brushing violently with the paste, remained obstinate and, to the jeers of her mother and Lily and Jim, used the toothpaste regularly every night after her tea, carefully wrapping it up in a piece of flannel together with the brush, and taking it up to her bedroom lest the envious Lily should, when her back was turned, experiment with it.

When Hilda turned distastefully against the hard yellow soap with which they all washed, bringing out instead a tablet of highly-scented pink soap she had bought at Mrs Starkey's, Mrs Winstanley became seriously alarmed.

"Spending your money on such foolishness," she remarked impatiently. "Ah'd as soon think o' weshing myself wi' money as use scented soap. Reckon it's aw reet for Miss Brown to use scented soap, but there's no call for you to go smelling like 'er. Miss Brown lives different from us, and dunna let me catch you buying any more on it. Whatever next, Ah wonder!"

*   *   *

As Hilda's thirteenth birthday drew nearer, the question of her future became grave and pressing. Lucy Stringer, coming to pay the monthly pound for her keep, talked to her earnestly about the undoubted advantages of going into service. It was only in this way, she stressed, that Hilda could immediately relieve her Grandma of the strain which the monthly pound and the cost of her clothes had placed upon her. Lucy pointed out that by going into service she would perhaps earn as much as five shillings a week, besides the cost of her keep. She could, therefore, become self-supporting immediately she left school. And to be self-supporting, Lucy continued sternly, was surely the aim of any right-thinking, well brought-up girl.

Hilda, however, cried so bitterly at the ugly prospect that even Lucy's hard face softened, and she promised to have a further consultation with Grandma Stringer to see what could be done. Mrs Winstanley, herself upset by Hilda's distress and fear, said she would have a talk with Joe. Perhaps, she half-promised, if Grandma Stringer would go on paying the five shillings a week while Hilda learnt the dressmaking, she and Joe might manage to find her in clothes. Mrs Winstanley, however, was uneasy as to whether Hilda had a natural bent for the dressmaking, in spite of the fact that at school her cross stitch and her button-holing had always been praised for neatness. It would, too, be a couple of years before she began to earn anything, and even then there would not be much scope in Moss Ferry and Kilnbrook. Florrie Woodville was going to be a dressmaker, and Hilda would have her as a rival. And Mrs Weatherhead, who so far had done all the professional dressmaking for the two villages, would last for a good many years yet. However, if Hilda wouldn't go into service, there was no other choice. Mrs Winstanley, talking it over very seriously with her husband, blamed the "book-reading" for Hilda's determination not to go into service. The book-reading had put all sorts of uppish ideas into her head. But she agreed with Joe that the mischief had been done, and there was no mending it now by putting Hilda to work at which she would never settle. After several further visits from Lucy Stringer, it was agreed that immediately Hilda left school she should be apprenticed to Mrs Ormston at Daneshead. Mrs Ormston was considered to be the last word in fashionable dressmaking, though nobody in Moss Ferry or Kilnbrook would have dreamt of being so disloyal as to have their dresses made by anybody but Mrs Weatherhead.

Lucy Stringer herself took Hilda to see Mrs Ormston, and it was arranged that she should be apprenticed to her for two years, and after that should stay on with her, receiving a small wage until she set up on her own as a qualified dressmaker in Moss Ferry. The nightmare of going into service over and done with,

Hilda now looked forward eagerly to the end of her school life
and the beginning of her new career as a dressmaker.

She left school a few weeks after her thirteenth birthday—when
it broke up for the summer holidays. Mr Woodville wrote out
a "character" for her, in which he informed all whom it might
concern that she had been a good and industrious scholar and had
reached Standard VII, the top standard at St Margaret's. He also
gave her a book—*Brave Dame Mary of Corfe Castle*—and
Maudie Holroyd, Mrs Pretty and Miss Askew gave her between
them a pretty wicker workbasket containing everything that she
was likely to need in her new life. With this, and the lady's companion which she had treasured for so many years, Hilda felt
herself to be thoroughly equipped for the glowing career which
now lay ahead of her.

*   *   *

Before beginning her apprenticeship with Mrs Ormston, Hilda
had one glorious week of complete freedom. She explained her
new work to Miss Brown at the Vicarage, and was not flattered
when Miss Brown said that both she and the Vicar had hoped she
would stay on there in daily service. Miss Brown seemed to have
no proper regard for Hilda's potentialities as a fashionable dressmaker. She pointed out at some length the material and spiritual
advantages of taking service under the Reverend James Black.
He was, said Miss Brown emphatically, the kindest employer in
all Lancashire.

"I don't know what your mother is thinking of to take you
from here for dressmaking," said Miss Brown severely. "And
you're not old enough to be the best judge yourself, Hilda. Why,
you can stay on here and have your food and five shillings a week.
Surely that's better than wasting two years earning nothing. And
it will be safe and regular," she added persuasively.

Hilda remained firm. To work at the Vicarage, of her own free will, for extra spending-money was a very different matter from working there, of necessity, as a servant. She thanked Miss Brown, awkwardly, for having been so kind to her. Miss Brown, perceiving that no blandishments would move her, bade her a chilly goodbye and made it disagreeably plain that from now on she took no further interest in her. Henceforth she was, in the eyes of the Vicarage, a misguided, heretic chapel-goer with ideas above her station. Folding up her sacking apron, Hilda walked home dejectedly, Miss Brown's cold stare as she finally left the kitchen having made her feel quite a criminal.

On the whole her work at the Vicarage had improved her. She had learnt easily to speak a fair imitation of Miss Brown's genteel speech. She now knew how to set a table neatly and accurately. She had discovered the pleasantness of toothpaste and scented soap, and the added lustre which daily and vigorous brushing gave to her hair. Miss Brown, whose one claim to physical attractiveness was her thick, glossy black hair, had often asked Hilda to brush it for her. She always brushed it for ten minutes every day, she confided to Hilda. After learning this astonishing piece of information, Hilda, to her mother's surprise, spent ten minutes every night brushing her own hair. She even volunteered to brush her mother's hair daily, flattering her by pointing out how much thicker it was, any road, than Miss Brown's.

She had learnt, too, the quiet, unhurried routine of the gentry's way of life. Every Saturday she had eaten her dinner with Miss Brown, and could now eat and drink and handle a knife and fork as expertly as that lady herself. She had discovered that the gentry ate strange combinations of food. They mixed a lettuce up with all sorts of things and called it a salad, instead of just eating it plain with bread and butter. And they broke up one egg after another and made them into an omelette. And they made their own coffee instead of buying it in a bottle, like her mother. Hilda used to grind coffee berries at the Vicarage every morning, and was impressed by the fact that the Vicar always drank coffee with his breakfast, and only had tea in the afternoon. And she knew for a positive fact that he took a bath every day of his life. Her mother did not at first credit this outrageous statement. She said he probably washed as far up as he could and as far down as he could, but nobody in their right senses washed themselves all over every day, even if cleanliness was next to godliness. There was a proper bathroom at the Vicarage and always plenty of hot water from the big kitchen range. And there was a W.C. by itself next door to the bathroom, with a chain that swilled the water round. Until she went to the Vicarage, Hilda had never seen an indoor closet: it was a luxury and a mark of gentility which made a greater impression upon her than all the other refinements put together.

*　　　　*　　　　*

Mrs Ormston lived at the far end of Daneshead. Hilda, who was to work there from half-past eight until six o'clock, set out excitedly for her first day. In a lidded wicker basket she carried her dinner and tea, the workbasket given her by the teachers, and the treasured lady's companion.

Mrs Ormston welcomed her heartily. She was a stout, middle-aged woman with a very plain, very red face and a high pile of fuzzy, grey-black hair. There were no signs of dressmaking about when Hilda arrived, except a full-sized dressmaker's "dummy" which stood in a corner of the kitchen with a half-made frock draped over it. As soon as she had taken off her hat and coat

Hilda was invited to have a cup of tea and then, to her surprise, was told to clear the table and to wash up. Mrs Ormston, noting her puzzled look, explained that all apprentices to the dressmaking, as a matter of course, were expected to help with the housework; that there would be plenty of time to learn her trade, and that, if she had it in her, she'd make a fashionable dressmaker out of her or die in the attempt.

While Hilda washed up the breakfast things in the small scullery leading out of the kitchen, Mrs Ormston went to do the bedroom. When the washing-up was finished and the things put away, Hilda was handed a large piece of emery paper and told to burnish the steel fender and fire irons in the kitchen. After this she was asked to sweep and dust the front room while Mrs Ormston busied herself in the kitchen. When the front room was finished, and Mrs Ormston had tidied up the kitchen, Hilda waited expectantly for the dressmaking to begin. Mrs Ormston, however, set her to peel potatoes, explaining that Mr Ormston came in to his dinner regularly just after twelve o'clock. Mr Ormston worked on the railway and did not like to be kept waiting. Mrs Ormston, bustling about the oven, asked if Hilda had brought anything for her dinner which would eat tastier for being hotted up. Hilda, touched by this thoughtfulness, drew from her basket a small meat and potato pie, and placed it beside the rice pudding already in the oven. The morning passed quickly and energetically and, while Hilda was laying the table for dinner, Mr Ormston came in and she was introduced. Mr Ormston was small and thin and wiry; his face was even redder than Mrs Ormston's and he had a big yellow weeping moustache that made him look smaller than he actually was. Mr Ormston did not say a single word all the time they were having their dinner. Hilda, having learnt at the Vicarage how to eat genteelly, was shocked when Mrs Ormston placed the rice pudding between herself and her husband so that both spooned it up noisily out of the original dish.

"Saves washing up," explained Mrs Ormston cheerfully as she caught Hilda's unguarded look. "Have a taste, Hilda. Go and get yourself a spoon."

Hilda, remarking that she was already full up, politely refused and found herself saying inside:

> Jack Sprat could eat no fat;
> His wife could eat no lean.
> And so betwixt them both, you see,
> They licked the platter clean.

Mr Ormston, after his wife had scraped the brown off the dish with a knife, picked up the dish and licked it round with his tongue till it was as clean as a well-washed egg. Mrs Ormston then brewed a pot of strong tea, and the three of them sat and enjoyed it. Mr Ormston, who had not yet spoken, got up, knocked out his pipe, licked the sugared dregs out of his cup, put on his cap and jacket, and, with a pleasant "Ah mun away now", went back to the railway.

Hilda, feeling, as she afterwards told her mother, slightly mazed, again washed up. After this job was over, Mrs Ormston produced a red serge skirt she was making and initiated Hilda into the art of oversewing. She herself became busy snipping and tacking at the half-made frock on the "dummy". The afternoon wore away pleasantly enough, Mrs Ormston occasionally making a professional remark and coming over now and again to see how Hilda was shaping with the oversewing.

At five o'clock she made another pot of tea, which Hilda drank with the bread and butter and cake she had brought in her basket. After this Mrs Ormston stopped dressmaking for the day and began to prepare Mr Ormston's tea. Again Hilda laid the table and, when Mr Ormston had finished, again washed up. By now it was six o'clock and time to go home, and Mrs Ormston, assuring her that she had not done so badly and had made a favourable impression on both herself and Mr Ormston, said she might go.

Walking home after her first day of real professional work, Hilda reflected gloomily on her prospects. She had spent a busy day, mainly doing housework. The sewing part had been easy, and she had never before seen two grown-up people eat their dinner out of the same dish. She related all the day's happenings to her mother, and expressed unhappy forebodings that at this rate she would never learn the dressmaking. Mrs Winstanley, however, reproved her for being impatient. She pointed out dramatically that everybody must learn to walk before they could run. All the same, she thought it very strange that Hilda had been given so much housework to do, and denounced the bad manners of both Mr and Mrs Ormston for eating out of the same dish—"same as if they was pigs or fowls".

*   *   *

As the weeks passed, Hilda became acutely uneasy and confided to her mother that she had no faith in Mrs Ormston being able to teach her the dressmaking. She spent all her mornings doing housework, sewing only for a few hours in the afternoon. She did a fair amount of plain hemming and joining-up seams, and was flattered when Mrs Ormston praised the neat finish of her button-holes. Once she was even allowed to make all the button-holes down the back of a handsome brown serge dress for one of Mrs Ormston's best customers. But for the rest she had not even been shown how to lay a pattern and to cut out. When customers came to be fitted, she stood by and handed pins to Mrs Ormston and threaded needles for her with tacking cotton. She admired the fearless way in which Mrs Ormston snipped pieces off here and there, and waited hopefully for the time when she would be allowed to do the same. But Mrs Ormston seemed to be in no hurry, and Hilda's uneasiness grew. The housework and the errand-running now began to bore her, and her hands were getting quite rough through the continual washing-up in soda water. When she was given thin silk material to sew, a strand sometimes caught on her fingers; once she puckered a whole length of material in this way and was mildly reproved for her clumsiness.

When, during a particularly slack week, Mrs Ormston set her to mending Mr Ormston's stockings and underwear, Hilda flared up. Red and crying she protested that she had been apprenticed to learn the dressmaking; that she had now been there for three months and hadn't learnt a thing that counted; and that she would not, in any circumstances, mend Mr Ormston's stockings and Mrs Ormston could do what she liked about it.

Mrs Ormston was flabbergasted at this shocking outburst. Her fingers itched to box her pupil's ears, but some instinct warned her that this would not mend matters. She had no fear of what Mrs Winstanley might say, but had no mind to face Lucy Stringer should that young woman decide to take Hilda's part. When she had calmed down, she reasoned with the crying girl, pointing out that the dressmaking was never learnt in a day, and that the cutting-out and fitting would all come in good time. She made no further attempt to get the stockings darned, but instead found Hilda some dusters to hem.

Mrs Winstanley was deeply worried when Hilda that night burst out with what had happened. Hilda, crying again, said she knew in her bones she would never learn the dressmaking from

Mrs Ormston, not if she stopped with her till her dying day. It suddenly dawned on Mrs Winstanley that, though Mrs Ormston could dressmake well enough herself, it might be that she wasn't up to teaching anybody else, and it certainly looked as though she would never teach Hilda.

The situation was grave, for Hilda's entire future was at stake. It was Aunt Susannah, paying a rare visit from Ancoats to Grandma Buckley, who made the sensible suggestion: a suggestion that sent Hilda's spirits rocketing, although it did not at first please Mrs Winstanley.

"There's big shops in Manchester", said Aunt Susannah, "where maybe Hilda could begin the dressmaking again. Proper Court dressmaking, too. And she would be paid a wage from the start. There's plenty of openings, and I reckon Hilda's nobbut wasting her time at Mrs Ormston's, and nothing coming in from it either. There's Lewis's in Market Street. And grand shops in St Ann's Square. Why, Hankinson & Sankey or Kirby Nicholson might give her a start. She's got a good school character, and I reckon if she was to write summat might come of it."

Hilda looked gratefully at Aunt Susannah and was all for writing there and then. The thought of going back next day to the dreary round at Mrs Ormston's became unbearable, and she made the daring suggestion that perhaps she needn't go back at all.

Her mother, however, was firm. She was to stop with Mrs Ormston until she had another place to go to; in any case nothing could be done about Manchester till her Grandma Stringer had been consulted. Mrs Ormston, too, would have to be properly approached and asked to release her. It would never do, went on Mrs Winstanley, to upset Mrs Ormston's feelings.

The next afternoon, Mrs Winstanley went over to Bridge

Farm and told of what had happened. She asked for Mrs Stringer's advice as to what was best for Hilda at this grave turn in her life.

"She'll never settle wi' Mrs Ormston after this. You know that as well as me and Joe. And any road Ah'm of our Susannah's way o' thinking that happen she'll do better for 'erself i' Manchester if she can get a good start there. She's no age yet to be going to a place like Manchester. But us 'as brought 'er up well and not to talk wi' strangers. Reckon it might turn out best that road."

Grandma Stringer considered the matter solemnly; but she made no comment until she had spread a substantial tea before her visitor. Then, for the first time since Mrs Winstanley had had charge of Hilda, she alluded to Hilda's mother. Of Hilda's real father she made no mention. Not even to her own husband, indeed not even to herself, had she ever admitted, since Hilda's birth, the fact that George Huntley had not begotten her.

"Ah knows she's headstrong, Mrs Winstanley. Our Maggie wor just the same and reckon Hilda takes after her. But she's got to settle some time. We canna look after her for ever. We've had a mort o' trouble over our Mary Ellen and her childer, and we dunna want any wi' Hilda. If she gets a place in Manchester happen she mun *stop* there. She was set on the dressmaking, and she's got to learn it. It's coming to summat, Ah mun say, when childer puts their betters to all this worritting o'er what they want to earn at. Ah'll take her to Manchester myself and see if Ah can place her. Reckon your Susannah's right about Hankinson & Sankey. There isn't a better shop i' Manchester. If Hilda gets a footing there, it'll be the making of her. There's no call for her to write her letters. Best to take her with me. If there's no opening in Hankinson's, reckon we can try other shops."

Hilda was beside herself with excitement when her mother reported the interview with Grandma Stringer. To work in a high-class shop in Manchester! She'd be the luckiest girl in Moss Ferry. She had no doubt at all that if Grandma Stringer meant to find her a place she would do it. It was as good as settled already.

A few days later, dressed in her Sunday best, she went to Manchester. Grandma was wearing her black beaded velvet cape and her best black bonnet with a purple ostrich feather. And all the way in the train she gave Hilda good advice. She was, said Grandma, to answer all questions put to her clearly and pleasantly; she was also to express her utmost willingness to work hard should she be given her chance.

To be free from Mrs Ormston for even a day was a pleasure in itself. To be spending the day in Manchester, with the dazzling prospect of coming there to work every day of her life, was almost smothering in its excitement. She had only once before been to Manchester. As a great and illegal treat, Mrs Winstanley had taken her and Lily during the school holidays one summer. Her mother had been scared out of her wits by the noise and the traffic and what she felt to be an enveloping wickedness. But nevertheless they had all enjoyed themselves till they were exhausted. Hilda remembered how they had spent hours, just walking through Lewis's big shop in Market Street. And how her mother had been afraid to make even the smallest purchase until Hilda and Lily, itching to spend some of their money, had begged that they might buy something to take back to Moss Ferry. In the end they both treated themselves to a length of white silk hair-ribbon, while their mother bought a white embroidered apron to wear in the afternoon. They had even gone into a teashop for their dinner, sitting self-consciously and very frightened at a tile-topped table. There was a printed list on the

table of several sorts of dinners, and Mrs Winstanley, determined
that there should be no stinting, plumped for steak-and-kidney
pudding with mashed potatoes and greens. And a cake apiece to
follow with a cup of tea. And for weeks afterwards she talked to
her husband and Grandma Buckley of the slummocky way the
pudding had been cooked. All crust, she explained resentfully,
and sad crust at that. Nobbut a spoonful o' meat amongst them.
And poor foreign stuff it was, too. And the greens fair running
wi' water and that gritty they set your teeth on edge. And she
discoursed for weeks on the black dirt of Manchester. The white
muslin frocks which Hilda and Lily wore were not fit for putting
on a second time even, whereas in Moss Ferry they could have
worn them clean and stiff for a month of Sundays. Nevertheless,
they had all thoroughly enjoyed the outing. And now Hilda
found herself in Manchester again, and, if her Grandma could
manage it, would be coming here every day of her working life!

When they came out of the station, Grandma Stringer headed
straight for Hankinson & Sankey's in St Ann's Square, as though
it was already settled that Hilda would begin there. But when
they turned into that solid, blackened, dignified place, and stopped
in front of Hankinson & Sankey's beautiful shop, she wavered.
They walked past it several times, Hilda hot and red with
nervousness. Then Grandma, settling her bonnet and cape, said
stoutly: "Well, reckon they canna eat us," and pushed through
the door, Hilda following closely and fearfully.

It was very cool and quiet in the shop, and they stood there
for a second, uncertain what to do next. But almost immediately
a gentleman in a black frock coat glided up and politely asked
Grandma what he could do for her. Grandma, no longer nervous,
asked firmly if she could have a word with the Mester. The
gentleman looked a little surprised, and Grandma, indicating

Hilda, explained the nature of their visit. At this the gentleman smiled, and said he was not sure. He would have to inquire if it was convenient. But in spite of his elegant Sunday clothes, Hilda observed that he did not give himself airs. He treated Grandma just as if she had gone there to buy something, and asked her to sit down while he sent to inquire. Grandma sat down by a counter, Hilda standing by, and both surveyed wonderingly the beautiful big shop. There was a rich-looking carpet all over the floor and covering the staircase as well. Behind the different counters were young ladies, all dressed alike in plain but smart black frocks. They made Hilda feel very stuffy and over-dressed in her Sunday frock of red serge trimmed with black velvet ribbon.

In a few minutes the gentleman came back and said that Miss Jackson would see them. And would they please go up the stairs into the Millinery and to the door marked "Private" at the far end of the room. Grandma thanked him for his trouble, and off they went. They found themselves in a long, high room, with windows all the way round, and more black-frocked young ladies standing about. One of these moved towards them inquiringly, but Grandma pointed to the door marked "Private" and made for it resolutely. In answer to her knock a voice called "Come in". A lady, also in black, and with lovely fair hair, was sitting at a desk. She motioned Grandma to be seated and asked what she could do for her. Grandma, producing Mr Woodville's testimonial of Hilda's scholastic abilities, handed it to the lady and explained that she wanted to get Hilda a good start in life. She related Hilda's stagnant three months with Mrs Ormston, and said that she was casting no reflection on Mrs Ormston, who was the best dressmaker in Daneshead, but evidently had no gift for passing on, for Hilda had made no headway there.

16

Miss Jackson, who had been reading the testimonial, looked up at this and surveyed Hilda closely. She then asked: "Are you quite sure Mrs Ormston has no gift for teaching? Perhaps you're not cut out for the dressmaking. Have you thought of that?"

Both Hilda and her Grandma were staggered. It had never occurred to anybody to doubt Hilda's capacity for becoming, in course of time and through hard work, a properly qualified dressmaker. Hilda, confused and humiliated, stammered out about the continual housework at Mrs Ormston's, and Grandma came loyally to her aid and bore witness to the truth of what she was telling.

Miss Jackson listened attentively, all the time looking at Hilda. She asked many questions, and ended up by demanding from Hilda an assurance that her heart was really in the dressmaking. "We are Court Dressmakers here," she explained proudly, "and only do the very best work. And you would have to be apprenticed to us for three years before beginning to earn anything." She turned to Grandma Stringer. "I think we could start her almost at once. They will soon find out in the workroom whether she has a natural bent for the work. Not every girl has, you know. Shall we say she is to start next Monday?"

Grandma looked put out. She thanked Miss Jackson for seeing them and said disappointedly: "Reckon Ah canna afford to keep her for three years without earning summat. And there'd be her fares, too. Ah had it in mind she could be started with a small wage. She didn't earn with Mrs Ormston, but that was only for two years, and no fares to find."

Miss Jackson considered thoughtfully. She again looked hard at Hilda, and then at Grandma.

"Well, it's our rule never to pay apprentices until they are out of their time. In fact it's the rule everywhere in dressmaking.

But perhaps we can arrange something. We want an errand-girl for the workroom. If Hilda likes to come as that, for a small wage, she could learn the dressmaking too. Of course she won't have quite the same standing as the properly apprenticed girls. And she won't have quite the same training. It might take her a year longer. But if she shows a natural bent for the work, I don't see why she shouldn't get on just as well. She would have to go out 'matching' and do odd jobs for me and be willing to make herself generally useful. We could pay her five shillings a week for the first year, then 7s. 6d. till she's taken on as an improver. If she shows real promise she'll be kept on with us."

Grandma turned to Hilda. "Reckon that sounds all right, Hilda. What dost say?"

Hilda agreed earnestly and looked gratefully at Miss Jackson. If she worked hard she might in time become a Miss Jackson herself. It was an end worth striving for, and Hilda made an inward vow to exert herself to the utmost in the service of her new employers.

It was settled that she was to start the following Monday morning. She was to bring her birth-certificate, said Miss Jackson; and on no account was she to enter by the front door. The front door was for customers only and those in the higher ranks of Messrs Hankinson & Sankey. The young ladies in the workroom used the side entrance. Miss Jackson also explained that Hilda could bring her own dinner and tea. There was a dining room in the basement for the use of the staff, and she could buy a cup of tea or cocoa there for a halfpenny. Her dinner-time would be half-an-hour, and a quarter-of-an-hour for tea. The hours were from nine o'clock to seven o'clock, and two o'clock on Saturdays, but of course no dinner-time was allowed on Saturdays. She might, however, bring something to eat in the workroom.

As they came out of the shop both Hilda and her grandmother made instinctively for the opposite side of the Square; and here they stopped for some minutes, staring across admiringly at the beautiful front of Hankinson & Sankey's. The workroom, Miss Jackson had told them, was at the very top of the building. They craned their necks upwards but nothing could be seen except a high stone balustrade that ran the entire length of the front.

As they left the Square, casting one last look at the shop, Grandma turned gravely to Hilda, and admonished her to make the most of this wonderful new chance of getting on in the world. "Ah dunna want to hear any more talk of onrest, Hilda Winstanley. And you take care to be a good girl to your mother and father. Mind, Ah'm not blaming you about Mrs Ormston. But if you dunna make headway at Hankinson & Sankey's, Ah winna answer for what'll become of you. So take heed, there's a good lass. Reckon we mun think of getting home, but we'll have a bite o' summat first."

Grandma led the way to the Central Market, and here, at a stall, they had a meat pie apiece and a good strong cup of tea. Hilda was disappointed. She had hoped for dinner again at a teashop, as with her mother. Grandma, however, knew all about the Market refreshments, and said the meat pies sold there were the best for miles. She strongly advised Hilda, when she came to work in Manchester, never to waste her money on food in a teashop. "All show and nowt to bite on," she concluded contemptuously.

When they arrived back at Kilnbrook Station, Grandma said they must ask about a season ticket. Hilda's former schoolmate, Peter Pettener, opened the wooden shutter of the booking office, where he was now firmly installed as junior clerk for the Cheshire Lines. The senior clerk, Mr Partington, was also the

station-master and, when necessary, the porter. Grandma looked
doubtfully at Peter. He was no age, she decided, to be entrusted
with the serious matter of Hilda's season ticket, and she demanded
the presence of George Partington. Mr Partington, called from
his tea, appeared and the great business of the ticket was completed. Hilda came under the heading of a half-timer and as such
was entitled to a special rate. The full rate would not have to be
paid till she was sixteen. Grandma handed over the 1s. 6d. for
the first week; after that Hilda would pay it herself out of her
wages. As soon as the precious ticket was in her hand, Hilda
wanted to get home quickly and show it to her mother. Grandma,
however, invited her to tea at the farm and, while she ate and
drank, Lucy Stringer, more iron-faced than ever, pointed out the
evils which would befall her if she did not apply herself heart and
soul to her new work. Unjustly, as was her way, she implied
that Hilda was naturally given to flightiness and unrest; and that
such painful weaknesses of character must now be stamped out
once and for all.

CHAPTER XVI

DRESSMAKING FOR THE COURT

During the whole weekend Hilda's excitement and fidgetiness grew, and her mother declared that if she didn't give over worriting they would all be taking leave of their wits. But at last Monday morning came. All through breakfast Mrs Winstanley earnestly impressed upon Hilda the importance of keeping herself to herself, for in a big place like Manchester danger lay everywhere. On no account, she stressed over and over again, was Hilda to let a stranger speak to her, either man or woman. She had heard tell that in the big towns women were every bit as wicked as men; always on the look out to entice young girls away from their homes to unimaginable horrors. She was to go straight from the station to Hankinson & Sankey's, looking neither to right nor left. And when her day's work was over, she was to make immediately for the station and the solid safety of Moss Ferry. Hilda, eager to be off, promised to take every care. She was wearing her Sunday frock, taken for weekdays before its appointed time, and her brown kid shoes. When she actually realised that she was sitting in the Manchester-bound train, travelling for the first time in her life entirely on her own, she found herself nearly crying with emotion. In her wicker basket was her dinner and tea; in her hand the magic passport to unlimited travel between Kilnbrook and Manchester.

Until the train stopped at Daneshead she was alone in the compartment, and she kept on looking at the piece of green and white cardboard. It meant that every Friday night, if it was her pleasure, she could get out at Daneshead and change her book at the Co-op. She was a Traveller! In her pocket was a whole shilling, to last her the week, for such comforts as cups of tea and cocoa. Mrs Henry Wood's novel, *The Channings*, lay unopened on her lap. For almost the first time in her existence she felt too restless to read. Instead she gazed out on the hideous landscape which lay between Daneshead and Manchester. It was pock-marked by the belching chimneys of the steel works and the soap works and the foundries which bit deep into the flat, grey-green country. Now and then, between the soaring chimneys and the smoke clouds, she could see a ship's red funnel on the Mersey, the only touch of warm colour in the drab scene. At last the train was drawing into Manchester, together with other trains on parallel platforms. Hundreds of other travellers got out, both ladies and gentlemen. Many of the gentlemen wore frock coats and silk hats, while the others were dressed in dark suits and bowler hats. And there seemed to be just as many young ladies too, all very neatly and quietly dressed. They all carried little leather cases, and Hilda became agonisingly conscious of her common wicker basket. It marked her out plainly as a newcomer to the civilised ways of Manchester, and she determined that out of her first week's wages she also would purchase a leather case.

Proudly she showed her season ticket at the barrier, and set out determinedly for St Ann's Square. She had never before walked alone among so many people and, remembering her mother's warning words, began to feel scared. Trams were clanging and swaying along, crowded to the platforms, and quite a number of horse cabs rattled past. With a good five minutes to spare, she climbed the narrow wooden staircase to Hankinson & Sankey's workroom. Nervously pushing open a greasy-looking door she found herself alone in a big, bare room. It was a great shock to see it so different from the richly furnished shop downstairs. There was no covering on the wooden floor. There were several very long, very wide tables, and a lot of dressmaker's dummies standing about, a white sheet draped over each. She walked to a window and looked out; but she could not see down into the Square. A church clock struck nine, and almost immediately she heard the clatter of hurrying feet up the stairs. A crowd of young ladies, all laughing and talking, burst into the room. Hilda, still wearing her hat and coat and clutching her dinner basket, stood there awkwardly, and for a second they all stared at her. Then several came up and smiled pleasantly and said they would show her where to hang her clothes, and that Miss Robinson would soon be along to take her in charge. They made her feel very countrified; they talked so much faster than the folk in Moss Ferry and it was quite a strain at first to make out what they were saying. One girl, whom they called Violet, took special charge of her. Violet asked her name and where she came from and how long the train journey took. The workroom was now fairly humming with talk. It quietened down a good bit when a short, grey-haired lady walked in and said a cheerful "Good morning" to everybody. Violet whispered to Hilda that this was Miss Robinson, the head fitter. She had sole charge of the workroom, said Violet, and was very easy to get on with; and taking Hilda's arm she presented her to Miss Robinson, who shook hands and said she hoped that Hilda would settle down comfortably with them all.

"Just sit down somewhere for a bit while I give out the work; then I'll have time to see to you."

Hilda found a stool and sat down to watch. All the tables now had girls sitting at either side. Miss Robinson went round each table in turn, giving everybody their instructions. The girls had put on pinafores, and soon they were all sewing; some by hand; some at treadle machines. Some sewed standing up, doing things to the frocks on the dummies. And one girl was ironing with a very large flat iron. Hilda could not keep her eyes off one particular dress of rich black velvet, on to the bodice of which Violet was sewing glittering golden sequins. It must be an evening dress, Hilda thought, for it had a low-cut neck and no sleeves. In her ignorance she immediately concluded that it was a Court Dress for some lady to wear at Buckingham Palace, London.

Miss Robinson, having set all her tasks, beckoned Hilda and explained what her work would be. First thing every morning she was to go down to Miss Jackson's office in the Millinery. She was to dust and tidy her desk and, when Miss Jackson arrived at half-past nine, button up her showroom frock and give her a good brushing-down. And if Miss Jackson wanted any errands done she was to do them. And she must never leave Miss Jackson without inquiring if there was anything else she could do for her. Miss Jackson was THE BUYER, and Hilda was given to understand that the entire world of Hankinson & Sankey revolved around her; indeed only existed because of her. It was therefore of the utmost importance that Miss Jackson should never be crossed. Even Mr Hankinson and Mr Sankey, added Miss Robinson gravely, would think twice before crossing Miss Jackson.

Frightened out of her wits, Hilda went down to Miss Jackson's room and was dusting vigorously when that lady arrived. She was beautifully dressed and smiled encouragingly as she observed Hilda's ingratiating nervousness.

"I hope you're going to like it with us, Hilda. Do everything you're told and you'll make your way all right. I'll change now into my showroom frock. It's hanging in the cupboard there."

Hilda tremblingly took out the long black cashmere dress and held it awkwardly while Miss Jackson took off the dress she had

221

arrived in. The showroom frock was very plain—not so much as a white frill round the high boned collar—and it fitted tight like a kid glove. Hilda buttoned it up and then pulled and smoothed until Miss Jackson was satisfied that there was not a single wrinkle to be seen. Her great mass of fair hair was now badly disarranged and she sat down in front of the cheval mirror and unpinned it. It fell below her waist and was thick and springy. She began to brush it, and Hilda, eager to be useful, asked if she might do this. She explained, as she brushed, about Miss Brown's hair at the Vicarage. Hilda brushed till her arms ached, Miss Jackson talking to her all the time and evidently pleased with the way she was managing her hair. Hilda told her all about her work at the Vicarage, and more about Mrs Ormston. Miss Jackson, however, seemed to be more interested in Miss Brown's hair than in Mrs Ormston, and gave Hilda a specially warm smile when, anxious to please, she said that Miss Brown's hair, thick though it might be, was altogether inferior in quality and abundance to Miss Jackson's. And Miss Brown did hers up so plainly too, Hilda chattered on; just a heavy knob at the back of her head instead of the handsome pile Miss Jackson affected. After this information Miss Jackson piled her hair up higher than ever, and fluffed it out in two great clouds over her temples. Hilda could not keep the admiration out of her eyes. Except for Queen Alexandra, she thought she had never seen anyone so beautiful and elegant as Miss Jackson; and when Miss Jackson thanked her and said she was to brush her hair for her every morning, she had never felt happier in her life.

She spent the rest of the morning idly, Miss Robinson explaining there was not much for her to do as yet, except sit and watch. It was surprising, said Miss Robinson, what a lot could be learnt through keeping one's eyes open and just watching.

At half-past twelve the girls clattered down to the dining-room. Violet kindly came up to Hilda and showed her where the W.C. was and the wash-basin. She then saw her into the dining-room and introduced her to Mrs Henshaw, who made the tea and cocoa. The dining-room was very dingy and was lit by gas. It had no proper window—only an oblong of thick green glass flush with the ceiling, on which you could hear the people treading outside. There were two long tables covered with white american cloth. Most of the girls had brought a hot dinner with them, and there was a cheerful rushing backwards and forwards as they fetched their dishes from the oven. Hilda, feeling for her shilling, asked timidly for a cup of cocoa, and established friendly relations with Mrs Henshaw. Mrs Henshaw, looking at her meat sandwiches, said good-naturedly: "Tell your mother to make you something I can hot up for you another day. It's none too warm, and a growing girl like you needs a proper dinner."

Hilda thanked her, and settled down next to Violet with her cocoa and sandwiches. Some of the girls had got *Home Chat* and other journals propped up in front of them and were oblivious to the buzz going on all round. Violet was talking to a friend across the table, but every now and again stopped to say a word to Hilda. Hilda, aware that it was bad manners to be seen listening to a conversation in which she had no part, tried to look as unreceptive as possible while she took in every word Violet and her friend said. They were discussing the theatre as easily and naturally as the folk in Moss Ferry talked about the chapel. Hilda, who had been told repeatedly by her mother that to enter a theatre was to be damned for ever, could hardly believe her ears. Violet was telling her friend that she and her mother were going to the Theatre Royal that very night.

"My mother never misses a new musical comedy," Violet

was saying. "And she always treats me, too. Of course we only go into the gallery, but you can see better from there, any road." She turned to Hilda. "Does your mother ever treat you?" she asked.

Hilda reddened. "No. My mother's never been to a theatre. Only a picture-theatre once at Ashton-under-Lyne. Our Jack's been though. He liked it and said he'd take me one Saturday, but my mother said no. She goes to chapel regular," added Hilda defensively.

Violet laughed, but not unkindly. "Well, reckon Manchester'll work wonders for you. We all go to chapel too—Congregational—but that's not to say we shouldn't go to the theatre. There's no harm to the theatre. You tell your mother that from me."

The clock showed a few minutes to one. The dinner-time had flown past, and Hilda had enjoyed every second of it. It was wonderful to be sitting there among grown-up girls, and for Violet she had already conceived a passionate devotion. And they were all so cheerful and friendly. And she had made the staggering discovery that girls brought up just as respectably as herself— regular chapel-goers—went to the theatre as a matter of course, and with their own mothers too!

In the afternoon Hilda was given the inside seam of a patterned ninon sleeve to oversew, and took immense pains to do it as neatly as she could. Her stitches showed no bigger than needle points, so carefully did she work. Miss Robinson told her not to be in a hurry over it; it didn't matter if she took all afternoon at it.

"We like to finish off our things as well inside as outside. That's the way you can tell a good dressmaker, Hilda. If a thing's worth doing at all it's worth doing well. So don't get flustered.

And if your hands get hot go and wash them. This is a frock for one of our best customers, Mrs Honeywell at Whalley Range."

Hilda glowed with pride as she began her work for the rich and esteemed Mrs Honeywell, and she loved the feel of the wispy ninon between her fingers. She noticed that other girls were sewing at similar material. When, in her ignorance, she remarked how funny it was for a lady to have more than one dress of the same material, Violet rocked with laughter. Then, sorry she had made fun, explained what a complicated business the making of a dress was. First of all Mrs Honeywell came to the shop downstairs and selected the material. Then she spent days, even weeks, in choosing a pattern. Then she came to be measured. Then the material was given to the cutter; after this it was tacked up. Then she had to be fitted by Miss Robinson before the dress was actually made up. Several girls, Violet continued, worked on different parts of it. There was, for instance, one girl who did nothing all day long but press, keeping two flat irons going for this purpose. Every seam was pressed flat as soon as it was finished. And when the dress was quite finished it was pressed all over.

Violet further explained that not all their customers were as easy to make for as Mrs Honeywell. "Some are regular tartars. Nothing's ever done right for them. They'd pick holes in a sieve soon as look at you." And she warned Hilda always to be very careful with her work, and to take just as much trouble with the oversewing of a lining seam as she did with the more showy parts of a garment.

Hilda's first day at Hankinson & Sankey's had passed quickly and happily. All that evening she kept her mother and father and sister in a state of delighted interest relating her experiences. She passed on Violet's message about the innocence of theatre-going, and her mother warned her to take no heed of such idle talk. The theatre, said Mrs Winstanley, was dark and damned, and Violet's mother should know better than take her girl to such places. When Hilda, standing up loyally for Violet, reminded her mother how much she had enjoyed the moving pictures at Ashton-under-Lyne, Mrs Winstanley flared up. She pointed out that the moving pictures were different. They said nowt. It never harmed anybody to look. It was hearkening to what was said in the theatre that was so harmful.

* * *

By the end of her first week, Hilda felt as though she had been with Hankinson & Sankey for years. For Miss Jackson and Miss Robinson and Violet, she was prepared to lay down her life. There was such a comfortable, friendly feeling in the workroom; and the young ladies who were properly apprenticed to the dressmaking, receiving no payment, did not show in the smallest way that she too was not one of them. Even the ugly train ride became a daily treat, for once settled in a corner seat she had her book to enjoy. And she now read over her dinner and tea. And her mother, now that she had become a professional worker, no longer interfered with her leisure in the evenings. She still liked to help occasionally with the washing-up, but Mrs Winstanley would only let her do the wiping. It was of the greatest importance that she should not again roughen her hands; the frocks made at Hankinson & Sankey's were altogether different from the serviceable serges made up by Mrs Ormston. Silks and satins and chiffons and velvets had to be treated with respect. Her mother even allowed her now to read her library book after chapel on Sunday nights—the most tremendous concession she had ever made.

Meanwhile she was kept quite busy in the workroom, continually running errands in the morning for Miss Jackson and Miss Robinson and some of the older girls. In the afternoon she was always given sewing to do. After she had rather bashfully explained to Miss Robinson that if she could do one thing better than another it was button-holing, she was, with many careful injunctions, and after first doing a sample button-hole on a waste piece of material, given some of this important work to do. Aware that great issues were at stake, she did her utmost and had her reward when Miss Robinson praised the result. And when she was entrusted with making the button-holes for a new frock for Mrs Honeywell, she felt that life had nothing sweeter to offer. She loved, too, being sent on errands into the shop below. While waiting for her pattern of material to be matched, she was able to observe the rich customers who came in. One morning she jumped when she heard one of the counter assistants say to her companion: "Mrs Honeywell's just come in and I know Mr Bishop is up with Mr Hankinson. Better send up and tell Miss Jackson." Mr Bishop was the shopwalker who usually attended to the ladies when they entered.

Hilda, on hearing the magic name, stared hard and asked the assistant to point out Mrs Honeywell. Having, as her very first sewing job, oversewn the inside seam of a diaphanous sleeve for that lady, she felt a personal and passionate interest in her.

"She's the tall lady with the puce boa. Miss Jackson always likes to see her when she comes in. Don't let her see you looking at her. It's rude to stare at a customer, you know. Not that Mrs Honeywell would complain. She's one of the nicest we've got."

Hilda blushed at the reproof and made a note to mind her manners. However, while the assistant was matching up for her, she could not help slewing her eyes round to the puce boa, so bright and soft and rich-looking.

She was sent out frequently to other big shops to match up sewing silks and coloured cottons, for Hankinson & Sankey did not deal in these. Best of all she liked being sent to Lewis's in Market Street. It was so big and, no matter what time she went there, always full of people moving up and down the aisles or buying at the many counters. Being in Lewis's was nearly as exciting as being in Market Street itself. There were almost as many people in the shop as in the street. Miss Robinson used to give her a card with "Hankinson & Sankey" printed on it, and it was gratifying the way the assistants hastened to serve her as soon as she handed it over. Once or twice, in lesser shops, Hilda came up against very superior young ladies who, if what she required was not immediately to their hand, could not be bothered to make a thorough search. When, however, she mentioned that it was required by Hankinson & Sankey, their stuck-up attitude vanished instantly and no trouble was too much for them.

The one and only thing she actively disliked about her daily routine was picking up the countless pins which the young ladies in the workroom dropped so continually and carelessly. They never stopped their work to pick up a dropped pin. Hilda was sometimes a whole hour going round the big room on this dull, back-aching job. Even so she counted it a small price to pay for the glory of becoming a Court dressmaker in the highest-class shop in Manchester.

*　　　　*　　　　*

After three months of work in the city, Hilda Winstanley's country roughness had smoothed down so much that she was nearly as lady-like as the girls in the shop and workroom. She now took immense pains over her personal appearance, keeping her hair bright and clean, and softening her hands several times a week with melted mutton fat. She had also attained to the dignity of wearing shoes as a matter of course, discarding for ever the more sensible and more serviceable boots. She bought herself a comb for her own absolute use, and even announced her intention of one day possessing her own hairbrush as well. At this suggested extravagance Mrs Winstanley protested, and said she could see no sense in having more than one hairbrush in the family, or comb either for that matter. It was just as senseless as having two scrubbing brushes. She bought pink scented soap in defiance of her mother's still hostile attitude to this luxury. And she began to find continual fault with their simple rough way of living at home. Although she loved her mother and father, their illiterate ways made her feel ashamed. They were startled and embarrassed when she announced that there was no reason why they shouldn't, both of them, learn to read and write. Impressed by her confident assurance that she could soon teach them, they consented to have a try. Very slowly and patiently she got them to learn the alphabet, making them draw the letters on a slate. But when she rummaged out an old spelling book and urged them to start learning simple words, trouble swelled up, and the climax came when she purchased a penny copybook for them to write in. Her father was the first to backslide. He had tried hard to master the fearful business of forming words, egged on by the reward which Hilda assured him would be his when he could write, easily and confidently, his own name—Joseph Winstanley. To say nothing, Hilda went on enticingly, of the pleasure that would also be his when he could settle down comfortably of a Sunday morning and read Jack's newspaper.

"Just fancy being able to read for yourself what Mr Joynson-Hicks says in the Free Trade Hall at Manchester. And you'll know all about what's going on everywhere."

17

But when he saw the neat ruled lines of the copybook he took fright. His kind red face hardened stubbornly, and with a hopeless gesture he pushed the copybook away from him.

"Nay, our 'Ilda. Reckon Ah should ha' learnt my schooling when Ah wor a lad. It'll never come easy to me now. What dost say, Mother?" and he turned appealingly to his wife.

"Reckon your father's reet, our 'Ilda. Us is too far gone for larning now. Nobbut a waste o' time. And it's not for *you*, 'Ilda Winstanley, to go setting yourself up above us," she added resentfully as Hilda impatiently gathered up the spelling and copybooks. "Us 'as done our best by you and dunna forget it. Ever since you started i' Manchester it's bin nowt else but airs and graces. Buying your own comb and using scented soap and finding fault wi' all our ways. Ah dunna know what's come o'er you; you're getting that finicky. Why canna you be more like our Lily and leave us be?"

Hilda at first made no answer. Her disappointment was bitter. She had tried hard to get them to learn, and here they were, losing heart and giving up at the first little difficulty. Forgetting for a moment all the care and affection they had given her for nearly fourteen years, she regarded them spitefully and, before she realised what she was about, the words were out of her mouth.

"Well—I'm glad you're not really my father and mother, any road. And I'm not going to live here all my life either. I'll run away as soon as I'm earning enough."

Mrs Winstanley, her face flaming, shouted out: "Shame on you, 'Ilda Winstanley! And after the way us 'as brought you up. Never made no difference atween you and our own. And that's God's truth if Ah never stir from this chair. Mark my words, if you dunna larn to 'umble yourself you'll come to a bad end. Burn in t'Lake of Fire for ever."

She began to cry, and Hilda, thoroughly scared, made as if to go out of the kitchen. Her father, however, headed her off and, for the first time in her life, smacked her savagely.

"That'll larn you to talk about running away. And to go onsettling your mother. And dunna let me 'ear you talk that road again. Dost hear me?" he asked threateningly.

Hilda, crying noisily and brimming over with self-pity, flounced upstairs, taking the offending copybooks with her. It would be nearly three years before she was earning enough to keep herself. Once she could do this, however, she resolved that nothing and nobody would stop her from leaving Moss Ferry. The enchanting prospect of living independently in lodgings in Manchester rose before her. Then, ashamed and uneasy at the way she had behaved, she began to make plans for coming to spend her weekends in Moss Ferry. She would, too, "make" for her mother. Plain, well-cut frocks with hardly any trimming. Her heart even warmed towards Lily and she decided generously that she would make for her as well, and, of course, would not charge anything.

CHAPTER XVII

"FAREWELL MANCHESTER!"

The happier Hilda became at Hankinson & Sankey's, the more dissatisfied she grew with her life at home. She became cheeky to her mother, and was continually provoking the stolid Lily and the uncouth Jim. Lily had announced her intention of working at Endicott's farm with her brother, and Hilda, proudly enrolled in the ranks of the professional workers, despised her heartily for her lack of ambition. But for her brother Jack she never lost her affection. He was not a bit like the other two, for he read a Sunday newspaper and could talk quite knowledgeably about politics. And he now took her quite often to tea at Edie's on Sundays. There was a free, slap-dash, cheerful atmosphere in Edie's home and always plenty of *Home Chats* lying around for her to dip into. And both Edie and her mother flattered her by expressing the hope that, when she was a duly qualified Court dressmaker, she would, as a great favour, "make" for them in her spare time on condition of course that they should pay her full money for her services.

Then one afternoon in the workroom, Miss Robinson announced that the time had come for her to begin the dressmaking proper. She was to be given her first lesson in cutting out, under the watchful guidance of Miss Robinson herself. The work was not important, only the sateen pocket of a skirt, but Hilda worked carefully, the big cutting-out scissors feeling like shears in her trembling hands. Miss Robinson, watching kindly, said it was all right and she had taken the first step up the ladder. It would all come to her in the proper time and there was no hurry. If there was one thing more important than anything else in the dressmaking, it was that there should be no *hurry*. No dress-maker living, Miss Robinson assured her, ever learnt her trade in a hurry. "Slow but sure" was the beginner's motto. Let Hilda always keep that in mind and she would end up all right.

On reaching home that night she burst out with her great news about the pocket. Her mother, however, did not even pause in her work of getting the tea. Setting the meal before her she said bitterly: "Reckon you'll not 'ave to put up wi' our ways much longer. Lucy Stringer's been here. You're to go to London, if you've a mind to. To your relations at London. Lucy wouldn't tell me owt else. But you're to please yourself about it—whether you stop wi' us or go to them that's never owned you till now."

Hilda stared at her mother, scarcely believing her ears. Her relations at London! So Sarah Dumbell was right after all, and she had proper relations at London. Perhaps her father himself. She had not for a long time believed that George Huntley was her father, in spite of Mrs Winstanley's fierce and renewed assurances to the contrary. Any road, they must be her father's relations, for Grandma Stringer had none in London.

Her face glowed. She could not quench the light in it, although she saw that her mother was making a great effort not to break down.

"But what about the dressmaking at Hankinson & Sankey's? I started my first cutting out today," and she related the story of the pocket.

Mrs Winstanley, perceiving from Hilda's face that Hankinson & Sankey, cutting out and all, was, together with Moss Ferry, already a thing past and done with, said resentfully: "Ah've told you what Lucy Stringer said. You're to go your own road, and reckon you will, too, or my name's not Lizzie Winstanley. And in a year or two you'd 'a bin bringing home a bit like t'others.

233

Well—eat your tea. Your father's fair mazed about it. He's not like us. He canna show 'is feelings. He feels it 'ere," and she placed her hands on the front of her bodice. "He's gone down to *T'Black Horse*, and Ah've never known him do that afore when it wasn't a Saturday neet. Reckon it'll cut 'im up if you go. But Lucy Stringer said you was to make up your mind of your own free will. It said that in the letter from them at London."

Hilda could think of nothing to say. She knew that she should at least pretend some sorrow at the prospect of leaving her home for good. But for the life of her she couldn't. Her mind fairly danced at the prospect of London. She returned, unconvincingly, to the question of her work with Hankinson & Sankey, but her mother interrupted savagely.

"Ah can see you're bent on going. It said in the letter you was to go in three weeks. You'd best tell Miss Jackson tomorrow and leave a week come Saturday. That'll give you a week getting your things ready. Lucy Stringer's buying you a basket for your clothes. Reckon you're satisfied at last. You've done nowt but find fault ever since you went to Manchester. If it 'adna bin for Sarah Dumbell you'd never 'ave started worriting. She'll come to a bad end and Ah hope Ah'm at 'er burying to see t'Owd Lad take 'er off."

*   *   *

Miss Jackson, when Hilda nervously told her of the letter from London, was very bad tempered and asked peevishly why she had troubled to start with them at all if she hadn't intended to stop.

"And you were getting on nicely, I hear. Miss Robinson spoke well of you only the other day."

Hilda, brushing Miss Jackson's hair more assiduously than ever, pointed out respectfully but reasonably that the leaving was not of her doing. Her relations at London had written to say she was to live with them, whereupon Miss Jackson, her natural good temper reasserting itself, sympathised with her at being torn so heartlessly from her home and work, and promised that she would explain the position herself to Miss Robinson.

All the workroom girls were most interested when it got round that young Hilda Winstanley was going to live in London with her well-to-do relations. For by this time Hilda had decided firmly that of course they must be well-off otherwise they could not afford to live in London. When the final Saturday morning came they all wished her the best of luck, and her special friend and patron, Violet, gave her a shell-surrounded pincushion to remind her always of her short though promising career as a Court dressmaker in the best shop in Manchester. Miss Jackson and Miss Robinson gravely shook hands with her and said they were sorry to be losing her. The leave-taking was over, and Hilda walked slowly and solemnly and happily down the steep wooden staircase into the solid beautiful dignity of St Ann's Square. She crossed over and stood again admiring the handsome façade of Hankinson & Sankey, reflecting that, except for the daily pin-picking, she had enjoyed every second of her time there. But she felt no sorrow at leaving. No sooner had she got to the corner and taken a last look back than it vanished from her life as completely as it vanished from her sight. There was now only one word in her mind: London.

*   *   *

In Moss Ferry and Kilnbrook, Hilda Winstanley was now an object of unparalleled interest and curiosity. With the single exception of the Reverend James Black, nobody in either village had ever been to London, where gold, they had always heard tell, was to be had for the asking, though the Vicar had made no mention of this glittering fact. Also the glamour of mystery enveloped her. People were eager to find out what sort of relations she was going to. And because both Grandma Stringer and Lucy kept close as oysters about them, people talked all the more among themselves and said they had always known that Hilda's mother, Maggie Stringer, had got herself into trouble at Warburton. And not with George Huntley either, even though he had wed her. Everybody was anxious to give her good advice, warning her in hushed tones that London was bigger even than Manchester and that she mustn't let herself be led away.

Going to Sunday School for the last time she felt that all the classes were concentrated on her instead of on their teachers, and her face burned when, in his closing prayer, the Superintendent mentioned her by name. He prayed for her passionately.

"We ask Thee, Lord Jesus, to take under Thy wing this lamb from our fold who is about to enter into the perils and temptations of life in a great city. Guide her, Oh Lord! and keep her feet in the paths of righteousness that she may serve Thee humbly and faithfully unto the end. And we ask Thee in Thy great mercy to bless and comfort those loved ones she leaves behind. May Thy loving kindness descend upon them and give them strength to bear their loss."

Before he dismissed the Sunday School, the Superintendent made a little speech, asking them all to include Hilda Winstanley in their nightly prayers, and pointing out what a faithful scholar she had always been. He then beckoned her forward and, trembling and self-conscious, she walked up to him. He held in his hand a beautiful bible, bound in soft black leather, with gilt edges and a blue silk marker. On behalf of the teachers of the United Methodist Chapel of Kilnbrook and Moss Ferry he presented this to her, and begged her earnestly, in the name of the Lord Jesus, to

let no day pass into night without reading a chapter of the Word.
Then, with tears in his eyes, he gravely shook hands with her, and
Hilda, proudly clasping her new treasure, was surrounded by
scholars and teachers wishing her happiness in the new life to
which she was going.

*   *   *

The following week was a busy one and slipped past very
quickly. Mrs Winstanley washed and ironed Hilda's simple
wardrobe, Hilda herself sewing on buttons and tapes and doing
any necessary mending. One afternoon they went, by special
invitation, to have tea with Grandma Stringer, and to fetch away
the rush basket that was to take Hilda's clothes. And as this was
such a special occasion Grandma had set out the tea in the front
parlour, a room Hilda had never before seen. It was big but
stuffy, and both Hilda and Mrs Winstanley thought it was very
grand. Grandma and Lucy regarded Hilda sternly all during tea,
pointing out the importance of her always being a good girl and
obeying her new relations implicitly. When Mrs Winstanley, who
was just as terrified of Grandma Stringer as Hilda was, asked
timidly and anxiously what sort of relations Hilda was going to,
Grandma replied mysteriously: "Hilda'll know soon enough.
But there's no call for you to worrit yourself, Mrs Winstanley.
She's going to a good home, that Ah do know." And with this
Mrs Winstanley had to be satisfied.

Hilda went also by invitation to say goodbye to Aunt Emma
and Uncle Fred in Daneshead, and also to Edie and her mother.
And Mrs Woodville asked her to tea. Everybody was very kind
and concerned for her, and all said they hoped she would send
them a picture-postcard when she arrived at London. The last
tea-party was at Grandma Buckley's, who reproached her for her
"onnatural" cheerfulness at leaving them. She urged Hilda never

to forget what a good home she was going from and to walk always in the fear of the Lord. And if it was the Lord's will that she, Grandma, was "took" before she saw Hilda again, she promised to make it her particular business to watch over her from Beyond. And would be waiting to lead her to the Lord when it was her time to go. Uncle Billy, lapsed from Grace, was slightly drunk. He kissed her and gave her a threepenny-bit, urging Grandma to give over moaning, pointing out that, as anybody could see, Hilda was a bit down.

The last night at home was one of bustle and hurry. Mrs Winstanley was feverishly anxious that all Hilda's clothes should be properly and neatly packed. Her father, so that she might have a bath in front of the fire, went to bed earlier than usual. While Hilda was washing herself, her mother urged her repeatedly always to remain a good girl. To be sure to say her prayers every night, to read in the Book daily, to obey her new relations absolutely, and to go to chapel every Sunday just as she had done in Moss Ferry.

"And write us a letter from London as soon as you're settled. And dunna forget that this is none of our doing."

She began to cry, and Hilda cried with her. Then she went on: "You've allus got us to come 'ome to if you dunna settle. Dunna forget that. Me and Joe 'as allus looked on you as one of our own, and allus shall. But you've allus bin that self-willed."

*   *   *

It had been arranged by Lucy Stringer that Hilda and her father should be on Manchester Central Station, by the Refreshment Room, at a given time next morning, where they would be met by one of Hilda's new relations. Jack, having got the time off from the foundry, was to go with them as far as Kilnbrook Station. Hilda had said goodbye to Jim the night before. The time came for her to take leave of her mother, who had refused to come to Manchester, saying that it would unsettle her. Her father, very neat in his Sunday blacks and bowler hat, had the rush basket in his hand.

Mrs Winstanley, reaching to the mantelpiece for her purse, gave Hilda a shilling for spending-money at London. Hilda said goodbye to Lily, and kissed her. She then turned to her mother. They clung to each other and cried, and her mother repeated again that this was none of their doing, and that whatever happened it was her home always. Mr Winstanley and Jack, standing by uneasily, said they must be off or they would miss the train. Mrs Winstanley, lifting a corner of her apron, wiped Hilda's face, set her hat straight, and fairly hustled her out of the kitchen. They were off. Various neighbours stood at their gates to wave as they passed. Grandma Stringer and Lucy were on the look-out at Bridge Farm, and Grandma added another shilling for spending-money. And now, on Kilnbrook Station, as the Manchester train pulled in, Hilda said goodbye to Jack and sent her love to Edie. Jack told her to buck up. "Me and Jim Hogben'll be coming to London for t'Cup Tie, and us'll watch out for you, our 'Ilda...."

And then the train was drawing in to Manchester. Hilda, her legs shaking, made for the big Refreshment Room, followed by her father. A tall lady was standing by the door, and some instinct told Hilda that this was her new relation. Seeing them advancing, the lady also moved forward and said pleasantly: "You're Hilda, aren't you? And Mr Winstanley? And I'm your Aunt Mildred."

She kissed Hilda and shook hands with Mr Winstanley.

"Our platform's over there and the train's in, but it doesn't start for ten minutes. We'd better get our seats, though."

She took Hilda's hand and they made for the London train. Hilda was immensely impressed by her new relation's distinguished appearance. She was dressed plainly and elegantly, just like Miss Jackson. And her talk was quite different from Lancashire talk. Indeed she talked so that you wouldn't know where she came from.

Aunt Mildred found an empty carriage, and Mr Winstanley placed Hilda's basket and Aunt Mildred's case on the rack. For a few minutes they stood on the platform, Hilda tongue-tied with nervousness and excitement; her father very stiff and with a stupid, unnatural look on his face. Aunt Mildred talked fast, and said she hoped Hilda would be very happy in London. She turned to Mr Winstanley and said they need never worry: Hilda was going to have a very good home and would be as well taken care of as she had been up to now. And of course she would write from time to time and let them know how she was getting on. And if ever they came to London they were to come and see her; she would send on the address.

They were shutting the carriage doors.

Aunt Mildred, an embarrassed look on her handsome face, said kindly: "Say goodbye to your father, Hilda. It's time we were getting in."

She shook hands with him again and then, moved by the misery in his face, assured him once more that there was no need to worry and she would see that Hilda wrote to them regularly.

Hilda kissed her father and followed her aunt into the compartment. He stood there, with a dazed look all over him, and seemed not to understand that they were almost off. The train began to move and she leant out. Her father, nearly choking in his effort to speak steadily, said in a whisper: "Dunna forget as you've allus got us, our 'Ilda. And you'll act as she says and send us a letter from London? Your mother's that cut up she'll not settle till us knows of your doings. And be a good girl." The train was moving faster but still he stood there, then turned and walked stolidly towards the entrance. Hilda watched him as long as she could but he did not once turn round.

Settling herself in the corner opposite Aunt Mildred, while the facile tears poured down her cheeks, he vanished from her mind as she gave herself up to thinking of the wonders that awaited her in the new rich life at London.